Jan 1977

Wayne — Hope you can make many good meals from this book. Love Mother

ANN SERANNE'S
Good Food
Without Meat

ANN SERANNE'S
Good Food Without Meat

by Ann Seranne

William Morrow & Company, Inc.   New York   1973

Dedicated affectionately to my patient friend,
Barbara Wolferman, who had to forego many a steak dinner
during the testing of these meatless dishes

Printed in the United States of America.

Library of Congress Catalog Card Number 72-9563

ISBN 0-688-00159-9

3 4 5 77 76

Contents

Introduction

What we eat is a matter of custom and habit. As late as the fifth century B.C., the Caucasians believed that their grandfather was immortalized if he were sacrificed and eaten by his progeny, that he lived on in the off-spring who consumed his roasted flesh. It was a disgrace to allow him to die a natural death. In prehistoric times, the eating of human flesh was taken as much for granted as the eating of animal flesh. Human brains and liver were considered great delicacies, human eyes, cheeks, thighs, and buttocks were considered the choice parts, and human blood was drunk avidly at victory celebrations.

In the historical cookbook, *Cooks, Gluttons and Gourmets* by Betty Wason, the author suggests that it may have been a mystic urge that caused primitive man to eat his ancestors, but that cannibalism has had its practical rationalizations as well. An eighteenth-century cannibal chief in Brazil explained, "When I have slain an enemy, it is surely better to eat him than to let him go to waste."

Mrs. Wason relates that "In the Upper Congo, as late as the seventeenth century, living men, women, and children were bought and sold frankly as articles of food. A century later, on the island of New Britain, human meat was offered in butcher stalls along with animal flesh. Savages on the Solomon Islands fattened women for a feast just like pigs; they ranked female flesh as preferable to that of dogs because 'dogs taste of otter.' " Yet the dog had been considered a succulent dish by nations considerably more advanced in civilization and in the culinary arts. The Greeks ate dogs. Hippocrates considered dog a light and wholesome supper dish, and the Romans prepared it in much the same manner as we prepare hare today.

Have we really evolved very far from these primitive customs? The offering of Grace before the host carves the blood-rare roast beef, the suckling pig with the rosy apple in its mouth, or the plump-breasted turkey is very reminiscent of the prayer that primitive man offered up to his god during the ceremony of sacrifice.

For many years now I have found myself questioning and criticizing the meat-eating society in which we live. As a person with a growing interest in Truth and in God-man relationships, I find it very difficult to condone the slaughtering of domesticated animals for human consumption. On the other hand, as a cook and a lover of good food, I cannot imagine foregoing the pleasure of such by-products of animal husbandry as eggs, milk, cream, butter, and cheese. Yet, we can't have one without the other. To be a true vegetarian one must restrict one's eating to vegetables, fruits, nuts, and legumes and wear only man-made shoes and clothing. But in trying to practice vegetarianism either as a protest against the slaughterhouses or for reasons of religion, one becomes involved in the complications of present-day ecology. To enjoy eggs, there must be hens raised to lay them, but for every female chick born there is a cock, and one cock can service an entire henyard. For every cow born, there is likely to be a bull. Modern methods of artificial insemination make the sperm of one prize bull available to farmers across the country.

What can we do with the excess cocks and bulls? Must we put them out to pasture and feed and care for them to a ripe old age? Or do we philosophize, like the Brazilian cannibal, that it is surely better to use them to feed the human race than to let them go to waste?

Perhaps in a few hundred years we will have evolved to a higher state of consciousness and, with the help of science, can and will become a race of vegetarians who recognize that every living animal cherishes the gift of life.

The monumental advances that have taken place in the field of genetics in the past twenty years bring this dream into the realm of possibility and, according to a recent article by Dr. Braxton B. Sawyer, has caused some of our leading scientists to predict that "within the next ten years it will be possible for a woman to walk into a kind of commissary which would contain day-old embryos in frozen packets labeled to describe the sex, physical characteristics, type of temperament and IQ likely to be present in the full-grown individual. After making a selection, she could take the packet to her physician and have the embryo implanted in her uterus where it will mature for nine months like a normally conceived pregnancy."

If this is to be our brave new world, then science can conceivably enable the farmer to control the sex of his farm animals to such an extent that he can produce mainly egg-laying hens and milk-producing cows, and there will be no excess cocks or bulls to go to waste.

Meanwhile there is a surprising number of young men and women who are having serious thoughts on the subject of vegetarianism. Many have already given up eating meat and have found that they have lost nothing in the way of health, vitality, and strength. There is a rapidly increasing number of restaurants operated by young people where only vegetarian dishes are served, and theirs is good food, it is satisfying food. These young people are gravely concerned with the rapid depletion of our soil and the fact that DDT, other dangerous chemicals, and synthetic hormones are found in animal flesh. But they have spiritual concerns as well, if not downright mystical ones. A recent article in *Time* magazine quoted California's Wheeler as saying, "When carrion is consumed, people are really greedy." It went on to say that "Others maintain that food is the determining factor in the biological conditions in man that produce wars, brutality, and narrow thinking."

The youth of today are not willing to remain within the emotional or intellectual confines of the past. They are seeking the truth and they are discovering the universal law of love, which works whenever it is applied. Their God did not create creatures with the capacity to feel pain, fear, friendship, and affection to be used for food.

Whether you eat meat or don't eat meat is a personal matter. If you can justify vegetarianism in your own mind, you will find this book useful. I do not consider it a strictly vegetarian cookbook, because I have used animal by-products lavishly in the recipes. And so, until the lion lies down with the lamb, it will serve best the budget-minded who find the price of good hamburger today staggering; those who wish to eat more simply, more lightly; and everyone who enjoys good honest food—meatless or not—delicious dishes made from beans, nuts, whole grains and cereals, pasta, and, of course, fruits and vegetables.

ANN SERANNE

SOUPS

Vegetable Soups

Soup can be an economical source of fine nutrition, either as an appetizer to begin a meal or as a satisfying main dish at luncheon or supper when accompanied by a hot bread and a salad.

Not all soups depend on a rich beef or chicken stock for their flavor. The wonderful raw vegetable soups of Spain—the Gazpacho-style soups, which you will find in the chapter on raw vegetables—are meatless, and the world-famous French onion soup, with its legendary restorative powers, served in the Paris markets, is frequently made with water. As a matter of fact, France has a great variety of delicate vegetable soups, hearty vegetable chowders, and unctuous bean purées which use only water or vegetable broth for the liquid. These are known as *maigre* soups, in the Lenten sense of "meatless" rather than lean, meager, or emaciated. There is nothing emaciated about the soups that follow. They are rich in the wonderful flavors that only fresh vegetables can give them. Some are actually lean, but only in calories, not in vitality; others are enriched with cream or with cream and eggs. So, it is with some truly noble soups, whose nobility lies in their simplicity, that we begin this meatless book.

POTAGE BONNE FEMME MAIGRE
(Leek, Potato, Onion, and Cabbage Soup)

Serves 6

BUY THE FRESHEST POSSIBLE

Bunch of leeks
3 medium potatoes
2 medium onions
1 small cabbage
Bunch of parsley

HAVE ON HAND	*COOKWARE*
Butter	Large soup kettle
Salt and pepper	Small skillet
Garlic	
Bread	

1. Discard the green leaves of *4 leeks*. Trim ends and wash very carefully to remove any sand. Chop the leeks. Peel and chop the *potatoes* and *onions*. Fill the tea kettle with *water* and bring to a boil.

2. In a large heavy soup kettle melt *2 tablespoons butter*. Cook the chopped vegetables in it over low heat for 3 minutes, stirring constantly. Add *8 cups boiling water* and *salt and pepper to taste*. Simmer gently for 30 minutes.

3. Meanwhile wash, core, and shred the *cabbage;* discard stems from *parsley* and chop it; peel and mince *1 clove garlic*.

4. Add cabbage, parsley, and garlic to the soup and continue to simmer for 30 minutes longer.

5. While the soup simmers, dice *2 slices of bread* and brown the cubes in *2 tablespoons butter* in a small skillet.

6. Ladle the soup into soup plates and sprinkle with croutons.

SOUP À L'OIGNON MAIGRE
(French Onion Soup)

Serves 6. Peel onions under running water and wear your sunglasses when you slice them. You won't cry.

BUY

6 large Spanish onions
Small loaf French bread

HAVE ON HAND

Garlic
Butter
Lemon
Black peppercorns

Salt
Parmesan, Gruyère, *or* Swiss cheese
Beer

COOKWARE

5-quart saucepan *or* soup kettle
Baking sheet
Individual earthenware casseroles

IN ADVANCE:

1. Peel and thinly slice the *onions.* Peel and mince *1 large clove garlic.*

2. In saucepan slowly melt *½ cup butter (1 stick).* Add the onions and garlic and stew over medium heat for 15 minutes, or until onions are wilted and transparent but not browned, stirring often to separate onion slices into rings.

3. Add *4 cups water, juice of ½ lemon, ½ teaspoon freshly ground pepper,* and *salt to taste.* Bring to a boil, then simmer for 30 minutes. Correct seasoning. Set aside and reheat when needed.

4. Meanwhile slice the *French bread,* place on baking sheet, and toast in hot oven or under broiler until golden on both sides. Grate a *heaping bowl of cheese.*

TO FINISH AND SERVE:

5. Preheat oven to 375° F. Stir *½ cup beer* into the hot soup. Ladle onions and liquid into earthenware casseroles and set casseroles on baking sheet. Top each serving with a slice of toast, sprinkle liberally with cheese, and dot with *butter.* Bake in the hot oven for 5 minutes, or until cheese melts and becomes crusty.

6. Serve *additional cheese and crusty bread* on the side.

A MINESTRONE is nothing more than a wholesome vegetable soup to which you may add practically any vegetable you happen to have around—hence there are as many variations of it as there are cooks in Italy. But always serve minestrone with a large bowl of freshly grated Parmesan cheese and slices of hot Italian bread.

MINESTRONE DI VERDURA
(Minestrone with Greens)

Serves 6. Here is a basic recipe to which you may add peas, string beans, zucchini, parsnips, turnips, cabbage—whatever and as much as you wish.

BUY

1 pound fresh lima beans *or* peas
1 head of escarole *or* romaine
¼ pound spinach
6 small beets
8-ounce box elbow macaroni *or* small pasta tubes

HAVE ON HAND	COOKWARE
2 stalks celery	Large soup kettle
2 small onions	Small skillet
1 carrot	
Salt	
Peppercorns	
Olive oil	
Dried marjoram	
Parmesan cheese	

1. Shell the *lima beans or peas.* Wash and chop the *escarole or romaine* and the *spinach.* Peel and dice the *beets;* chop *2 stalks celery;* peel and chop *2 small onions* and *1 carrot.*

2. Place the lima beans, escarole, spinach, beets, and celery in a large pot. Add *1½ teaspoons salt, ¼ teaspoon freshly ground pepper,* and *enough water to cover* the vegetables. Cover pot and bring liquid to a boil. Reduce heat and simmer for 10 minutes.

3. In skillet, heat *2 tablespoons olive oil* and in it sauté the onions and carrot until onions are soft. Add to the hot vegetables, along with *¼ teaspoon marjoram,* and simmer for 30 minutes.

4. Meanwhile grate *½ cup cheese* and set aside. Cook the macaroni less than al dente, drain, and stir into soup. Simmer for 5 minutes, uncovered.

5. Serve in hot soup bowls with grated Parmesan sprinkled on top.

QUICK MINESTRONE

Serves 4 to 6

BUY

1-pound can Italian-style tomatoes with basil
1 pint tomato juice
1-pound can garbanzos *or* chick peas
Small loaf Italian bread

HAVE ON HAND	*COOKWARE*
Garlic	Large saucepan
Small onion	
2 stalks celery with leaves	
1 medium carrot	
Parsley	
Salad oil	
Sage	
Pepper	
Salt	
Instant rice	
Grated Parmesan cheese	

1. Peel and mince *1 clove garlic* and *1 small onion*. Slice *2 stalks celery with leaves*. Peel and chop *the carrot*. Chop *2 tablespoons parsley*.

2. In saucepan sauté garlic, onion, and celery in *2 tablespoons oil* until onion is tender.

3. Add the *tomatoes, tomato juice,* and the carrot; drain the *chick peas,* and add them along with *a pinch of sage, ⅛ teaspoon pepper,* and *salt to taste*.

4. Bring to a boil. Then add *½ cup instant rice* and the chopped parsley, and simmer for 5 minutes. Serve with a bowl of *grated Parmesan cheese,* and *a loaf of hot crusty Italian bread*.

VEGETARIAN BORSCHT

Serves 4 to 6

BUY

1 small cabbage
3 medium carrots
1 parsnip
3 medium beets
8-ounce can tomato purée
8-ounce container dairy sour cream
Bread

HAVE ON HAND

1 medium onion
Garlic
3 medium potatoes
Cooking oil
Bay leaves
Salt and pepper

COOKWARE

Large heavy saucepan

1. Peel and chop *1 onion.* Remove any discolored outer leaves from *cabbage;* quarter, and discard thick core. Shred cabbage. Peel the *carrots, parsnip,* and *beets* and cut into thin julienne strips. Peel *1 large clove garlic* and mince. Peel and dice the *potatoes.*

2. In heavy saucepan heat *2 tablespoons cooking oil.* Add the prepared onion, carrots, parsnip, and beets, and sauté for 5 to 8 minutes, or until onion is golden, stirring frequently. Add *6 cups water,* the garlic, *2 bay leaves,* potatoes, and the *tomato purée.* Bring liquid to a boil, season to taste with *salt and pepper,* and simmer for about 45 minutes, or until vegetables are soft. Add shredded cabbage and simmer for 15 minutes, longer.

3. Serve with hot crusty bread and top each serving with a big dollop of sour cream.

POTAGE SANTÉ
(Soup for the Health)

Serves 6. Salad greens of almost any kind may be used in this soup.

BUY

2 heads lettuce *or* romaine
1 bunch scallions
A handful fresh spinach
Bunch water cress

HAVE ON HAND

Butter
Salt and pepper
Lemon

COOKWARE

Large heavy saucepan

1. Fill the tea kettle and set to boil.

2. Wash the *lettuce or romaine.* Use only the outer leaves, reserving the hearts for salad. Shred the outer leaves. Trim, wash, and chop the *scallions.* Wash *spinach* and *water cress,* and discard any thick stems.

3. In heavy saucepan melt *2 tablespoons butter.* Add the scallions and cook over low heat, stirring constantly for 5 minutes. Add the lettuce, spinach, water cress, *6 cups boiling water,* and *salt and pepper to taste.* Simmer, uncovered, for about 30 minutes.

4. Just before serving, add *lemon juice to taste.*

VEGETABLE GUMBO

Serves 2 or 3

BUY

1 pound zucchini
Parsley
1-pound can stewed tomatoes
10-ounce package frozen okra

HAVE ON HAND	*COOKWARE*
Onion	2-quart saucepan
Celery	
Butter	
Bay leaf	
Salt and pepper	
Dried basil	
Cayenne	
Raw rice	

1. Peel and mince *1 small onion.* Chop *enough celery to measure* ½ *cup.* Wash, trim, and slice the *zucchini.* Chop *2 tablespoons parsley.*

2. In saucepan melt *2 tablespoons butter* and in it sauté the onion and celery for 5 minutes. Stir in *tomatoes with the liquid* and *1 cup water.* Add *1 bay leaf,* ½ *teaspoon salt, or to taste,* ⅛ *teaspoon pepper,* ½ *teaspoon basil,* and *a good dash cayenne.* Bring to a boil, then simmer over low heat for 15 minutes.

3. Add zucchini and *2 tablespoons raw rice,* and simmer for 10 minutes. Add *okra* and parsley and cook over low heat for 10 minutes longer. Serve steaming hot.

Chowders & Bisques

Next in line are some soups which, although basically *maigre,* become a little fatter in calories with the addition of heavy cream. These are the simplest kind of creamed soups; seasoned with nothing more than salt and pepper, they allow the wonderful flavor of fresh vegetables to come through. You may add a favorite herb, fresh or dried, if you wish. Tarragon and dill are always great soup herbs, but you may prefer a little sweet marjoram or a bay leaf. Milk or a mixture of milk and cream may be substituted for the heavy cream, but the soup will not be quite so delicious.

These soups may be either chunky or smooth. If you purée the vegetables in a food mill or a blender, the soups fall into the category of vegetable bisques; if you leave the vegetables in small pieces, they are classified as vegetable chowders. Either way, garnish them with chopped parsley, chives, dill, or celery leaves.

CREAM OF CELERY SOUP

Serves 2 or 3

   BUY

Head of fresh celery
8-ounce container heavy cream

   HAVE ON HAND   *COOKWARE*

Onion   Saucepan
Salt and pepper   Electric blender

   1. Wash and slice thinly *enough fresh celery to measure 2 cups.* Peel and mince *1 small onion.*

   2. Put the vegetables in a saucepan with *2 cups water* and *salt to taste.* Bring to a boil and simmer for about 15 minutes, or until celery is tender. Set aside until ready to serve, or blend vegetables and liquid in an electric blender and return to saucepan.

   3. When ready to serve, chop a *few celery leaves* for garnish. Return the soup to a simmer. Stir in the *heavy cream;* heat, stirring constantly, until steaming hot. Add *lots of freshly ground black pepper,* and serve each portion with a topping of chopped celery.

   VARIATIONS: In place of the celery use any one of the following vegetables or a combination of them: sliced carrots or parsnips; chopped fresh broccoli or cauliflower; freshly shucked peas or lima beans; sliced zucchini or summer squash; peeled and diced winter squash, sweet potatoes, or white potatoes; chopped fresh mushrooms; a 10-ounce package of frozen chopped spinach or baby limas.

CURRIED CREAM OF ZUCCHINI SOUP

Serves 4

BUY

1 pound fresh young zucchini
8-ounce container heavy cream
Chives

HAVE ON HAND

Butter
Shallots *or* green onions
Garlic
Curry powder
Salt
White pepper
Milk

COOKWARE

Medium saucepan

1. Wash, trim, and slice *zucchini* thinly. Put into a saucepan with *2 tablespoons butter, 2 tablespoons minced shallots or green onions, 2 cloves garlic,* peeled and minced, *1 teaspoon curry powder, ½ teaspoon salt,* and *¼ teaspoon white pepper.* Cook over low heat for 5 minutes, shaking pan frequently.

2. Add *½ cup water* and simmer for 10 minutes, stirring occasionally.

3. Rub vegetables through a food mill or purée in blender.

4. Return to saucepan and stir in the *cream* and *1 cup milk.* Carefully reheat and serve hot, or chill and serve cold, with *chopped chives* on top.

LEEK AND POTATO SOUP

Serves 4. This is a peasant soup from France, and is always served steaming hot for supper. It was originally made with water and cream, but when it was refined by Louis Diat in America, he substituted a rich chicken stock for the water, puréed the vegetables, and served the soup cold—the result was the popular "vichyssoise."

BUY

2 large leeks
8-ounce container heavy cream
Chives

HAVE ON HAND	COOKWARE
Medium onion	Large saucepan
Butter	
3 medium potatoes	
Salt	
Black peppercorns	

1. Trim root ends from *leeks*. Cut off and discard most of the long green stems, leaving just the palest part of the green above the white part. Slit leeks lengthwise from stem end, then turn and slit once more. Rinse well, separating the leaves, under cold running water. Dry, then chop into small pieces. Peel and chop *1 medium onion*.

2. Sauté the chopped leeks and onion in *3 tablespoons butter* for 5 minutes, without letting them brown.

3. Meanwhile peel and dice *3 medium potatoes*. Add the potatoes to the onions and leeks along with *3 cups water;* bring to a boil, then simmer for 15 minutes, or until potatoes are tender. Season with *salt* and *freshly ground black pepper*. Stir in *cream* and bring just to a boil. Serve hot with *chopped chives*.

VICHYSSOISE DIAT

Serves 8

BUY

Bunch of leeks
5 medium potatoes
1 quart milk
1 pint heavy cream
Chives

<table>
<tr><td>*HAVE ON HAND*</td><td>*COOKWARE*</td></tr>
</table>

HAVE ON HAND	*COOKWARE*
1 medium onion Butter 1 quart chicken broth (*or* use water) Salt	Large heavy saucepan

1. Discard all of the green parts from *4 large leeks;* wash the remaining white parts thoroughly and carefully, for they are often full of sand, and slice. Peel and slice *1 medium onion.* Peel and thickly slice the *5 potatoes.*

2. In a large heavy saucepan melt *½ stick (¼ cup) butter,* and in it sauté the leeks and onion until the onion is golden. Add the potatoes and *1 quart chicken broth or water;* bring to a boil, then simmer for 35 minutes, or until potatoes are very tender. Rub soup through a strainer or food mill, or blend it 2 cups at a time in an electric blender.

3. Return the puréed soup to the saucepan and stir in *3 cups milk* and *1 cup of the cream.* Add salt to taste, and bring to a boil, then cool and once again rub through the strainer. Chill.

4. Stir in *remaining cup of cream,* and serve garnished with *chopped chives.*

BLUSHING VICHYSSOISE

Serves 6

BUY

Leeks
8-ounce container heavy cream

HAVE ON HAND	*COOKWARE*
Potatoes Carrots Milk Salt White pepper	Large saucepan

1. Peel and dice *enough potatoes to measure 2 cups*. Scrape and slice *enough carrots to measure 1¼ cups*. Trim, wash carefully, and slice the *white part of 2 leeks*.

2. Put all the vegetables in a saucepan and add *2 cups water* and *1 teaspoon salt*. Bring to a boil, then simmer for 25 minutes, or until vegetables are very tender.

3. Rub liquid and vegetables through a food mill, or purée in an electric blender. Pour into a mixing bowl. Stir in *1 cup milk, a dash of white pepper,* and the *heavy cream*. Cool, then chill.

4. Before serving, shred a *little raw carrot*. Serve the soup icy cold with a garnish of the shredded carrot on top.

QUICK CORN CHOWDER

Serves 4

   BUY

1-pound can cream-style corn

   HAVE ON HAND   *COOKWARE*

Onion   Saucepan
Green pepper
Butter
Milk *or* light cream
Salt
White pepper

1. Peel and chop *enough onion to measure ½ cup*. Seed and chop *enough green pepper to measure ½ cup*.

2. In saucepan melt *2 tablespoons butter,* and in it sauté onion and green pepper over low heat for 10 minutes, or until onion is tender but not browned.

3. Add *corn, 2 cups milk or light cream,* and *salt* and *white pepper to taste*. Mix well and heat to serving temperature.

SIMPLE AND SIMPLY DELICIOUS
CREAM OF TOMATO SOUP

Serves 4

BUY

1 pint cream (light *or* heavy)
1-pound can stewed tomatoes

HAVE ON HAND	*COOKWARE*
Salt	2 small saucepans
Peppercorns	
Parsley, chives, *or* fresh sweet basil	
Dry vermouth (optional)	

1. Heat *cream* in a saucepan until scalding hot.

2. In another saucepan, heat *stewed tomatoes* and season to taste with *salt* and *freshly ground black pepper*.

3. Chop 2 *tablespoons parsley, chives, or sweet basil.*

4. When ready to serve, stir the tomatoes into the hot cream. Serve with a garnish of the chopped parsley or chives or basil. *A last-minute dash of dry vermouth* will give this soup an unusual extra bit of flavor.

CREAM OF FRESH ASPARAGUS SOUP

Serves 6

BUY

1 bunch fresh asparagus (1 pound)
8-ounce container heavy cream

HAVE ON HAND	COOKWARE
1 medium onion	3-quart saucepan with lid
Butter	Small saucepan
Chicken broth *or* water	
Salt and pepper	
Mace	
Milk	
Lemon	

1. Snap off tough white portion of *asparagus stalks* and discard. With vegetable peeler, strip scales off stalks to remove any sand lurking beneath. Soak in cold water for 5 minutes. Drain and cut off tips. Set tips aside and cut remaining stalks into 1-inch lengths. Peel and chop *1 medium onion.*

2. In saucepan melt *2 tablespoons butter,* and in it sauté the onion for 5 minutes. Add *all the asparagus except the tips* and *2 cups chicken broth or water.* Season with *salt and pepper to taste,* and *a dash of mace.* Bring to a boil, cover, and cook over low heat for 30 minutes.

3. Meanwhile put *asparagus tips* in a small saucepan. Cover with boiling salted water and simmer for 10 minutes. Drain, reserving the *liquid,* and set aside.

4. Force cooked asparagus stalks and their liquid through a sieve, or purée a couple of cups at a time in an electric blender. Return to saucepan. Measure reserved liquid from the tips; if necessary, add *milk* to measure 2 cups. Add to soup. Stir in *1 teaspoon lemon juice.* Cool soup and then chill.

5. Just before serving, stir in the *cream* and the asparagus tips.

SPINACH SCHAV

Serves 6

BUY

10-ounce package frozen chopped spinach
Pint dairy sour cream
2 cucumbers

HAVE ON HAND　　　*COOKWARE*

Salt and pepper　　　Saucepan
Lemon

1. Put *spinach* into saucepan with *2 cups water* and *1 teaspoon salt* and ¼ *teaspoon pepper*. Bring to a boil, then simmer for 10 minutes.

2. Remove from heat and stir in *juice of 1 lemon*. Cool and chill.

3. Stir in the *sour cream* and *2 cucumbers,* peeled, seeded, and chopped.

VEGETABLE STEW WITH CHEESE

Serves 4

BUY

1 large ripe tomato *or* 8-ounce can whole tomatoes
1 bunch parsley
Cheddar cheese, aged
1 pint heavy cream

HAVE ON HAND　　　*COOKWARE*

Potatoes　　　Saucepan with cover
1 medium onion
Celery
1 medium carrot
Salt
White peppercorns

1. Peel and dice *enough potatoes to measure 2 cups*. Peel and dice *1 medium onion*. Wash and slice *1 large stalk celery with leaves,* and *1 medium carrot*.

2. Put all the prepared vegetables in a saucepan with *1 cup boiling water or enough to cover,* and *1 teaspoon salt*. Cut stems off bunch of *parsley;* set aside the leaves; tie the stems with string and add them to the saucepan. Cover and simmer vegetables for 15 minutes.

3. While vegetables are cooking, peel, seed, and chop the *tomato;* also chop ½ *cup parsley leaves*. Shred ¼ *cup cheddar cheese*. Set aside.

4. Remove parsley stems and discard. Add the parsley leaves and cheese to the soup. Add *lots of freshly ground white pepper,* and gradually stir in the *heavy cream.* Heat to serving temperature. Just before serving stir in the chopped tomato. Remove soup from heat, and let stand for 2 minutes before serving.

Soups Thickened with Flour

Another type of creamy vegetable soups is thickened with a little flour or cooked potato before the cream is added. If such soups are made with water, which allows the full flavor of fresh vegetables to come through, they are still known as *maigre.* You may, however, use part or all chicken broth—or, better still, use the cooking liquid from mild-flavored vegetables, such as peas, asparagus, carrots, string beans, and so on if the vegetable is specified in the recipe. The first recipe below takes advantage of any vegetable left over from dinner the previous day.

CREAM OF LEFTOVER-VEGETABLE SOUP

Serves 4

BUY

8-ounce container cream

HAVE ON HAND

1 small onion
Butter
Flour *or* leftover potatoes
Chicken *or* vegetable broth
    (optional)

COOKWARE

Saucepan

1 cup leftover cooked vegetable *or*
    a combination of leftovers
    (spinach, carrots, cauliflower,
    broccoli, Brussels sprouts, celery,
    asparagus, peas)
Celery salt
Salt
White pepper
Parsley, chives, *or* celery leaves

1. Peel and mince *1 small onion*, and sauté in *3 tablespoons butter* over low heat for about 5 minutes, or until onion is tender.

2. Stir in *3 tablespoons flour or ½ cup cooked potatoes*, then gradually stir in *1½ cups water or broth*. Add the *leftover vegetable (or vegetables)*, and *½ teaspoon celery salt*. Bring to a boil, then simmer for 10 minutes.

3. Purée the soup in a food mill, or blend 2 cups at a time in an electric blender. Return purée to saucepan, and stir in the *cream* and *salt and white pepper to taste*.

4. Chop *a little parsley, chives, or celery leaves*. Serve the soup hot or cold, sprinkling each serving with a little of the chopped garnish.

POTAGE SAINT GERMAIN

Serves 8

BUY

2 pounds unshelled fresh peas
8-ounce container heavy cream

HAVE ON HAND

Parsley
Carrot
Onion
Potato
Butter

Flour
Vegetable broth (optional)
Salt and pepper

COOKWARE

2 large saucepans
1 lid

1. Chop *2 tablespoons parsley* and set aside. Wash and shell *peas,* reserving the *pods.* Scrape and slice *1 carrot.* Peel and slice *1 onion* and *1 potato.* Put these vegetables, with the pods of the peas, into a large saucepan with *2 tablespoons butter.* Cover and braise over low heat for 10 minutes.

2. Sprinkle the vegetables with *2 tablespoons flour* and add *6 cups water or vegetable broth.* Bring liquid to a boil, then cover and cook over low heat for 10 minutes. Strain the liquid through a sieve, pressing through as much of the soft vegetables as possible into a clean saucepan. Stir in *salt and pepper to taste.* Add the peas and simmer for 8 minutes, or until peas are tender. Add the *cream* and chopped parsley.

MUSHROOM BISQUE

Serves 4. This soup is just as good if it is not blended to a purée. Just change its name to "chowder."

BUY

½ pound fresh mushrooms
8-ounce container heavy cream

HAVE ON HAND   *COOKWARE*

Onion   Saucepan
Butter
Flour
Chicken broth (optional)
Salt
White pepper
Dry sherry
Sour cream (optional)

1. Wash *mushrooms* and trim stem ends. Slice caps and mince stems. Peel and mince *1 medium onion.*

2. In saucepan melt *3 tablespoons butter,* and in it cook the onion over low heat until onion is tender. Add the mushrooms, and continue to

cook over low heat for 10 minutes, or until mushrooms are tender, stirring frequently.

3. Stir in *3 tablespoons flour*. Gradually stir in *2 cups water or broth, ½ teaspoon salt, or to taste,* and *¼ teaspoon white pepper*. Simmer for 30 minutes. Purée in an electric blender and return to saucepan.

4. Stir in *heavy cream* and *2 tablespoons sherry* and heat to serving temperature. Serve with a topping of *sour cream,* if desired.

CUCUMBER MINT SOUP

Serves 4. This is a cool treat for blistering summer days.

BUY

3 firm cucumbers
Bunch of fresh mint
8-ounce container heavy cream

HAVE ON HAND	*COOKWARE*
Medium onion	Saucepan with cover
Butter	
Cooking oil	
Flour	
Chicken broth (optional)	
Salt and pepper	

1. Peel *1 cucumber* and slice. Wash *a second cucumber;* this time leave on the green skin but trim the ends; slice the cucumber. Peel and slice *1 medium onion.*

2. Put all of the cucumber and onion slices in the saucepan with *2 tablespoons butter, 1 tablespoon cooking oil,* and *3 tablespoons water.* Cover and cook over low heat for 30 minutes, or until vegetables are tender.

3. Stir in *3 tablespoons flour* and *2 cups water or broth,* and *salt and white pepper to taste.* Continue stirring over moderate heat until the liquid begins to boil. Remove from heat, then rub through a strainer or food mill, or blend 2 cups at a time in an electric blender. Return soup to the saucepan.

4. Stir in *¾ cup cream* and *1 tablespoon chopped fresh mint*. Either heat and serve, or cool, then chill, and serve on a bed of crushed ice.

5. Garnish each serving with *a little shredded cucumber* and *a sprig of mint*.

CREAM OF TOMATO SOUP

Serves 4

BUY

5 large ripe tomatoes
Small can tomato paste
1 pint heavy cream
Fresh dill

HAVE ON HAND   *COOKWARE*

Medium onion   Saucepan with cover
Garlic
Salt and black pepper
Flour
Sour cream (optional)

1. Wash *tomatoes* and peel *1 medium onion*. Slice *4 of the tomatoes* and the onion into the saucepan. Add *1 teaspoon minced garlic, ¼ cup cold water,* and *a sprinkling of salt and pepper*. Cover and cook over low heat for 12 minutes.

2. Remove tomato mixture from heat, then stir in *2 tablespoons tomato paste, 3 tablespoons flour,* and *1½ cups water*. Return to heat; cook, stirring, until soup comes to a boil.

3. Rub soup through a strainer or food mill, or blend 2 cups at a time in an electric blender.

4. Let the soup cool to room temperature, then stir in *1½ cups cream* and *2 tablespoons finely chopped dill*. Peel the *remaining tomato,* discard seeds, and chop the flesh. Add to the soup and chill for several hours.

5. Serve in bowls surrounded by crushed ice. Top if desired with *a dollop of sour cream,* and garnish with *a sprig of dill*.

Soups Thickened with Eggs & Cream

Here we come to a group of wonderful soups that are still creamier than the preceding ones, thickened and enriched by means of both egg yolks and cream. And we begin with my favorite of ALL soups, French sorrel soup. One of the truly great soups of the world, it is made from the common garden weed known as sour grass. Sorrel is a perennial and so easy to grow that everyone with a square yard of earth in a sunny spot should sprinkle some sorrel seeds in early spring. The plants will supply your table constantly with the sour leaves until frost and will return again the next year. I doubt that any food chemist has analyzed it for vitamins and minerals, but I'm sure that anything as good as this soup must be good for you!

CREAM OF SORREL SOUP

Serves 4. Spinach may be used in place of the sorrel leaves, and if you flavor the soup just before serving with the juice of a lemon, the flavor will come close—close and yet so far.

BUY OR HARVEST

½ pound fresh sorrel leaves (2 large handfuls)
8-ounce container heavy cream

HAVE ON HAND

Onions *or* shallots
Butter
Chicken broth (optional)

Salt

Black peppercorns   *COOKWARE*

1 egg yolk   Saucepan

1. Wash and pick over *sorrel leaves*. Drain well. Cut out and discard the coarse center stem from the larger leaves and shred the sorrel thinly.

2. Peel and mince *1 small onion (or 4 shallots)* and sauté in *½ stick (¼ cup) butter* for 3 or 4 minutes, or until onion is transparent. Add the shredded sorrel to the saucepan, and cook for 5 minutes, or until the sorrel is wilted, stirring frequently.

NOTE: As fall approaches and you do not want the sorrel remaining in the garden to get frostbitten, harvest it and prepare it to this point in the recipe. The wilted sorrel-and-butter mixture freezes well and will allow you to enjoy a bowlful of this fabulous soup during the winter months. Cool the sorrel mixture, spoon into freezer bags, and seal. Defrost when desired and continue . . .

3. Add *2 cups water or chicken broth, ½ teaspoon salt, some freshly ground black pepper,* and bring to a boil. Simmer for 15 minutes.

4. When ready to serve, combine the *heavy cream* with *1 egg yolk* and *½ cup of the hot soup;* gradually stir this into the remaining soup. Cook the soup over low heat for 2 minutes, stirring rapidly and being careful not to let it boil. Serve immediately.

TCHORBA
(Sour Lettuce Soup)

Serves 6. Sour soups, such as Sorrel Soup, are beloved in most countries in Europe. From Bulgaria, comes this one made with lettuce and vinegar.

BUY

2 small heads tender young lettuce
Bunch green onions
Head of garlic
8-ounce container heavy cream
Parsley

HAVE ON HAND	*COOKWARE*
Chicken *or* vegetable broth (optional)	Saucepan
Salt and pepper	
Vinegar	
2 egg yolks	

1. Wash *lettuce,* separating the leaves. Shred leaves into the saucepan. Add *6 cups broth or water* and bring to a boil.

2. Meanwhile wash and mince *6 green onions,* using as much of the green stalks as possible. Peel and mince *6 cloves garlic.* Add onions and garlic to the simmering lettuce and simmer for 10 minutes.

3. Add *1 teaspoon salt, ¼ teaspoon pepper,* and *2 tablespoons vinegar;* simmer for 5 minutes longer.

4. Just before serving combine *2 egg yolks* and *½ cup heavy cream* with *½ cup of the hot broth.*

5. Remove soup from heat and slowly stir in the egg-cream mixture.

6. Sprinkle each portion with *chopped parsley.* Serve immediately.

WHITE TURNIP SOUP

Serves 6

BUY

1 pound white turnips
1 large sweet onion
8-ounce container heavy cream
Parsley

HAVE ON HAND	*COOKWARE*
Butter	Saucepan
Vegetable broth (optional)	
Salt	
White pepper	
Bread	
2 egg yolks	

1. Put kettle of water (or enough vegetable broth for 6 cups) on heat to boil. Peel and chop the *turnips* and *sweet onion*.

2. In heavy saucepan melt *2 tablespoons butter*. Add chopped vegetables and cook, stirring constantly, for 3 minutes. Add *6 cups boiling water or vegetable broth* and *salt and white pepper to taste*. Crumble in *4 slices bread* and bring soup to a boil. Simmer over low heat for 30 minutes, or until vegetables are very tender.

3. Meanwhile chop *4 tablespoons parsley* and set aside. Rub the soup through a strainer, or blend 2 cups at a time in an electric blender, and return to saucepan. Return soup to a boil.

4. Just before serving, combine the *2 egg yolks* with the *heavy cream* and a *little of the hot soup*. Remove soup from heat and gradually stir in the egg yolk mixture. Correct seasoning with salt and pepper. Pour into soup cups. Sprinkle each serving with chopped parsley.

VARIATIONS: Use radishes or cauliflower in place of the turnips.

CHEESE SOUP

Serves 6

BUY

½ pound aged Cheddar cheese
Heavy cream

HAVE ON HAND	*COOKWARE*
Garlic	Heavy saucepan
Butter	
Flour	
Dry white wine *or* dry vermouth	
Milk	
White pepper	
Nutmeg	
2 egg yolks	

1. Shred the *cheese* and set aside. Peel and crush *1 clove garlic*.

2. In heavy saucepan melt *2 tablespoons butter*. Add garlic and cook over low heat for 3 minutes without letting the garlic brown. Discard garlic. Add *2 tablespoons flour* and stir to make a smooth paste. Cook for 2 minutes, stirring constantly.

3. Gradually stir in *½ cup dry white wine, 2½ cups milk, ⅛ teaspoon white pepper,* and *a dash of freshly grated nutmeg;* cook, stirring, until sauce is smooth and slightly thickened. Add cheese and cook over moderate heat, stirring occasionally, until cheese is melted.

4. Combine *2 egg yolks* and *½ cup heavy cream.* Stir a *little of the hot soup* into the egg mixture, then stir gradually into the soup. Cook over low heat for 2 to 3 minutes, stirring constantly, without letting soup boil. Serve immediately.

Bean Soups

No flour or potatoes are needed to thicken bean soups, for the beans themselves provide body and substance.

CURRIED LIMA BEAN SOUP

Serves 4

BUY

10-ounce package frozen baby lima beans
Bunch of green onions
8-ounce container light cream
Chives *or* parsley, for garnish

HAVE ON HAND	*COOKWARE*
Butter	Saucepan with cover
Curry powder	Food mill *or* electric blender
Salt	
White pepper	
Marjoram	
Chicken broth (optional)	
Milk	

1. In saucepan combine *lima beans, ⅓ cup sliced green onions, 2 tablespoons butter, 1 teaspoon curry powder, ½ teaspoon salt, ⅛ teaspoon white pepper, ¼ teaspoon marjoram,* and *1 cup water or chicken broth.* Bring to a boil, partially cover, and simmer for 15 minutes, or until beans are tender.

2. Press vegetables and liquid through a food mill, or purée in an electric blender. Return to saucepan and stir in *1 cup milk* and *1 cup cream.*

3. Reheat to serving temperature, or chill and serve cold. Either way, garnish each serving with *chopped chives or parsley.*

KIDNEY OR BLACK BEAN SOUP

Serves 4 to 6

BUY

1 pound dried kidney beans *or* black beans
1 large Spanish onion
Container sour cream

HAVE ON HAND	*COOKWARE*
Salt	Large heavy kettle
Coarsely cracked pepper	8-inch skillet
Bay leaves	
Garlic	
Cooking oil	
Red wine vinegar	
Water, milk, *or* light cream	

1. Wash the *beans* and put them into a large kettle with *4 quarts water*. Let them soak overnight.

2. Next day, bring beans to a boil in the same water. Add *1 tablespoon salt, 1 teaspoon coarsely cracked pepper,* and *1 bay leaf.* Simmer for 2 hours, or until beans are very tender, adding water, if necessary, to keep beans covered at all times.

3. Discard bay leaf. Rub beans and liquid through a strainer or food mill, or purée 2 cups at a time in an electric blender until smooth. You should have 6 to 7 cups thick purée, the amount depending on how rapidly the beans boiled and how much of the liquid evaporated.

4. Peel and finely chop the *large onion* and *1 large clove garlic.* Heat *½ cup cooking oil* in a skillet, and in it simmer the onion and garlic for about 10 minutes, or until onion is transparent.

5. Add onion-garlic mixture plus the pan oil to the purée. Then add *2 tablespoons red wine vinegar.* Thin with about 2 cups *water, milk, or light cream*—the amount depending on the consistency desired. Correct the seasoning with salt and pepper.

6. Heat to serving temperature. Serve with a big dollop of *sour cream* in each plate.

VARIATION: Substitute a 1-pint 7-ounce jar of cream-style schav for the water, milk, or light cream. An interesting change. Try it!

DUTCH PEA SOUP
(Snert)

Serves 6 to 8

BUY

1 pound green split peas
Bunch of leeks
1 large celery root
2 medium onions
Bunch of celery
8-ounce container heavy cream

HAVE ON HAND	*COOKWARE*
Chicken broth (optional)	Large heavy kettle
Salt	
Coarsely cracked pepper	
Butter	

1. Wash the *split peas,* and put into the kettle with *2½ quarts water or part water and part chicken broth.* Bring to a boil and simmer for 30 minutes.

2. Meanwhile discard green stalks from the *leeks,* then trim the white parts, wash thoroughly to remove any sand, and chop. Peel and chop the *celery root* and *onions.* Chop *enough celery stalks with the leaves to measure 1 cup.* Add these vegetables to the peas and liquid, along with *2 teaspoons salt* and *1 teaspoon pepper.* Simmer for 30 minutes longer, or until peas are very tender.

3. Just before serving stir in *3 tablespoons butter* and the *heavy cream.*

LENTIL SOUP

Serves 6

BUY

1-pound box lentils
8-ounce can whole tomatoes
2 medium potatoes *or* 1 large Idaho baking potato

HAVE ON HAND	*COOKWARE*
1 medium onion	Large saucepan with cover
Garlic	
2 large stalks celery with leaves	
Butter	
Salt and pepper	
Beer	

1. Wash the *lentils* thoroughly. Peel and chop *1 medium onion, 1 clove garlic,* and the *2 large stalks of celery.*

2. In saucepan stew the onion, garlic, and celery in *2 tablespoons butter* over low heat for 10 minutes, or until onion is tender.

3. Add *8 cups water,* the *tomatoes, with juice, 1½ teaspoons salt, ¼ teaspoon pepper,* and the lentils. Partially cover and cook over low heat for 2 hours.

4. Meanwhile peel and dice the *potato.* Cover with cold water and set aside.

5. Rub the soup through a strainer or food mill, or blend 2 cups at a time in an electric blender. Return to the saucepan and add *1 cup beer.* Drain the potatoes and add them to the soup. Bring soup to a boil, then simmer for 20 minutes, or until potatoes are tender. Correct seasoning and serve hot.

NAVY BEAN SOUP

Serves 6

BUY

1-pound box navy *or* pea beans
3 medium onions
2 carrots
Bunch of celery
8-ounce can stewed tomatoes
Parsley

HAVE ON HAND

Garlic
Bay leaves
Salt
Black peppercorns
1 potato

COOKWARE

Large saucepan

1. Pick over *beans,* discarding any shriveled or discolored ones. Put beans in a saucepan with *2½ quarts water* to soak overnight.

2. Next day add the *3 onions,* peeled and chopped, the *carrots,* scraped and diced, *2 cups chopped celery with leaves, 1 clove garlic,* peeled and minced, the *tomatoes, 2 bay leaves, 1 teaspoon salt,* and *a good grinding of black pepper.* Bring liquid to a boil, then simmer for 2 hours, or until beans are very tender. Discard bay leaves.

3. Peel and dice the *potato* finely. Add potato to the soup and cook for 10 minutes longer, or until potato is mushy. Add *½ cup minced parsley* and serve.

BLACK BEANS AND RICE

Serves 6

BUY

1 pound black beans (kidney beans may be substituted)

HAVE ON HAND	COOKWARE
Onions	Large saucepan
Celery	
Garlic	
Lemon	
Cayenne pepper	
Salt	
Coarsely ground black pepper	
Raw rice	
Dry sherry	
Parsley	

1. Wash *beans* well and soak overnight in water to cover. Next day drain *beans* and add *2 quarts cold water, 1 medium onion,* peeled and chopped, *½ cup chopped celery,* and *1 clove garlic,* peeled and minced. Bring water to a boil and simmer beans for 3 hours, or until very soft.

2. Rub beans and liquid through a strainer or food mill, or blend 2 cups at a time in an electric blender. Return bean purée to saucepan, and add *juice of 1 lemon, ¼ teaspoon cayenne pepper,* and *salt and pepper to taste.* Cook over low heat for 30 minutes, stirring occasionally.

3. Meanwhile cook *½ cup rice* according to recipe on page 191.

4. Just before serving, stir in *½ cup dry sherry.* Ladle the soup into

large soup plates; add a heaping tablespoon cooked rice to each serving, and sprinkle the rice with *minced onion and parsley*.

Fruit Soups

The Scandinavians are fond of a variety of fruit soups, which they serve either hot or cold, according to the season. Sometimes they present them as a first course, but more often as a dessert. Either way, these soups are certainly healthful, flavorful, and different—one can take advantage of fresh fruits in season or use dried fruits during winter months. For lunch on a broiling hot summer day, I prefer them (served icy cold on a bed of crushed ice) to a fruit salad. Fresh rhubarb, black cherries, fresh peaches, or apricots are excellent fruits to use. Since fruit varies in acidity, you will have to add sugar to taste, but avoid making the soups overly sweet. Use your own imagination, too, with such fruits as blueberries, raspberries, fresh plums, diced apples, or a combination of several fruits.

The first soup is a basic recipe. If raspberries are used, the soup must be strained to remove the seeds.

SWEET CHERRY SOUP

Serves 6

BUY OR PICK

1 quart sweet cherries

HAVE ON HAND

Stick cinnamon
Sugar

Cornstarch *or* instant tapioca	
Lemon	*COOKWARE*
Cognac *or* kirsch	Large saucepan

1. Wash the *cherries,* and then pit them over the saucepan in order to collect the cherry juice. Add *1 quart boiling water,* and *1 stick cinnamon.* Simmer for 20 to 30 minutes, or until cherries are tender.

2. Stir in *sugar to taste.*

3. Combine *2 tablespoons cornstarch or instant tapioca* and *¼ cup cold water;* stir into the soup. Return to a simmer and cook, stirring, until juice is clear and thickened. Remove from heat and cool a little. Then add *juice of ½ lemon* and *2 tablespoons cognac or kirsch.* Chill and serve very cold.

SCANDINAVIAN CREAMED FRUIT SOUP

Serves 8

BUY

Box of pitted dried prunes
Box of dried apricots
1 pint light cream

HAVE ON HAND	*COOKWARE*
Lemon	Large heavy saucepan
Salt	Small saucepan
Sugar	
Cornstarch	
Sherry *or* cognac	
Butter	
Flour	
Eggs	
Vanilla extract	

1. Put *1½ cups prunes* and *1½ cups apricots* into a heavy saucepan and add *2 quarts boiling water.* Let the fruit soak overnight.

2. Add to the fruit and juice the *grated rind of ½ lemon* and *a pinch of salt;* bring to a boil, then simmer for 20 minutes.

3. Combine *½ cup sugar, 2 tablespoons cornstarch,* and *½ cup sherry (or 2 tablespoons cognac),* and gradually stir this into the hot fruit mixture. Cook for about 10 minutes, stirring occasionally. Remove from heat. Cool, then pour into serving bowl and chill.

4. Meanwhile, make the cream topping: In small saucepan melt *2 tablespoons butter,* then stir in *4 tablespoons flour.* Cook, stirring, until this roux bubbles. Gradually stir in *1½ cups light cream,* and cook, stirring, until mixture is smooth and thickened. Continue to cook over low heat for 10 minutes longer, stirring occasionally.

5. Beat *2 eggs* with a *little of the hot sauce* until light, then stir into *remaining sauce.* Stir in *1 tablespoon sugar* and *1 teaspoon vanilla.* Remove from heat and pour into a small serving bowl. Chill.

6. Serve the soup and cream separately, and let each person top his portion with a big dollop of the cream.

HOT PURÉED FRUIT SOUP

Serves 6

BUY

1-pound 14-ounce can purple plums, apricots, *or* peaches, in heavy syrup
Heavy cream

HAVE ON HAND

Brown sugar
Cornstarch
Lemon
Butter
Rum
Cinnamon

COOKWARE

Large saucepan

1. Drain *fruit;* reserve *1 cup of its liquid.* Pit fruit, if necessary; then press through food mill, or blend in blender, to make a purée.

2. In saucepan combine ¼ *cup brown sugar, 1 tablespoon cornstarch,* the *cup of reserved liquid,* and *1 teaspoon lemon juice.* Bring to a boil and cook, stirring constantly, until soup is smooth and slightly thickened.

3. Stir in puréed fruit and heat to steaming.

4. Stir in *1 tablespoon butter, 2 tablespoons rum,* and *½ cup heavy cream.* Cook, stirring, until butter melts.

5. Ladle into serving bowls, and top with *sprinkling of cinnamon.*

APPETIZERS THAT DOUBLE AS LUNCHEON DISHES

Quiches & Tarts

An appetizer can mean a dish of nuts; a platter of crisp raw vegetables; a creamy dip; a bowl of green and ripe olives and another of bright radishes; half of an avocado, cantaloupe, or papaya; or one of the many other simple foods which are discussed in the chapter on raw foods and salads. An appetizer can also be eggs with any one of a number of zesty mayonnaise sauces, or a cooked vegetable, such as an artichoke, leeks, or fresh asparagus vinaigrette, or one of those piquant vegetable combinations— the *ratatouilles, capalatinas,* or the *à la grecque* dishes—or a soup, of course, either hot or cold, or a fondue. All these have found a place in other chapters of this book.

In fact, almost any savory dish, if served in small enough quantity, can serve as an appetizer. So, rather than make this a comprehensive chapter on appetizers, I have collected here some rather special hot savories which also can double as excellent meatless luncheon dishes.

The first group includes a variety of savory custard tarts, the progenitor of which was undoubtedly the famous specialty from the French province of Lorraine; known as the *quiche Lorraine,* it consists of a hot flaky crust filled with a rich, velvety cheese custard containing bits of crisply cooked bacon or ham. A little finely chopped onion or bits of mushroom or truffles make good substitutes for the meat, even if they are not traditional. Fortunately, there are no substitutes for the fresh eggs and cream and good butter and honest cheese which go into these recipes. Rich? Yes, but the best. Just cut the slices a trifle small and serve with a water cress and Belgian endive salad, delicately flavored with lemon juice and vegetable oils, and a glass of chilled white wine.

Both the crusts and the fillings of these tarts can be made in advance, and assembled and baked when needed. Since they deserve the finest pastry that can be made, this chapter begins with how to make a flaky butter pie crust. If you want to double the quantities, go ahead. Divide the dough in two; then roll out one half, and freeze the other half for another tart another day; or line 2 pie plates—one to bake, and one to freeze.

If you have had trouble rolling out pie crust, chances are that you have not been using the indispensable canvas pastry cloth and a knit stockinette for your rolling pin. These can be saturated with flour to keep the dough from sticking without adding too much additional flour to your dough. They are inexpensive and available at most five-and-dime stores. They make pastry-making a cinch.

FLAKY PIE CRUST

For a 1-crust pie

HAVE ON HAND	COOKWARE
Flour	9-inch pie plate
Salt	
Butter	
1 egg	

THE DOUGH:

1. Into a small mixing bowl measure *1 level cup flour*. There is no need to sift it. Add *½ teaspoon salt*. Make a well in the center of the flour and into this well slice *1 stick (½ cup) butter* taken directly from the refrigerator, NOT from the freezer.

2. Separate *1 egg;* reserve the white for another use, and dump the *yolk* on top of the butter. Add *1 tablespoon cold water.*

3. With one hand, squeeze the center ingredients into a paste; then gradually knead in the flour until all ingredients are incorporated into a hard rough paste.

TO ROLL OUT:

4. Place your pastry canvas on a worktable. Dust the canvas and the stocking on your rolling pin generously with flour, rubbing it in well with the palm of your hand. With the heel of your hand, press the dough onto the floured canvas, making a circle about ½ inch thick. Now turn the dough to coat the other side with flour. Begin to roll out the dough into a thin circle. Roll from the center of the circle to the outer edge, changing the direction of the rolling pin with each roll. Turn over the circle of dough frequently, making sure that the canvas is lightly coated with flour. If your dough sticks badly, crumble it into a ball and begin again.

LINING THE PIE PLATE:

5. When the dough is rolled out as thinly as possible into a circle about 1 inch larger than your pie plate, place the floured rolling pin across the dough, but a little off center. Flip the wider side of the dough over the rolling pin. Now you're ready to transfer it to your pie plate. Hold the rolling pin at each end, with your thumbs on the dough, and slide pin and dough over the pie plate, a little off center, so that the edge of the dough under the rolling pin rests about 1 inch beyond one edge of the plate. Then flip the dough covering the rolling pin over the other side of the plate. Remove the rolling pin, and gently ease the circle of dough down into the plate, letting it cover the bottom and sides quite loosely. Pat it gently into place with your finger tips.

FLUTING THE EDGE:

6. Trim off edge of pastry with kitchen scissors, leaving ½ inch overhanging. Fold the overhanging edge under itself, thus making a double edge of the dough; press it firmly onto rim of pie plate, still keeping the dough lining the sides of the plate quite loose. Even a slight bulge just below the rim is an asset; since the dough shrinks in the baking, the bulge will keep the pastry from pulling away from the rim. Now push your left forefinger against the outer edge of the pastry rim, and pinch the inside edge of the pastry rim against the forefinger with your other thumb and forefinger. Repeat all around the rim.

7. Chill pastry until ready to bake.

TO PARTIALLY BAKE:

8. Preheat oven to 450° F. Prick bottom and sides of pie shell with tines of a fork. Bake in center of the preheated oven 8 to 10 minutes, or until pastry is set and is beginning to brown around the edges. Remove from oven to cool.

TO COMPLETELY BAKE:

Prick the shell. Bake in preheated oven for 12 to 14 minutes. Remove from oven to cool.

FOR A SEED CRUST:

When pastry is partially rolled into a circle, sprinkle each side generously with *poppy, sesame, caraway,* or *sunflower seeds,* using about *2 tablespoons* in all, then roll the seeds into the dough.

FOR AN HERB CRUST:

Add *1 tablespoon chopped fresh parsley, dill,* or *tarragon—or 1 tea-*

spoon of the dried herb—to the egg-butter mixture before kneading in the flour.

CREAM CHEESE FLAKY PASTRY

For 2 one-crust pies. Another excellent rich, flaky pie dough is made with a mixture of cream cheese and butter.

BUY

8-ounce package fresh cream cheese

HAVE ON HAND	*COOKWARE*
Butter (2 sticks)	Two 9-inch pie plates
Flour	

1. Remove the *cream cheese* and *2 sticks butter* from the refrigerator and let soften for half an hour at room temperature.

2. Slice cream cheese and butter into a mixing bowl, and beat with wooden spoon, or electric beater, until blended and fluffy.

3. Stir, or beat, in *2 level cups flour* (no need to sift), and mix until blended. Chill for at least 3 hours before rolling out and lining pie plate. Cut dough in half. Use half and freeze half, or line two plates and bake one shell and freeze the other. For fluting the edge and baking the shell, see page 50.

QUICHE AU FROMAGE

Serves 6 for lunch, 8 as an appetizer

BUY

½ pound fresh mushrooms
½ pound unprocessed Swiss or Gruyère cheese (imported is best)
1 pint cream

HAVE ON HAND	*COOKWARE*
Ingredients for pastry	9-inch pie plate
Butter	Skillet
6 eggs	
Dry mustard	
Salt and pepper	

IN ADVANCE:

1. Make and partially bake *a 9-inch pie shell.* Cool.

2. Wash, trim, and dry *mushrooms;* slice or dice them. Shred the *½ pound of cheese.* You should have about 2 cups. Set aside.

3. In skillet melt *2 tablespoons butter,* and in it sauté the mushrooms over moderate heat for 5 minutes, stirring frequently. Remove from heat and spread over bottom of partially baked crust. Sprinkle the mushrooms with the shredded cheese.

4. Separate *6 eggs,* reserving the whites for another use, and drop the *yolks* into a mixing bowl. Sprinkle with *½ teaspoon dry mustard* and *¼ teaspoon each salt and pepper.* Gradually beat in *1½ cups cream.*

TO BAKE:

5. Preheat oven to 350° F. Place the prepared pie plate on a baking sheet and pour in the custard. Bake in center of the preheated oven for 35 minutes, or until custard is barely set in center. Remove from the oven and let cool for 10 minutes before cutting and serving. Serve warm or at room temperature.

NOTE: Leftover quiche may be reheated in a 250° F. oven for 10 to 15 minutes. It's better warm than when served directly from the refrigerator.

LEEK AND MUSHROOM TART

Serves 6 for lunch, 8 as an appetizer

BUY

6 large leeks
½ pound fresh mushrooms
8-ounce container heavy cream

HAVE ON HAND	*COOKWARE*
Ingredients for pastry	9-inch pie plate
Salt	Saucepan
Butter	Skillet
Freshly ground black pepper	
Flour	
Grated Parmesan cheese	

IN ADVANCE:

1. Make and partially bake *a 9-inch pie shell*. Cool.

2. Trim root ends of the *leeks* and discard green leaves. Split lengthwise and wash thoroughly, then cut crosswise into 1-inch pieces. Cook in *boiling salted water to barely cover* for 20 minutes, or until almost tender. Drain, reserving *the liquid*.

3. Wash, trim, and dry *mushrooms*. Slice thinly and set aside.

4. In skillet melt *2 tablespoons butter,* and in it sauté the sliced mushrooms for about 5 minutes, stirring frequently, or until cooked. Sprinkle mushrooms with *¾ teaspoon salt* and *lots of pepper*. Sprinkle *3 tablespoons flour* over the mixture and stir well. Gradually stir in *1 cup of the reserved leek liquid* and *½ cup heavy cream*. Cook, stirring, until sauce is smooth and thickened. Stir in the leeks and set aside, partially covered.

TO BAKE:

5. Preheat oven to 350° F. Place pie shell on a baking sheet, and pour in the creamed leeks and mushrooms. Sprinkle with *¼ cup grated Parmesan cheese*. Bake in the center of the preheated oven for 20 minutes. Remove from oven and serve hot.

EGG AND SPINACH TART

Serves 6

BUY
1 pound fresh spinach
8-ounce container sour cream
8-ounce container heavy cream

HAVE ON HAND	*COOKWARE*
Ingredients for pastry	9-inch pie plate
Nutmeg	Large saucepan with cover
Whole-wheat bread	Small skillet
Parmesan cheese	
Butter	
6 eggs	

IN ADVANCE:

1. Make and partially bake *a 9-inch pie shell*. Cool.

2. Wash *spinach* and discard coarse stems and any discolored leaves. Lift spinach directly from water into a large saucepan and cook over high heat, covered, for 5 minutes, or until wilted. Drain well and chop coarsely. Spread spinach over bottom of partially baked pastry and sprinkle with *a pinch of nutmeg*.

3. Crumb *enough bread slices to measure ¾ cup*. Grate *4 tablespoons Parmesan cheese*. Melt *2 tablespoons butter*. In a small bowl toss bread, cheese, and butter together lightly. Set aside.

TO BAKE:

4. Preheat oven to 350° F. Make 6 nests in the spinach; break *1 egg* into each nest. Combine the *sour cream* and *½ cup heavy cream* and pour over the eggs and spinach. Sprinkle with the bread crumb mixture.

5. Bake in the preheated oven for 25 minutes. Serve hot.

QUICHE CIBOULE

Serves 6 for lunch, 8 as an appetizer

BUY

2 large bunches green spring onions
½ pound imported Swiss *or* Gruyère cheese (2 cups, grated)
1 pint light cream *or* half-and-half

HAVE ON HAND	*COOKWARE*
Ingredients for pastry	9-inch pie plate
Butter	Large skillet
Parmesan cheese	
4 eggs	
Salt and pepper	

IN ADVANCE:

1. Make and partially bake *a 9-inch pie shell.* Cool.

2. Wash and trim *green onions,* leaving on the tender green tops; chop *enough to measure 1 cup, firmly packed.* Sauté onions in *3 table-spoons butter* for 5 minutes, or until wilted. Spread on bottom of pie shell.

3. Shred the *Swiss or Gruyère cheese,* and grate *enough Parmesan cheese to measure ¼ cup.* Set aside.

4. Beat *4 eggs* with *¼ teaspoon each salt and pepper.* Stir in *1½ cups light cream or half-and-half* and the shredded cheese.

TO BAKE:

5. Preheat oven to 350° F. Place partially baked pie shell on a baking sheet and fill with the cheese mixture. Sprinkle with the *grated Parmesan.* Bake in the preheated oven for about 40 minutes, or until nicely browned and set.

6. Cut into wedges and serve hot or warm.

ITALIAN GREEN PEPPER TART

Serves 6 for lunch, 8 as an appetizer

BUY

3 long pale-green Italian frying peppers (¾ pound)
6 ounces mozzarella cheese
8 ounces creamed cottage cheese
8-ounce container heavy cream

HAVE ON HAND	*COOKWARE*
Ingredients for pastry	9-inch pie plate
Butter	8-inch skillet
Salt	
Coarsely cracked pepper	
Eggs	

IN ADVANCE:

1. Make and partially bake *a 9-inch pie shell.* Cool.

2. Wash *green peppers,* and discard stems and seeds. Cut into strips ½ inch wide and about 3 inches long. In 8-inch skillet, sauté the peppers in *2 tablespoons butter* for 8 minutes, or until wilted, stirring frequently.

3. With slotted spoon, spread peppers on bottom of partially baked pie shell, then sprinkle with *½ teaspoon salt* and *¼ teaspoon coarsely cracked pepper.* Dice the *mozzarella cheese* and sprinkle over the peppers.

4. Combine *3 eggs,* the *creamed cottage cheese,* and *½ cup heavy cream.* Set aside.

TO BAKE:

5. Preheat oven to 350° F. Place pie shell on baking sheet. Pour cream-cheese-egg mixture over peppers in pie shell and bake in the preheated oven for 45 minutes.

6. Cut into wedges and serve very hot.

ZUCCHINI TART

Use *¾ pound zucchini,* washed and sliced, in place of the peppers.

CAULIFLOWER TART

Serves 6 for lunch, 8 as an appetizer

BUY

¾ pound imported Swiss cheese
8-ounce container heavy cream
Medium head cauliflower

HAVE ON HAND

Ingredients for pastry
Dry bread crumbs
3 egg yolks
Milk
Salt and pepper
Butter

COOKWARE

9-inch pie plate
Saucepan

IN ADVANCE:

1. Make and partially bake *a 9-inch pastry shell*. Cool.

2. Shred the *cheese*—you should have about 3 cups. Mix the cheese with *½ cup dry bread crumbs*, the *heavy cream, 3 egg yolks, ½ cup milk, ½ teaspoon salt, and ¼ teaspoon pepper*. Set aside.

3. Wash *cauliflower* and discard leaves surrounding the head. Cut out and discard the heavy center core and break the cauliflower into bite-size flowerets. Cover with *lightly salted boiling water* and simmer for 15 minutes, or until barely tender. Drain well, then empty cauliflower into pie shell.

TO BAKE:

4. Preheat oven to 350° F. Place pie shell on baking sheet and spoon cheese mixture on top. Dot with *2 tablespoons butter*. Bake in the preheated oven for 30 minutes, or until cheese is lightly browned. Serve hot.

CABBAGE TART

Use *1 small head cabbage*, coarsely shredded (about 1 quart), in place of the cauliflower.

BROCCOLI TART

Use *1 bunch fresh broccoli* in place of the cauliflower.

BRUSSELS SPROUT TART

Use *1 quart Brussels sprouts* in place of the cauliflower.

CELERY TART

Use *1 quart coarsely diced celery* in place of the cauliflower.

Luncheon Soufflé Rolls

Another delicious appetizer—and one which doubles as a delicate luncheon dish—is a savory roll made of a soufflé mixture that is baked in a jelly roll pan and then is allowed to deflate. This fallen soufflé is then spread with a filling and rolled lengthwise like a jelly roll. It may be made early in the day and reheated before serving. Or it may be refrigerated for one to two days, and then reheated. Or you can freeze it and transfer it to the oven directly from the freezer. It will stay fresh in the freezer for several weeks. You may find the soufflé roll a bit difficult to manipulate; see page 305 for a detailed description of how to handle it easily.

The fillings may be made of eggs, cheese, vegetables, or almost any creamed seafood or poultry mixture.

SOUFFLÉ ROLL

Serves 4 for lunch, 6 to 8 as an appetizer

HAVE ON HAND	COOKWARE
Oil	10 x 15-inch jelly roll pan
Waxed paper	Small saucepan
Parmesan cheese	
Butter	
Flour	
Milk *or* half-and-half	
Salt and pepper	
5 eggs	

1. *Oil* the jelly roll pan, line with waxed paper, and oil the paper.

2. Preheat oven to 350° F.

3. Grate *6 tablespoons Parmesan cheese* and set aside.

4. In small saucepan melt *2 tablespoons butter*. Stir in *3 tablespoons flour*. Gradually stir in *1 cup milk or half-and-half*, and cook, stirring, until sauce is smooth and thick. Stir in *½ teaspoon salt, ¼ teaspoon pepper*, and the grated cheese. Remove from heat.

5. At intervals, break *each of the 5 eggs* carefully, emptying the *whites* into a mixing bowl, and beating *each yolk* into the sauce before adding another. Return sauce to heat; cook, stirring rapidly, for 1 minute.

6. Beat egg whites until stiff but still glossy. Beat a big spoonful of the egg whites into the yolk mixture. Now fold the egg yolk mixture gently but thoroughly into the remaining beaten whites.

7. Spread the batter onto the prepared pan evenly and well into the corners.

8. Bake in the preheated oven for exactly 15 minutes.

9. Remove soufflé from oven, cover with waxed paper, and let cool.

10. Make the desired filling; see the three recipes immediately following.

11. To ready the roll for filling, first run a knife around the edge of the pan. Flip the soufflé over onto a long sheet of waxed paper and gently remove the pan, starting at one end and working toward the other. Next, carefully remove the waxed paper from the bottom of the soufflé. You may need the help of a thin knife for, if you didn't oil the waxed paper thoroughly or fold the egg whites completely into the egg yolk mixture, you may have little spots that stick. This won't hurt the final dish at all. Just be persistent.

12. Spread the filling evenly over the soufflé. Then roll the soufflé lengthwise, using the paper underneath to help guide the roll forward. Wrap in foil, sealing the ends well.

BAKE AND SERVE or REFRIGERATE or FREEZE.

TO BAKE:

13. Preheat oven to 350° F. Place the foil-wrapped roll on a baking sheet and bake in the preheated oven for 20 minutes if freshly made or if refrigerated; for 40 to 45 minutes if frozen.

14. Unwrap, slice, and serve hot. Garnish with a dab of sour cream if desired.

CURRIED-EGG FILLING—for Soufflé Roll

HAVE ON HAND

6 eggs
Onion (preferably green scallions)
Dill weed
Dry mustard
Salt and pepper
Curry powder
Mayonnaise
Lemon

1. Hard-cook the *eggs* (page 147). Shell and cool in cold water. Drain and chop.

2. Put chopped eggs into mixing bowl. Add *2 tablespoons finely chopped onion, 1 teaspoon dill weed, ½ teaspoon dry mustard, salt to taste (about ½ teaspoon), ¼ teaspoon pepper, 1 teaspoon curry powder, 6 tablespoons mayonnaise,* and *2 teaspoons lemon juice.* Mix to a moist spread.

MUSHROOM CREAM FILLING—for Soufflé Roll

BUY

¾ pound fresh mushrooms
8-ounce container heavy *or* sour cream

HAVE ON HAND   *COOKWARE*

Medium onion   Skillet
Butter
Flour
Salt
Freshly ground black pepper

1. Wash, trim, and slice the *mushrooms*. Peel and finely chop the *onion*.

2. Sauté onion in *3 tablespoons butter* for 5 minutes, or until tender but not brown. Add mushrooms and cook over moderate heat for 5 minutes, or until tender and most of moisture is cooked away, stirring frequently. Stir in *2 tablespoons flour*. Stir in *¾ cup cream, salt to taste,* and *a good sprinkling of pepper*. Cook, stirring, until mixture is thick.

SPINACH FILLING—for Soufflé Roll

BUY

10-ounce package frozen chopped spinach
6 ounces Swiss *or* Gruyère cheese
8 ounces cream cheese *or* ricotta cheese

HAVE ON HAND	*COOKWARE*
Medium onion	Skillet
Butter	
Salt and pepper	
Nutmeg	
3 eggs	

1. Thaw *spinach* and drain well. Peel and chop *1 medium onion*. Dice the *Swiss or Gruyère cheese*.

2. In skillet heat *3 tablespoons butter,* and in it sauté onion for 5 minutes, or until transparent. Add spinach, *½ teaspoon salt, some freshly ground black pepper,* and *a pinch of nutmeg*. Cook over low heat for 5 minutes, stirring frequently. Remove from heat and stir in *3 eggs,* the diced cheese, and either the *cream cheese* or *ricotta cheese*.

Egg Rolls & Blintzes

We couldn't possibly leave out recipes for Egg Rolls. The first step is making the "skins," and that's a lot of fun. The skins freeze well if you want to keep a supply on hand.

EGG-ROLL SKINS

Makes 36

HAVE ON HAND	*COOKWARE*
Flour	Small skillet *or* crêpe pan, about
4 eggs	6 inches in diameter
Salt	Deep skillet
Butter	

1. In mixing bowl combine *2 cups flour, 2 cups water, 4 eggs,* and *1 teaspoon salt* to make a thin batter.

2. Pour batter into a small pitcher and stir occasionally.

3. Heat a small skillet or crêpe pan and brush lightly with *butter.* Pour in about *2 tablespoons of the batter,* and IMMEDIATELY lift the pan up over the heat and, at the same time, tip it over the pitcher, rotating the pan so that the bottom becomes covered with a thin layer of batter and any excess drains back into the pitcher.

4. Hold the pan over moderate heat for 30 seconds, or until the thin layer of batter, or the "skin," is set, but not brown.

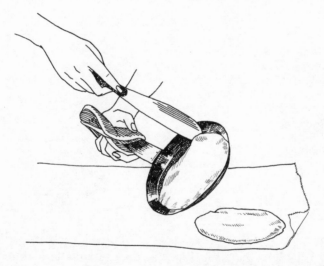

5. Shake out the skin onto a long sheet of waxed paper. Now repeat the process, but first heat the pan again thoroughly, for it is the heat of the pan that sets the batter and cooks the skin without browning it. Line up skins side by side on the waxed paper.

6. When all the skins have been cooked, place another sheet of waxed paper over them. Roll them in the papers so they will stay moist until ready to fill or freeze.

TO FREEZE THE SKINS:

Stack the cool skins with squares of waxed paper between them. Wrap in freezer paper, label, and freeze. To defrost, remove from freezer about 30 minutes before using.

TO MAKE EGG ROLLS

1. Make *desired filling;* see the two recipes immediately following.

2. Combine *1 tablespoon flour* and *2 tablespoons water.*

3. Place about *2 tablespoons of filling* on each skin. Brush edge of skin all around with the flour mixture. Fold in two sides, then roll in a small cylinder. Press the flap edge lightly against the roll in order to seal it.

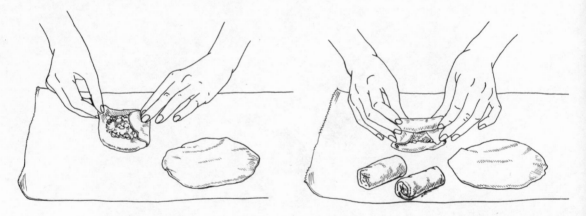

4. Pour *cooking oil* to the depth of about 1 inch in a deep skillet, then heat to very hot (365° F.). Place a few egg rolls at a time in the hot oil; fry, turning once, for about 3 minutes, or until crisp and brown on all sides.

5. Drain on absorbent paper and keep warm in a 250° F. oven until ready to serve. Serve with *Chinese mustard.*

Egg-roll fillings traditionally include either seafood or meat, but here are a couple of meatless variations which make no pretense at being traditional, but are delicious. The first contains soybean curd; you can use either *tofu,* which is packed in water, or *yakidofu,* which is baked. Both types of bean curd are available in cans at Oriental grocery stores or at health-food shops.

SPINACH EGG ROLLS

Makes 18

BUY

10-ounce package frozen chopped spinach
Bunch scallions
4 large mushrooms
5-ounce can water chestnuts
Small jar preserved *or* candied ginger
8-ounce can soybean sprouts
8-ounce container cottage *or* ricotta cheese

HAVE ON HAND   COOKWARE

Soy *or* peanut oil   Skillet
Cornstarch
Salt
Sugar
Soy sauce
18 egg-roll skins

    1. Defrost *spinach* and drain in a sieve, pressing out as much of the liquid as possible. Set aside.

    2. Slice *2 scallions, including tender part of the green stalks.* Wash, trim, and slice *mushrooms.* Drain and chop *water chestnuts* and *2 large pieces ginger.* Drain *soybean sprouts.*

    3. In skillet heat *1 tablespoon cooking oil,* and in it sauté scallions and mushrooms for about 5 minutes, or until vegetables are tender. Stir in *1 teaspoon cornstarch, 1 teaspoon salt, ½ teaspoon sugar,* and *1 tablespoon soy sauce.* Add the spinach and bean sprouts, and cook, stirring, for 2 minutes longer. Remove from heat and stir in the *cheese,* water chestnuts, and ginger. Cool and chill.

    4. Fill the *skins,* roll, and fry (page 64).

MEATLESS EGG ROLLS

Makes 24

BUY

5-ounce can water chestnuts
8-ounce can bamboo shoots
Bunch of green onions
Head of celery
8¾-ounce can soybean curd
4-ounce can mushroom stems and pieces

HAVE ON HAND

Salt
Soy sauce
2 eggs
24 egg-roll skins

1. Chop the *water chestnuts, 2 pieces bamboo shoots, 4 green onions,* and *1 cup celery.*

2. Drain the *soybean curd,* crumble into a mixing bowl, and drain again if necessary. Add the chopped vegetables, *1 teaspoon salt, 2 table-spoons soy sauce, 2 eggs,* and the can of *mushroom stems and pieces,* well drained. Mix well.

3. Fill the *24 skins,* roll, and fry (page 64).

BLINTZES

Egg-Roll Skins are used to make the popular appetizer known as blintzes, and blintzes serve also most palatably as a luncheon dish. *Makes 12*

BUY

8-ounces cottage *or* ricotta cheese
4-ounce can shredded toasted almonds (see Note below)
8-ounce container sour cream

HAVE ON HAND	*COOKWARE*
2 egg yolks	Skillet
Salt	
12 egg-roll skins, fresh *or* defrosted	
1 egg (optional)	
Butter	
Sour cream	
Jam *or* jelly	

1. In mixing bowl combine the *cheese, 2 egg yolks, ¼ cup almonds,* and a *little salt to taste.*

2. Place *1 spoonful cheese mixture* in the center of *each skin.* Fold sides over and roll. Seal edge with a *little beaten egg or some remaining batter.* Chill until ready to cook.

3. Heat *¼ cup butter* in a skillet. Place blintzes in it and sauté over low heat until browned on all sides.

4. Serve hot with *sour cream* and a *little jam or jelly.*

NOTE: You can vary the flavor of this filling by omitting the almonds and substituting *2 tablespoons chopped chives or parsley.*

Crêpes & Other Savory Dishes

Crêpes are just as much fun to make as Egg-Roll Skins. The chief difference is that they are browned lightly on both sides. Crêpes to be stuffed for savory dishes contain no sugar. Otherwise they are exactly the same as those used for desserts. Freeze them the same way as for Egg-Roll Skins (page 64).

THE CRÊPES

Makes 24

HAVE ON HAND	*COOKWARE*
Butter	Small skillet *or* crêpe pan,
3 eggs	5 to 6 inches in diameter
Milk	
Flour	
Salt	
Brandy *or* cognac	

1. Melt *1 tablespoon butter* over low heat, and set aside in warm place.

2. In mixing bowl beat *3 eggs* well. Gradually beat in *1½ cups milk.* Gradually stir in *1 cup flour* and *a pinch of salt,* and continue to stir until batter is smooth. Batter should be just thick enough to coat a spoon.

3. Stir in the melted butter and *1 tablespoon brandy or cognac.* Let the batter stand for 1 to 2 hours before using it, stirring occasionally. Pour into 1-quart measuring cup or pitcher.

4. Heat the skillet until very hot. Crêpes must cook quickly or they will be tough. Put *½ teaspoon butter* in the pan, and swirl the pan to coat bottom and sides with butter.

5. As soon as the butter stops foaming and begins to turn golden brown, raise pan from heat (use pot holder), pour in *about 2 tablespoons crêpe batter,* and again swirl the pan in a circular motion to spread batter evenly and thinly over the bottom. This must be done quickly—before the batter has a chance to set.

6. Return pan to heat and cook crêpe for about 1 minute, or until set and brown on one side. Turn with a spatula and brown other side.

7. Turn crêpe out onto absorbent paper to cool. Repeat until batter is used.

8. When cool, cover the crêpes with waxed paper and roll until ready to fill.

CRÊPES AU FROMAGE

Serves 6 for lunch, 12 as an appetizer

BUY

½ pound imported Swiss *or* Gruyère cheese
8-ounce container heavy cream

HAVE ON HAND

Ingredients for Hollandaise Sauce
   (page 134)
Dry white wine *or* vermouth
Cornstarch
Milk
12 crêpes, freshly made *or* defrosted

COOKWARE

1-quart saucepan
Oblong baking dish

IN ADVANCE:

1. Make *Hollandaise Sauce* and let cool.

2. Shred the *cheese* and put it into the saucepan with *½ cup dry white wine*. Cook over low heat, stirring constantly, until cheese is melted and mixture is smooth.

3. Combine *2 teaspoons cornstarch* and *1 tablespoon milk*. Stir into cheese mixture and cook, stirring, until it comes to a boil. Keep warm over hot water.

4. Arrange crêpes on worktable. Spread each with *about 1½ teaspoons of the cheese mixture* and roll up like a small jelly roll. Arrange rolls side by side in a buttered oblong baking dish or lasagne pan.

TO FINISH:

5. Preheat oven to 425° F.

6. Whip *½ cup cream* and fold into the Hollandaise Sauce.

7. Bake crêpes in the preheated oven for 8 to 10 minutes, or until bubbling hot. Remove from oven and spoon a ribbon of sauce crossways over the crêpes. Return to oven for 1 to 2 minutes, or until sauce is lightly browned.

GNOCCHI PARISIENNE

Serves 6. These delicate dumplings are another favorite appetizer, but they are also hard to top as a hot luncheon dish.

HAVE ON HAND	*COOKWARE*
Butter	2-quart saucepan
Salt	Large kettle
Cayenne pepper	2-quart au gratin *or* baking dish
Flour, all-purpose	Pastry bag and #12 pastry tube
Dry mustard	
Parmesan cheese	
4 eggs	

1. In saucepan combine *4 tablespoons butter, 1 cup water, ¼ teaspoon salt, ⅛ teaspoon cayenne pepper.* Bring slowly to a boil.

2. Meanwhile combine *1 cup all-purpose flour, ½ teaspoon dry mustard,* and *4 tablespoons grated Parmesan.*

3. When liquid is boiling rapidly, dump in flour mixture all at once, and, stirring rapidly with a wooden spoon, raise the pan a few inches above the heat; continue stirring for 30 seconds, or until the paste comes away from the sides of the saucepan and forms a rough ball in the center.

4. Beat in *4 eggs, one at a time,* beating vigorously after each addition until, after the last one, the paste is very shiny. This may be done with an electric beater if you wish.

TO COOK THE GNOCCHI:

5. Measure *4 quarts water* into the large kettle, add *1 tablespoon salt,* and bring to a boil.

6. Meanwhile spoon the paste into a pastry bag fitted with a large plain pastry tube (No. 12). When the water is boiling, reduce heat so it barely simmers. Hold the bag over the boiling water and press out the paste. As the paste is extruded, cut off 1-inch lengths with a knife, letting them drop into the simmering water. They will sink to the bottom, but as they puff and cook they will rise to the surface of the water and float. Cook the gnocchi for about 15 minutes, or until firm, constantly spooning the hot water over them so they remain moist on all sides.

7. Use a slotted spoon to lift the gnocchi out of the simmering water, and place them on paper toweling to drain.

8. Arrange them in a buttered baking dish, cover the dish with waxed paper, and refrigerate.

TO FINISH:

When needed, the gnocchi may simply be sprinkled with *hot melted butter* and *grated Parmesan cheese,* and browned and heated under the broiler. Or they may be sauced with Mornay Sauce as follows:

9. Remove gnocchi from refrigerator. Preheat oven to 350° F. Butter the au gratin dish.

10. Spread *a thin layer of Mornay Sauce* in the dish. Arrange the gnocchi in the dish, and cover with the *remaining sauce.* Bake in the preheated oven for 15 to 20 minutes, or until sauce is bubbling hot.

MORNAY SAUCE

Makes about 2½ cups

HAVE ON HAND	COOKWARE
Milk	Small saucepan
Bay leaves	1-quart saucepan
Onion	
Peppercorns	
Parmesan cheese	
Gruyère *or* Swiss cheese	
Butter	
Flour	
Salt	
Cayenne pepper	
Heavy cream	
Dry mustard	

1. Heat *2 cups milk* to steaming hot in small saucepan with *1 bay leaf, a slice of onion,* and a *few peppercorns.* Grate *3 tablespoons Parmesan cheese,* and shred *1 tablespoon Gruyère or Swiss cheese.* Set these items aside.

2. In a larger saucepan melt *4 tablespoons butter*. Stir in *6 table-spoons flour, ¼ teaspoon salt*, and *a dash of cayenne pepper*. When mixture begins to bubble, remove it from the heat and strain the hot milk into it. Return saucepan to heat and bring to a boil, stirring vigorously.

3. When sauce is smooth and thickened, stir in *2 tablespoons butter*, bit by bit, *½ cup heavy cream, a pinch of dry mustard*, the grated Parmesan and the shredded Gruyère or Swiss cheese. Keep sauce hot over low heat for 5 to 10 minutes.

GOUGÈRE

Slice this cheese puff for an appetizer, or for an accompaniment to soup or salad at lunchtime.

BUY

¼ pound imported Gruyère *or* Swiss cheese
Small wedge of Italian Parmesan cheese

HAVE ON HAND	*COOKWARE*
Butter	2-quart saucepan
Flour	Baking sheet
Cayenne pepper	
Dry mustard	
Salt	
5 large eggs	
Milk	

1. Shred the *Gruyère or Swiss cheese* (you will need enough for 1 cup) and grate *2 tablespoons Parmesan cheese*. Set aside.

2. Combine *1 cup (less 1 tablespoon) flour with ⅛ teaspoon cayenne, ½ teaspoon dry mustard*, and *¼ teaspoon salt*.

3. In saucepan combine *1 cup water* and *½ stick butter*. Bring to a boil over medium heat. When liquid is boiling rapidly, dump in flour mixture all at once, and stir rapidly with a wooden spoon until mixture is smooth and forms a ball in center of the pan.

4. Remove saucepan from heat, and beat in *4 of the eggs,* one at a time, beating well after each addition until a smooth, glossy paste is formed. You can do this in an electric mixer if you wish. Fold in *1 cup shredded cheese and the Parmesan.* Refrigerate paste until ready to bake.

TO BAKE:

5. Preheat oven to 375° F. Butter the baking sheet lightly, and with the tip of a finger trace on it a circle 9 inches in diameter. Spoon the paste over the perimeter of the circle, forming a ring about 2 inches wide and 1 inch high.

6. Beat *1 egg* lightly with *1 tablespoon milk,* and brush over surface of the paste.

7. Bake in the preheated oven for 45 minutes, or until well puffed and golden brown, with no tiny beads of moisture appearing on the surface. Prick the ring in several places with a cake tester or wooden pick to release the steam. Then reduce oven temperature to 300° F. and bake for 10 to 15 minutes longer.

8. Cut into wedges and serve hot.

CROSTINI

If all the preceding recipes are just too much for you, try this easy and delicious finger appetizer. It won't quite make it as a luncheon dish, but it is great served hot as an accompaniment to a salad.

HAVE ON HAND　　　　*COOKWARE*

Sandwich bread　　　　Large skillet
Mozzarella cheese
Salt and pepper
Butter

1. Using a biscuit or cooky cutter, cut slices of *sandwich bread* into rounds about 2½ inches in diameter. Slice the *mozzarella cheese* and cut out half as many cheese rounds as you have bread rounds.

2. Place a cheese round on half of the bread slices, and sprinkle lightly with *pepper and salt*. Cover each with a second bread round, press firmly together, and chill.

3. Just before serving, sauté the crostini in *foaming butter* in a large skillet until lightly browned on both sides.

4. Keep hot in a 250° F. oven until ready to serve.

VEGETABLES—MAIN DISHES
& SIDE DISHES

Vegetables for Vegetables' Sake

How does one do justice to vegetables within the confines of a single chapter? The ways to cook them, the variations and interesting combinations are endless and could fill many books, let alone just one chapter.

I can therefore touch only briefly on the wonderful world of vegetables, giving you a few favorite dishes, stews, and casseroles that are so good one can easily make an entire meal of them with crisp hot bread or homemade muffins.

Select the freshest, youngest vegetables you can buy. There are a few vegetables, such as baking potatoes, in which quality improves with size, and a few others, such as turnips, onions, and parsnips for the soup pot, in which maturity adds dignity, but, in general, the younger and fresher a vegetable is, the more succulent and flavorful. Good vegetables and salad greens are well worth the trouble it takes to seek out a reliable greengrocer who carries a large selection and keeps his produce moist and cool. They are worth many trips to country roadside stands during the growing season and the fall harvest. Once you have bought them, it is up to YOU to keep them moist and fresh in the refrigerator until you are ready to cook them.

Fresh vegetables are powerhouses of vitamins and minerals IF they are not boiled to death in massive quantities of water. To insure minimum loss of nutrients, either steam them, or cook them in the least amount of water for the least amount of time it takes to make them just fork tender.

HOW TO COOK MOST VEGETABLES
FOR BEST FLAVOR

Wash scrape, peel, trim, or otherwise prepare vegetables carefully. Leave small young vegetables whole or halve them. Slice larger vegetables or cut into thin julienne strips.

Use a heavy saucepan with a tight-fitting lid. Put the prepared vegetables into it with *2 to 3 tablespoons butter* and *an equal amount of water.* Cover tightly and steam over moderate heat, shaking the pan occasionally, for no more than 5 to 8 minutes, or until just tender.

Empty vegetables into a warm serving dish, and sprinkle with *salt and pepper* (try white pepper for a change some time). *A squeeze of lemon juice* is good on such vegetables as cabbage, spinach, cauliflower, or Brussels sprouts.

Vegetable Dinners

BASIC VEGETABLE DINNER

Serves 6. Serve with hot crusty French bread or garlic bread. Begin with the basic vegetables that are included in a New England boiled dinner: potatoes, carrots, whole onions, celery. If beets or cabbage are used, they should be cooked separately. From there you can go on to a great variety of other vegetables, depending on the best and freshest available. This dinner provides a bonus—about 2 quarts of rich vegetable broth.

BUY

Basic vegetables: potatoes, carrots, onions, celery
Leeks (if possible)
1-pound, 12-ounce can whole tomatoes
A selection of *long-cooking* vegetables, such as: yellow turnips, parsnips,
   celery root, Jerusalem artichokes, winter squash, pumpkin
A selection of *quick-cooking* vegetables, such as: beets, cabbage, zucchini,
   summer squash, peas, green beans, cauliflower, broccoli, Brussels
   sprouts, eggplant, kohlrabi, mushrooms, white turnips, okra
Fresh parsley, dill, tarragon, *or* chives

HAVE ON HAND	COOKWARE
Garlic	5- to 6-quart kettle
Olive oil	
Butter	
Salt	
Bay leaves	
Lemon	
Coarsely ground pepper	
Dried marjoram *or* tarragon	
Dry white wine (optional)	
Cayenne pepper	

1. Peel and coarsely chop *2 medium onions* and *1 clove garlic.* Wash
and chop *3 outer stalks with leaves from a bunch of celery* and *2 leeks.*

2. In the kettle, heat *2 tablespoons each olive oil and butter* and in
it sauté the prepared vegetables until lightly browned. Add *tomatoes
with liquid, 1 tablespoon salt, 2 bay leaves, 1 lemon, sliced, ½ teaspoon
coarsely ground pepper, ½ teaspoon marjoram or tarragon,* and *4 quarts
water (or 3 quarts water and 1 bottle dry white wine).* Bring to a boil,
then simmer for 30 minutes.

3. While broth is simmering, prepare the *long-cooking vegetables:*
Peel potatoes and onions and leave them whole. Scrape carrots and leave
them whole, too, or cut in half lengthwise. Cut *remaining stalks of the
bunch of celery* into 6 lengthwise slices. Peel any other long-cooking
vegetables and cut into large chunks. You should have about 2 quarts of
cut-up vegetables in all. Add them to the simmering broth and simmer
for 1 hour.

4. Meanwhile prepare the *quick-cooking vegetables,* and cut into bite-
size slices or chunks.

5. When the long-cooking vegetables are almost tender, add the quick-cooking vegetables and return broth to a simmer. Correct seasoning of the broth with salt, add a *little cayenne,* and continue to simmer for 15 to 20 minutes.

6. To serve, spoon the vegetables out of the pot into a large tureen, then moisten them with a *little of the pot liquor.* Sprinkle with *chopped parsley,* or serve with *melted butter* to which is added *chopped parsley, dill, tarragon,* or *chives.*

NOTE: The remaining pot liquor makes an ideal vegetable broth. It will keep in the refrigerator for 3 or 4 days, or can be poured into containers and frozen.

HORSERADISH CREAM SAUCE

Makes 1½ cups. For a Vegetable Dinner New England style.

In saucepan melt *3 tablespoons butter.* Add *3 tablespoons flour* and cook, stirring, until mixture is blended and bubbling. Remove saucepan from heat, add *1 cup of the hot vegetable broth,* stirring vigorously. Return to heat and cook, stirring, until sauce is smooth and thick. Stir in *½ cup cream* and *fresh grated or preserved horseradish to taste (from ¼ to ½ cup).*

AÏOLI SAUCE

Makes 1 cup. For a Vegetable Dinner French style.

Peel and mash *5 or 6 large cloves garlic* and beat into *1 cup mayonnaise.* (If you have an electric blender, put garlic and mayonnaise into blender jar, stir to combine, and blend at high speed for 10 seconds.)

SKORDALIA SAUCE

Makes 2 cups. For a Vegetable Dinner Greek style.

Cook *4 large potatoes* in boiling water until very soft. Drain and mash with *8 peeled and crushed cloves garlic.* Gradually beat in *1 cup olive oil, juice of 2 lemons,* adding the olive oil and lemon juice alternately in very small amounts, stirring briskly. Season to taste with *salt and pepper,* and continue to stir in rotary motion until sauce is stiff enough to hold its shape.

VEGETABLE DINNER INDIAN STYLE

Tie in a small cloth bag *a small piece root ginger* and *1 tablespoon each coriander and fennel seeds.* Add the spice bag to the simmering broth (step 2 of Basic Vegetable Dinner), and simmer for 20 minutes. Discard spice bag before adding vegetables. When vegetable dinner is cooked, serve with:

CURRY SAUCE

Makes about 1 quart

In saucepan heat *4 tablespoons butter,* and in it sauté *1 small minced onion, 1 minced clove garlic,* and *2 tablespoons curry powder* for 2 to 3 minutes. Stir in *4 tablespoons flour.* Gradually stir in *3 cups of the hot vegetable broth* and cook, stirring, until sauce is slightly thickened. Stir in *3 tablespoons seedless raisins* and *3 tablespoons chopped pistachio nuts,* and simmer for 15 minutes, stirring frequently. Add *salt and cayenne pepper to taste,* and just before serving stir in *½ cup heavy cream.*

GHIVETCH

Serves 6. This is a traditional Romanian vegetable casserole which is baked in a moderate oven until most of the liquid has evaporated and the vegetables are tender. One does not eat it immediately, but rather allows it to cool so that the vegetables have time to blend and ripen. It is then served cold or at room temperature, or it may be reheated before serving. I hesitate to give a specific recipe for this dish, for it all depends on what vegetables are in season. In the spring, take advantage of the young fresh peas, tender new carrots and potatoes, stalks of asparagus, slim green beans. In the fall months you can use as many of the root vegetables as you can find and combine them with both hard and summer squashes, cabbage, cauliflower, and so on.

Here is just one version. Use your imagination for many others.

BUY
Selection of vegetables in season

HAVE ON HAND	COOKWARE
4 or 5 large tomatoes, fresh or canned	Heavy 4-quart casserole or clay pot
Onions	Skillet
Garlic	
Butter	
White wine *or* chicken broth	
Salt and pepper	
Olive *or* corn oil	

1. Fill the large casserole or clay pot with a *large selection of vegetables,* such as: sliced *carrots* and *parsnips;* peeled and diced *potatoes; Jerusalem artichokes;* a small *eggplant,* peeled and diced; a *green pepper,* seeded and cut into strips; *half a head of cabbage or cauliflower,* cut into chunks; *a summer squash* or *a couple of zucchini,* sliced; *sliced stalks of celery or fennel,* or *a celery root,* peeled and diced; *an acorn or butternut squash,* peeled, seeded, and cut into chunks.

2. To the mixed vegetables add *4 or 5 tomatoes,* fresh or canned, cut into sections.

3. Now peel and slice *2 large onions* and *2 large cloves of garlic.*

4. In a skillet heat ½ *stick butter,* and in it sauté the onions and garlic until lightly browned. Add ½ *cup white wine and* ½ *cup water, or 1 cup chicken broth,* and *salt and pepper to taste.* Bring to a boil. Add ½ *cup olive oil or corn oil,* and bring again to a simmer. Pour the hot broth and the onions and garlic over the vegetables in the casserole.

5. Cover casserole tightly and bake in a preheated 350° F. oven for 30 to 40 minutes, or until most of the liquid has evaporated.

6. Remove from oven, and LET COOL to room temperature before serving, or before reheating.

Mixed Deep-Fried Vegetables

FRITTO MISTO

In Italy, quick-fried foods are a specialty. They may be served as a simple first course, as an accompaniment to a main dish, or as a meal in themselves. *Fritto Misto,* or mixed fry, is an impressive array of bite-size tidbits—a variety of meats, fish, cheeses, and vegetables—quickly fried to golden crispness in deep fat. It is a dish which invites you to use your imagination in selecting the plain, unusual, and exotic foods that you choose to serve. If you wish, you may certainly make the assortment strictly vegetarian by eliminating such traditional items as chicken livers, thin slices of veal, veal kidneys, sweetbreads, and so on. A *Fritto Misto* of only vegetables and cheese is a delicious simple dish.

Prepare the ingredients well in advance. This leaves only the quick cooking to be done when it is time to eat. Everything should be cut or broken into bite-size pieces. Cauliflowerets, broccoli, carrot sticks, string beans, Brussels sprouts, and other hard vegetables should be parboiled in salted water for about 5 minutes, then well-drained. Eggplant and green peppers should be cut into julienne strips; they need no precooking. Cut Camembert, Gruyère, or Swiss cheese into squares or strips.

BUY

A variety of vegetables and cheeses, and other foods if you wish

HAVE ON HAND	*COOKWARE*
Salt and pepper	Frite pan *or* deep-fat fryer
Flour	Baking sheet
Cayenne pepper	
2 eggs	
Beer or milk	
Vegetable oil	
Lemons	
Parsley	

1. Prepare the *foods to be fried* as described in introduction to recipe. Sprinkle them lightly with *salt and pepper,* cover with transparent film, and refrigerate until ready to cook.

2. In mixing bowl, combine *1½ cups flour, 1 teaspoon salt,* and *⅛ teaspoon cayenne pepper.* In another small bowl combine *2 eggs, 1 cup beer or milk,* and *2 tablespoons vegetable oil.* Stir liquid ingredients into dry ingredients to make a smooth batter. Cover and refrigerate until ready to use. Stir frequently during use.

3. To cook: Fill a frite pan or deep-fat fryer one-third full of vegetable oil. Lower the basket into the pan and heat the oil to 365° F.

4. Dip a couple of pieces of each of the foods into the batter and fry for about 2 minutes, or until golden brown. Raise the basket and let the excess oil drain off. Empty fried tidbits onto a baking sheet lined with absorbent paper, and keep warm in a low, 200° F., oven until ready to serve; or serve them to one person at a time. Garnish with *wedges of lemon* and *sprigs of parsley.*

TEMPURA

If you choose to deep fry such vegetables as sliced lotus root, *shiitake* mushrooms, snow peas, water chestnuts, bamboo shoots, and soybean curd, the method is the same as for *Fritto Misto* in the preceding recipe, but you will be leaving Italy far behind and entering the fascinating world of Japanese cuisine. Japanese *tempura* does not mean simply batter-fried butterflied shrimp; it encompasses a large assortment of edible plain and exotic tidbits, which generally do include shrimp as well as oysters and small boneless pieces of fish.

Tempura is served hot, with one or more traditional dipping sauces. These sauces include a fish stock called *dashi,* which is distilled from seaweed and dried bonito.

TEMPURA SAUCE

Combine *1 cup dashi or dashi substitute* (see following recipes), *¼ cup soy sauce,* and *¼ cup saki* (rice wine). Serve in small individual dipping bowls.

DASHI
(Japanese Fish Stock)

BUY

Small square seaweed (*kombu*)
Package dried bonito (*kanakatsuo* or *katsuobushi*)

Wash *seaweed* and put it into a saucepan with *4 cups water.* Bring water to a boil and boil for 2 minutes. Remove seaweed. Add *4 tablespoons bonito* to the rapidly boiling liquid, remove saucepan immediately from heat, and let liquid settle for 1 minute. Strain off the stock; this is dashi.

DASHI SUBSTITUTE

Combine *½ cup beef bouillon, or broth or water in which mushrooms have been simmered,* with *2 tablespoons sherry or saki, 2 tablespoons sugar,* and *¼ cup soy sauce.* Use this mixture in place of the dashi in Tempura Sauce.

SWEET AND SOUR DASHI SAUCE

In small saucepan, combine *½ cup dashi or dashi substitute, ½ cup water, 2 teaspoons soy sauce, ½ teaspoon salt, 2 tablespoons cider vinegar, and ½ teaspoon sugar.* Cook and stir over moderate heat until mixture simmers and becomes clear.

DEEP-FRIED SOY-BEAN CURD

BUY	*HAVE ON HAND*
8 ¾-ounce cans (drained weight) baked soybean curd (*yakidofu*)	1 egg white
Fresh ginger root	Fresh bread

1. Drain *bean curd*. Each can contains three ½-inch-thick slices, 4 x 2 inches. Place the curd between plates with a heavy weight on top for 1 hour to press out excess liquid, then cut each slice into 8 oblongs 2 inches long and ½ inch wide.

2. Peel the *ginger root,* wrap in transparent film, and refrigerate.

3. Crumb *2 slices white bread.* Combine *1 egg white* and *1½ teaspoons water.*

4. Dip the pieces of bean curd into the diluted egg white, then roll in bread crumbs.

5. Fry curd in *deep oil,* heated to 365° F., for 2 minutes or until lightly browned.

6. Drain on absorbent paper, and serve hot with a spoonful of Sweet and Sour Dashi Sauce and a sprinkling of grated fresh ginger. Serve with Tempura.

Vegetables from Artichokes to Zucchini

ARTICHOKES

One of the vegetables that many people seem to be puzzled about preparing is the artichoke, which is such a delicious vegetable served either hot or cold, as an appetizer, luncheon dish, or salad course.

Buy fresh-looking green globe artichokes with tightly closed leaves. Cut the stem off each artichoke close to the bottom to give it a steady base on which to sit. Remove a row or two of the large outer leaves, for these are tough and fibrous and have little edible meat in them. Then, with a heavy sharp knife, slice off about 1 inch from the top of the artichoke, or trim the prickly point off each leaf with kitchen scissors.

TO COOK:

Stand the artichokes on their bases in a large kettle and just cover with *cold water*. For *4 to 6 artichokes*, add *1 tablespoon salt*, the *juice of ½ lemon* and, if desired, *a cut clove of garlic*.

Bring liquid to a boil, cover kettle, then simmer over low heat for 45 minutes. When a leaf is pulled easily from the base, or a fork easily penetrates the bottom of the artichokes, they are cooked. Turn off the heat and let them rest in the hot water until ready to serve. They will keep hot for at least half an hour.

With a slotted spoon lift the artichokes, one at a time, out of the water; drain them upside down on a cake rack set into the sink. Squeeze each one gently to drain it completely before setting it upright on a serving plate. Serve hot or cold.

When artichokes are served cold, they are generally accompanied by Sauce Vinaigrette (page 127) or Garlic Mayonnaise (page 149). When served hot, they are equally good with these same sauces or with a hot butter-lemon juice sauce seasoned with salt and pepper, and, often, with finely minced garlic.

TO EAT ARTICHOKES:

Pluck off a leaf and dip into the sauce. Eat only the tender base of each leaf, scraping off the soft pulp with the teeth, until you come down to the choicest morsel, the artichoke bottom. This is covered with tiny leaves folded tightly around furry filaments known as the choke. Cut or scrape away the choke; then cut the artichoke bottom into bite-size pieces, and dip these into the sauce before enjoying each delicious bite.

ARTICHOKES BRAISED WITH VEGETABLES

Serves 4

BUY

4 globe artichokes
1 head lettuce
1 pound fresh peas *or* 2 cups canned
1 head celery
1 small head fennel
1 carrot
8 small new potatoes
1 large ripe tomato

HAVE ON HAND

Butter
Garlic
Dry white wine
Salt
Coarsely ground pepper

COOKWARE

Large heavy casserole with cover

1. Trim stems from the *artichokes,* remove 2 rows of lower outer leaves, and cut off 2 inches from tops. Separate the leaves, wash well, and scoop out the pale yellow leaves and the furry choke from center of the artichokes with a metal spoon.

2. *Butter* the casserole. Wash and shred the *lettuce,* and arrange in the bottom of the dish. Place the artichokes upright on the bed of lettuce.

3. Shell the *peas,* or drain the canned. Remove outer stalks from the *celery* (and reserve for Creamed Celery with Toasted Almonds or some

other use). Chop the heart of celery. Chop the *fennel,* scrape and slice the *carrot,* and peel the *potatoes.* Cut the *tomato* into wedges. Peel and mince *1 clove garlic.* Fill the center of the artichokes with the peas. Then surround the artichokes with the celery, fennel, carrot, potatoes, and tomato. Sprinkle with the *minced garlic.*

4. Add *1 cup dry white wine, 2 cups water, 2 teaspoons salt,* and *½ teaspoon coarsely ground pepper.* Place casserole over heat and bring liquid to a boil. Then cover and cook over low heat for about 1 hour, or until artichokes are tender.

5. Serve one artichoke per person; surround it with some of the vegetables and moisten with some of the cooking liquid.

Note: Any remaining liquid makes a wonderful broth for meatless soups or casseroles.

BROCCOLI AU GRATIN

Serves 4. Other vegetables, such as white turnips, cabbage, parsnips, carrots, kohlrabi, Jerusalem artichokes, cauliflower, or Brussels sprouts, may be substituted for the broccoli.

BUY

1 bunch broccoli, about 1½ pounds
8-ounce container heavy cream

HAVE ON HAND	COOKWARE
Salt	2-quart saucepan
Milk	Shallow baking dish
Butter	Small saucepan
Flour	1½-quart saucepan
White pepper	
Parmesan cheese, grated	
Bread crumbs	

1. Discard lower tough portions of broccoli stalks, and cut stalks and flowerheads into thin slices. Put the slices into the large saucepan with *2 cups water* and *½ teaspoon salt.* Bring liquid to a boil and simmer for

10 minutes, or until broccoli is just fork-tender. Drain well and empty broccoli into a shallow baking dish.

2. In the small saucepan heat *2 cups milk* to simmering.

3. In the medium saucepan melt *6 tablespoons butter.* Stir in *6 tablespoons flour,* and cook, stirring, until mixture bubbles. Remove saucepan from heat and let mixture cool for a moment. Then add the hot milk, all at once, and stir vigorously with a wire whisk or wooden spoon until sauce is smooth. Return to heat; cook, stirring well from bottom and sides of pan, for about 3 minutes, or until sauce is thickened. Stir in *cream, a dash of white pepper,* and about *1 teaspoon salt or to taste.* Pour sauce over broccoli.

4. Combine *2 tablespoons grated cheese* and *½ cup bread crumbs.* Sprinkle crumbs over surface of the sauce and dot with *2 tablespoons butter.* Set aside until ready to cook.

5. To bake: Preheat oven to 375° F. Bake the broccoli for 20 minutes, or until the top is crusty and golden and the sauce is bubbling.

SWEET AND SOUR RED CABBAGE

Serves 6 to 8

You need a large saucepan for this dish, for it's amazing how much shredded cabbage you'll get from one head. This does wilt considerably as it cooks. The recipe may be halved, but you might as well cook the whole head of cabbage while it is fresh, rather than reserving half of it; the cooked dish is just as good reheated for another meal.

BUY

1 crisp red cabbage, medium size
2 tart apples

HAVE ON HAND

1 medium onion
Sugar, granulated *or* brown
Cooking oil
Red wine vinegar

Caraway seeds
Salt and pepper
Dry red wine *or* water
Lemon

COOKWARE

5-quart saucepan *or* kettle, with cover

1. Remove any discolored or wilted leaves from *cabbage*. Quarter cabbage and discard white core. Shred cabbage finely. You'll have about 8 cups.

2. Chop *1 medium onion*. Peel, quarter, core, and slice the *apples*.

3. Measure *4 tablespoons sugar* and *4 tablespoons oil* into saucepan or kettle. Place over moderate heat and cook until sugar turns caramel in color. Turn heat to low, add onion and cook until onion is golden, stirring frequently.

4. Add the shredded cabbage, the sliced apples, *4 tablespoons vinegar, 1 teaspoon caraway seeds, 2 teaspoons salt, ½ teaspoon pepper,* and *1 cup dry red wine.* Bring to a boil, then cover and cook over low heat for 40 minutes, stirring occasionally.

5. Correct seasoning with *salt*. Add a *little more sugar* if cabbage is not sweet enough, and *a squeeze of lemon juice* (a good last-minute addition to many vegetables).

VITAMIN CARROTS

Serves 4. You may use this recipe for 1½ quarts of any shredded root vegetable such as parsnips, white or yellow turnips, celery root, kohlrabi, Jerusalem artichokes, and so on.

BUY

10 large fresh carrots

HAVE ON HAND

Butter
Salt
White peppercorns

COOKWARE

1½-quart casserole

1. Wash, scrape, and shred the *carrots*.

2. Preheat oven to 350° F.

3. Put the carrots into the casserole and add *1 stick butter, a sprinkling of salt, lots of freshly ground white pepper,* and *½ cup water.*

4. Cover the casserole tightly and bake in the preheated oven for 30 minutes.

BRAISED CELERY OR BELGIAN ENDIVE

Serves 4

BUY

2 heads Pascal celery *or* 8 roots of Belgian endive

HAVE ON HAND	COOKWARE
Butter	Large heavy skillet
Salt	
Pepper	
Lemon	
Parmesan cheese	

1. Remove the coarse outer stalks of the *celery* and the large celery leaves from the top, and reserve for the soup pot. Wash the remaining head well and cut into quarters lengthwise. Or, if using *endive,* trim the root ends, and wash.

2. In skillet melt *2 tablespoons butter,* and in it arrange the stalks of celery or endive. Sprinkle with *½ teaspoon salt* and *¼ teaspoon pepper.* Add the *juice of 1 lemon* and *1 cup water.* Bring liquid to a boil, cover tightly, and cook over low heat for about 40 minutes, or until most of the moisture has cooked away.

4. Remove endive or celery to serving dish and pour over any butter and juices left in the skillet. Serve with *grated Parmesan* on the side.

CREAMED CELERY WITH TOASTED ALMONDS

Serves 6

BUY

1 head of celery
Bunch of green onions
1 container light cream
Toasted slivered almonds

HAVE ON HAND	*COOKWARE*
Butter	10-inch skillet with cover
Flour	
Milk	
Salt and pepper	
Worcestershire sauce	

1. Wash and trim the *celery* and separate into stalks. Cutting on the diagonal, thinly slice enough stalks to measure 4 cups. Wash and trim *green onions* and cut about 4, including green tops, into 1-inch diagonal pieces. They should measure about ½ cup.

2. In large skillet melt *4 tablespoons butter*. Add celery slices and toss them until coated with the melted butter; then cover and cook over low heat, stirring occasionally, for 10 minutes. Do not overcook. The celery should remain crisp.

3. Stir in the green onions, then cover and cook for 5 minutes.

4. Sprinkle the vegetables with *2 tablespoons flour*. Gradually stir in *1 cup milk,* and cook, stirring, until sauce has thickened and simmered for 1 minute.

5. Stir in *½ teaspoon salt, a good dash pepper, ½ teaspoon Worcestershire sauce,* and *½ cup light cream*. Heat to simmering.

6. Spoon into serving dish and sprinkle with *½ cup toasted almonds*.

FRESH FROM THE CORN PATCH

Whether you buy fresh corn from a local roadside stand or at your market, be sure the kernels are plump and shiny—then waste no time in getting it home and into the pot. If it is not going to be cooked immediately, dip the ears, husks and all, into cold water, wrap them in a towel, and store in the refrigerator.

Don't strip the corn of its husks until the water is boiling. And don't be like the bride who was in tears when her husband arrived home for dinner, because she had been boiling sweet corn all afternoon and couldn't get it tender. Corn should NEVER be boiled, only simmered for a brief time. Corn kernels are plump with corn milk. When the milk is boiled it will curdle and the corn is going to be tough.

CORN ON THE COB

Bring a large kettle of water to a rapid boil. Shuck *fresh ears of sweet corn* and drop them into the boiling water. This will stop the boiling. Allow the water to come back to a simmer, then turn off the heat, cover the kettle, and let the corn poach in the hot water 5 to 8 minutes. Actually, it may remain in the water longer without drastic deterioration, as the water will gradually cool.

It's quite permissible to serve one round of ears and allow the rest to remain in the hot water for second servings. It's better to keep it moist and warm than to allow it to cool and dry on the table. Serve the corn with *sweet butter* and *salt and pepper* on the side.

CORN COOKED IN CREAM

Cut *enough fresh corn kernels from the cobs to fill a small casserole. Butter* the casserole, fill with the corn, and sprinkle with a *little salt and freshly ground pepper.* Pour over *enough cream to almost cover the corn,* and top with *buttered crumbs*. Bake in a preheated 375° F. oven for 30 minutes, or until the top is browned.

VARIATION: Substitute *unpeeled yellow squash,* cut into ½-inch-thick slices, for the corn.

CORN PURÉE

Cook *fresh ears of corn* in simmering water for 5 minutes only. Plunge ears into cold water to cool them enough to make them easy to handle. Cut down through the rows of kernels with a sharp knife, splitting each kernel open. Then press out the corn purée or pulp with the back of the knife or with the side of a fork.

To *each cup of corn purée* add *2 tablespoons butter* and *salt and pepper to taste.* Cook over steaming water, stirring constantly, until purée is hot. Serve immediately.

FRESH CORN PUDDING

Serves 3 or 4

HAVE ON HAND	COOKWARE
2 cups corn purée (see preceding recipe)	1½-quart casserole
Butter	2-quart saucepan
Flour	
Thin cream *or* half-and-half	
Salt	
Black peppercorns	
3 egg whites	

1. Preheat oven to 375° F. *Butter* the casserole.

2. In saucepan melt *2 tablespoons butter*. Stir in *2 tablespoons flour.* Gradually stir in *1½ cups thin cream or half-and-half,* and cook, stirring, until sauce is thickened.

3. Stir in *2 cups corn purée, 1 teaspoon salt,* and *freshly ground pepper to taste.* Heat just to a simmer.

4. Beat *3 egg whites* until stiff but not dry. Fold into the corn mixture. Pour into the prepared casserole and bake in the preheated oven for 40 minutes.

EGGPLANT PARMIGIANA

Serves 4. This recipe may be doubled. Serve with salad and crusty bread.

BUY

1 medium eggplant
1 green pepper
8-ounce can tomato sauce
6- *or* 8-ounce package mozzarella cheese

HAVE ON HAND

Onion
Garlic
Flour
Salt and pepper
Olive oil
Parmesan cheese, freshly grated

COOKWARE

10 x 6 x 1½-inch baking dish
8-inch skillet

1. Peel and slice the *eggplant* ½ inch thick. One medium eggplant should give you 8 nice thick slices. Sprinkle slices with salt, stack them one on top of the other, and place a heavy weight on top for half an hour to draw out any bitter juices.

2. Meanwhile peel and chop *enough onion to measure ½ cup.* Seed and chop about *enough green pepper to make ½ cup.* Peel and mince *1 large clove garlic.* Set vegetables aside.

3. Measure *¼ cup flour, ½ teaspoon salt,* and *¼ teaspoon pepper* onto a piece of waxed paper, and mix well. Wash eggplant slices and dry between paper towels. Coat slices on both sides with the flour mixture.

4. Measure *½ cup olive oil.* Pour *2 tablespoons of this oil* into skillet, and heat to moderate temperature. Sauté the eggplant, over moderate

heat, about 2 slices at a time, until golden on both sides. Add oil to skillet as needed. Drain eggplant on absorbent paper.

5. Add *any remaining oil* to skillet, and in it sauté the onion, green pepper, and garlic over low heat for 5 minutes. Stir in *tomato sauce,* and simmer for 5 minutes. Correct seasoning with *additional salt and pepper.*

6. Spoon *half the sauce* into the baking dish, and top it with the eggplant slices. Cover with *slices of mozzarella cheese,* and spoon *remaining sauce* on top. Sprinkle with *3 tablespoons freshly grated Parmesan.* Set aside until ready to bake.

7. Preheat oven to 350° F. Bake the eggplant, uncovered, in the moderate oven for 30 minutes.

CURRIED EGGPLANT

Serves 6. Serve over cooked rice.

BUY

2 pounds eggplant
1 green *or* red sweet pepper
4 ripe tomatoes

HAVE ON HAND	COOKWARE
Onions	Large heavy skillet, with cover
Garlic	
Butter	
Turmeric	
Powdered ginger	
Dried red pepper	
Salt	

1. Wash and peel the *eggplant* and cut into 2-inch cubes. Peel and thinly slice *2 large onions* and *2 cloves garlic.* Wash, seed, and chop *½ green pepper (or ½ red sweet pepper).* Peel and slice the *tomatoes.*

2. In skillet melt *4 tablespoons butter.* Add the eggplant cubes, *1 teaspoon turmeric, ½ teaspoon powdered ginger,* and *¼ teaspoon dried red pepper.* Sauté over moderate heat, stirring frequently, for 10 minutes.

3. Add onions, garlic, chopped green or red sweet pepper, and *1 cup water,* and cook over high heat until most of the water has evaporated.

4. Add the tomatoes and *salt to taste.* Mix well, cover tightly, and cook over very low heat for 15 minutes, or until vegetables are tender, shaking the skillet occasionally.

VEGETABLE BROTH WITH BRAISED LEEKS OR ZUCCHINI

Makes about 1 quart

BUY

7 large fresh leeks *or* 4 medium zucchini
1-pound can whole tomatoes *or* 6-ounce can tomato paste

HAVE ON HAND

Onion
Garlic
Celery
Carrot
Parsley
Butter
Salt and pepper
Bay leaves
Lemon
Thyme
Dry white wine *or* dry vermouth (optional)

COOKWARE

Heavy 10-inch skillet *or* chicken fryer, *or* wide top-of-the-stove casserole

1. Peel and coarsely chop *1 medium onion* and *1 clove garlic.* Wash and chop *2 outer stalks celery with leaves.* If you are not using zucchini, also wash and chop the *white part of 1 leek.* Scrape and chop *1 carrot,* and chop *¼ cup parsley.*

2. In the heavy pan heat *2 tablespoons butter,* and in it sauté the prepared vegetables until lightly browned. Add *entire contents of the can of tomatoes or 2 tablespoons tomato paste, 1 teaspoon salt, ¼ teaspoon pepper, 1 bay leaf, 2 slices lemon, ¼ teaspoon thyme,* and *2 quarts water or 7 cups water and 1 cup dry white wine or dry vermouth.* Bring liquid to a boil, partially cover the pan, and simmer for 40 minutes.

3. If leeks are used, discard the root ends and any withered outer leaves from the *remaining leeks*. Cut off tough green stalks, leaving the leeks no more than 6 inches long. Slit the tops of the leeks lengthwise; then wash thoroughly under cold running water, spreading leaves apart to remove any sand trapped in them. If *zucchini* are used, trim them at both ends, then slice them thickly.

4. Add the leeks or zucchini to the simmering broth, and partially cover the pan. Simmer leeks for 40 minutes; zucchini for 20 minutes.

5. Remove the leeks or zucchini, and serve hot with melted butter, or chill and serve covered with Sauce Vinaigrette (page 127).

6. Strain the broth. It will keep in the refrigerator for 4 or 5 days. Or pour into freezer containers and freeze for future use.

BREADED MUSHROOMS

Serves 4. A marvelous hot appetizer before almost any meal, or a good vegetable accompaniment to a sauced dish.

BUY

24 medium mushrooms, about 1 ounce each (1½ pounds)

HAVE ON HAND	*COOKWARE*
Salt	10-inch skillet
Pepper	
1 egg	
Flour	
Cornflake crumbs	
Butter	
Tartar sauce	

1. Wash the *mushrooms* and trim off their stems close to the caps. Reserve stems for another recipe. Drain the mushrooms, cap side up, on absorbent paper, and sprinkle lightly with *salt and pepper*.

2. Beat the *egg* in a shallow dish with *1 tablespoon water*.

3. Roll the mushrooms in *flour* to coat them evenly, then coat them evenly in the *egg mixture*. Place mushrooms on waxed paper covered with *cornflake crumbs*. Sprinkle them well with more crumbs, and turn mush-

rooms over and around to coat them heavily. Set coated mushrooms aside for 30 minutes or longer to dry.

4. When ready to cook, melt *4 tablespoons butter* in skillet. Place mushrooms in the hot butter, cap side down, and sauté over moderate heat for about 3 minutes, or until brown and crisp. Turn and continue to cook for about 3 minutes longer, or until brown and crisp on both sides.

5. Serve with *tartar sauce.*

MUSHROOMS PAPRIKASH

Serves 4

BUY

1 pound fresh mushrooms
8-ounce container sour cream

HAVE ON HAND

1 small onion
Butter
Paprika (preferably Hungarian)
Salt
Cayenne pepper
Milk *or* light cream (optional)

COOKWARE

10-inch skillet with cover

1. Clean, trim, and slice the *mushrooms.* Set aside.

2. Peel and finely chop *1 small onion,* then sauté in *4 tablespoons butter* until golden.

3. Sprinkle the onion with *1 tablespoon paprika, ½ teaspoon salt,* and *⅛ teaspoon cayenne pepper.* Add mushrooms, cover, and cook over low heat for 6 to 8 minutes.

4. Stir in the *sour cream,* bring to a boil, and turn off heat. If not ready to serve, reheat to simmering before serving. If sauce is too thick, stir in a *little milk or light cream.* Correct seasoning with *salt* and serve.

OKRA is not a popular vegetable throughout America, except in the Southern states where it is used extensively in stews, soups, and gumbos. Yet it is delicious simply boiled and served with lemon butter, or creamed, scalloped, pan-fried, or batter-fried. Okra teams naturally with tomatoes, onions, and corn.

OKRA TOMATO STEW

Serves 4

BUY

1 pound young fresh okra
3 large ripe tomatoes
Bunch of green onions
1 green pepper

HAVE ON HAND	*COOKWARE*
Salt	Large heavy skillet
Vegetable oil	
Flour	
Pepper	

1. Wash the *okra* thoroughly. Trim the stem ends, but do not cut the pods. Drop the okra into a saucepan of *boiling salted water* and boil for 10 minutes, then drain.

2. Peel and coarsely chop the *tomatoes*. Peel and chop ½ *cup green onions*. Seed and chop the *green pepper*.

3. In skillet heat *2 tablespoons vegetable oil,* and in it sauté onion and green pepper for 5 minutes, or until green pepper is wilted. Stir in *1 teaspoon flour, 1 teaspoon salt,* and ¼ *teaspoon pepper.* Add the tomatoes and okra, and cook over low heat for 30 minutes, stirring occasionally.

THE BEST FRIED ONION RINGS

If you decide to make these, make a lot. Store what you don't eat in freezer bags and freeze.

Large sweet *or* mild onions   Heavy deep skillet *or* frite pan
Milk
Flour
1 quart vegetable oil
Salt

1. Slice *large sweet* or *mild onions* ¼ inch thick, and separate the slices into rings. Soak rings in *milk to cover* for 1 hour. Drain well and dry between sheets of absorbent paper.

2. Shake a handful of the onion rings at a time in a paper bag containing a *little flour*. Remove the onions and shake off the excess flour (a good way to do this is to place the floured rings in a colander and then shake the colander, tossing the rings, over a piece of waxed paper). Excess flour may be reused.

3. In a heavy deep skillet or frite pan, heat *1 quart of vegetable oil* to 375° F. Add a couple of handfuls of the floured onion rings at a time to the hot oil, and fry until golden brown and crisp. With a slotted spoon scoop them out onto a baking sheet lined with several thicknesses of absorbent paper to drain. Sprinkle with *salt* and keep warm in a very low oven until ready to serve.

TO HEAT FROZEN DEEP-FRIED ONION RINGS:

Empty the frozen onion rings onto a baking sheet lined with absorbent paper. Heat and crisp in a 350° F. oven for 10 minutes.

GARDEN PEAS À LA FRANÇAISE

Serves 6

BUY

2 pounds young green peas
1 head lettuce
12 small white onions

HAVE ON HAND	*COOKWARE*
Parsley	2-quart saucepan, with tight cover
Butter	
Thyme	
Sugar	
Salt and pepper	
Butter	

1. Shell the *peas*. Wash and shred the *lettuce*. Peel the *tiny onions*. Chop *1 tablespoon parsley*.

2. In saucepan melt *2 tablespoons butter*. Add peas, lettuce, onions, *a pinch of thyme*, the parsley, *1 teaspoon sugar*, *½ teaspoon salt*, and *¼ teaspoon pepper*.

3. Cover pan tightly, and simmer over low heat for 25 minutes, or until peas are tender, adding *a spoonful of water* from time to time if necessary.

4. Just before serving, stir in *1½ tablespoons butter*.

NIKA HAZELTON'S KARTOFFELRÖSTI

Serves 4

BUY

2 pounds potatoes

HAVE ON HAND	*COOKWARE*
Butter	Large saucepan
Salt	Large heavy skillet, with cover

1. In large saucepan boil *potatoes* in their jackets until tender. Cool and peel. Shred or cut potatoes into thin julienne strips.

2. In a large heavy skillet, heat *4 tablespoons butter*. Gradually add the potatoes and sprinkle with *¾ teaspoon salt*. Cook over low heat, turning frequently with a spatula, until potatoes are soft and yellow.

3. Press potatoes with the spatula into a flat cake. Sprinkle with *2 tablespoons hot water*. Cover and cook over low heat until potatoes are crusty and golden at the bottom, about 15 to 20 minutes. Shake the pan

frequently to prevent scorching and, if necessary, add a little more butter to prevent sticking.

4. Turn out, crusty side up, onto a hot serving dish. Serve immediately.

VIENNESE RAHMKARTOFFEL

Serves 4

Preheat oven to 300° F. Cook *12 new potatoes* in their jackets in *boiling water* until just fork tender. Drain, and as soon as they are cool enough to handle, peel them and cut into slices. Generously *butter* the bottom of a 1½-quart casserole. Put a layer of potatoes in the casserole and dot with *butter.* Sprinkle with *finely chopped garlic* and cover with *sour cream.* Repeat the layers until all potatoes are used. Sprinkle the top with *dry bread crumbs,* dot again with *butter,* and bake in the preheated oven for 30 minutes.

PUMPKIN should by no means be restricted to pies. There are countless other ways to cook this first cousin to the cucumber. It may be seasoned and baked, boiled in salted water, or steamed, and served with melted butter in exactly the same way as the many varieties of winter squash— the acorns, butternuts, and Hubbards. As a matter of fact, pumpkin and winter squash are interchangeable in most recipes.

The seeds of the pumpkin and the hard-skinned squash are hard and should be removed along with the fibrous tissue found in the center when the vegetable is cut.

BAKED PUMPKIN WITH WALNUTS

Serves 6. Sweet potatoes or butternut squash may be substituted for the pumpkin.

BUY

A small pumpkin

HAVE ON HAND	*COOKWARE*
Medium onion	1 large saucepan with cover
Salt	1 small saucepan
Butter	1½-quart casserole
Flour	
Light cream *or* half-and-half	
1 egg	
Orange	
Walnut meats	
Cracker crumbs	

1. Peel, seed, and thinly slice *2 pounds pumpkin* (enough slices to fill a heaping quart container). Peel and chop *1 medium onion*.

2. Put the pumpkin, onion, *1 cup water* and *1 teaspoon salt* into the large saucepan; bring to a boil, then cover and simmer for 15 minutes, or until tender. Drain and mash well with a fork or potato masher.

3. Preheat oven to 325° F. *Grease* the casserole.

4. In small saucepan melt *2 tablespoons butter*. Stir in *2 tablespoons flour*. Gradually stir in *1 cup light cream or half-and-half*, and cook, stirring constantly, until sauce is smooth and thickened. Remove from heat and stir in pumpkin, *1 egg, 1 tablespoon grated orange rind, 2 table-spoons orange juice,* and *½ cup chopped walnuts*.

5. Turn the pumpkin mixture into the prepared casserole, and sprinkle with *¼ cup fine cracker crumbs*.

6. Bake in the preheated oven for 35 minutes, or until lightly browned.

PIQUANT SPINACH

Serves 2 or 3

BUY

1½ pounds fresh spinach
8-ounce container dairy sour cream

HAVE ON HAND	*COOKWARE*
Salt	Large kettle with lid
Coarsely ground black pepper	
1 lemon	

1. Wash *spinach* well and discard coarse thick stems. Pick up by handfuls from sinkful of water, shake to remove excess water, and put into kettle. Cover and cook over moderate heat for 8 to 10 minutes, or until just wilted, tossing the leaves occasionally with a long two-tined fork. Remove from heat.

2. Drain spinach well, pressing out as much of the liquid as possible with the back of a spoon.

3. Cut through spinach in the kettle several times in different directions to chop it coarsely. Add *a light sprinkling of salt, a good sprinkling of coarsely ground black pepper, ½ cup sour cream, and 1 tablespoon lemon juice.* Heat, tossing spinach with the fork until combined with the sour cream and steaming.

BAKED GLAZED SWEET POTATOES

Serves 6. These may be cooked in a skillet on top of the stove if preferred.

BUY

3 pounds sweet potatoes

HAVE ON HAND	*COOKWARE*
Salt	2-quart shallow baking dish
Butter	
Light brown sugar	
Corn syrup	
1 large juicy orange	

1. Peel *potatoes* and cut into thin julienne strips. Drop the strips as they are cut into *heavily salted water.* Let them soak for 1½ hours.

2. An hour before serving, melt *4 tablespoons butter* in a baking dish.

Drain and add potatoes. Sprinkle potatoes with *1 cup brown sugar, ½ cup corn syrup,* and the *grated rind and juice of 1 orange.*

3. Preheat oven to 350° F.

4. Place potatoes in the oven and bake for 35 to 50 minutes, or until glazed and tender.

WHEN VINE-RIPENED TOMATOES are in the markets, enjoy them while you can. For the purest flavor, peel and slice them thickly and serve them with nothing more than a sprinkling of coarse salt and some freshly ground pepper. Or serve them *vinaigrette* (page 127) with a touch of chopped fresh tarragon, chives, or sweet basil.

Stuffed tomatoes make excellent luncheon dishes. To serve cold: First wash the tomatoes and remove the skins. (The skins of vine-ripened tomatoes should strip off easily; if not, dip them briefly, one at a time, into a saucepan of boiling water, then slip off the skin.) Cut a thin slice from the stem end, scoop out the core and seeds, and fill the centers with your favorite salad mixture or with cooked, diced vegetables moistened with mayonnaise.

Hot stuffed tomatoes are also delicious, but are only as good as the tomatoes themselves. So don't waste your time using the pale, hot-house excuses sold in the markets during most of the cold winter months. Make the following tomato recipes only with ripe, farm-grown fruit—and fruit they are, not vegetable.

TOMATOES PORTUGAISE

Serves 6. Marvelous served with scrambled eggs.

HAVE ON HAND	COOKWARE
6 large ripe tomatoes	Large heavy skillet
Shallots *or* green onions	
Garlic	
Fresh parsley	
Olive oil	
Salt	
Peppercorns	

1. Peel *tomatoes* and cut in half crosswise. Squeeze gently to remove seeds and excess moisture, then chop coarsely. *Chop 2 tablespoons shallots or green onions.* Peel and mince *1 large clove garlic.* Chop *¼ cup parsley.*

2. In heavy skillet heat *¼ cup olive oil.* Add tomatoes and cook for 5 minutes, or until tomatoes are slightly soft. Add the shallots or green onions and the garlic, and simmer for a few minutes longer, or until most of the moisture is cooked away. Sprinkle with parsley, *salt,* and *freshly ground pepper.*

GREEN TOMATOES WITH CREAM GRAVY

Cut *green (or mostly green) tomatoes* into thick slices. Coat slices with *flour* and sprinkle with *salt and pepper.* Melt *a chunk of butter* in a large skillet, and in it sauté the tomato slices until lightly brown on one side. Sprinkle with a *little light brown sugar,* and brown them on the other side, adding *more butter* if necessary. Pour *1 cup heavy cream* over the browned tomato slices, and bring to a simmer. Remove tomato slices to serving platter, cook the cream rapidly for 2 minutes, stirring in all the nice brown bits from bottom and sides of the pan, and pour over the tomatoes.

ITALIAN STUFFED TOMATOES

Serves 4

HAVE ON HAND	COOKWARE
4 large ripe tomatoes	Baking pan
Parmesan cheese	
Fresh bread	
1 egg	
Salt and pepper	
Olive oil	
Garlic	
Large black olives, pitted	
Butter	

1. Cut a thin slice from top of *each tomato,* scoop out the seeds, and place the tomatoes upside-down on a rack to drain.

2. Preheat oven to 450° F. Grate *4 tablespoons cheese* and set aside.

3. Crumb *2 thick slices fresh bread,* and mix the crumbs with *1 egg, salt and pepper to taste, 2 tablespoons olive oil,* and *2 minced cloves garlic.*

4. Fill the center of each tomato with some of the crumb mixture, then press *1 olive* into the center of each. Arrange in baking pan. Sprinkle with cheese, dot with *butter,* and bake in the hot oven for 10 to 15 minutes.

TOMATOES PROVENÇALE

Serves 4

HAVE ON HAND	*COOKWARE*
4 large ripe tomatoes	Baking sheet
Salt and pepper	
Bread	
Garlic	
Parsley	
Butter	

1. Do NOT peel the *tomatoes.* Wash and cut in half crosswise. Arrange the halves, cut side up, on a baking sheet and sprinkle with *salt and pepper.*

2. Preheat oven to 450° F.

3. Meanwhile crumb *enough bread to make ½ cup crumbs,* then mix the crumbs with *1 clove garlic,* peeled and minced, *2 tablespoons chopped parsley,* and *4 tablespoons melted butter.*

4. Sprinkle the tomatoes with the crumb mixture, and bake them in the hot oven for 10 to 15 minutes, or until the crumbs are golden brown.

MASHED TURNIPS WITH BLACK ONIONS

Serves 4

Peel and thinly slice *2 large Spanish onions*. In a heavy skillet melt ¼ *pound (1 stick) butter*. Add the onions and let them cook over very low heat for about 1 hour, stirring frequently, until the onions are very brown. These are called "black" onions.

Meanwhile, peel *2 large rutabaga turnips*. Cut into large dice, and cook in *boiling salted water* until tender. When onions are "black," drain and mash the turnips rather coarsely. Season with *salt* and *plenty of freshly ground black pepper*. Pile the turnips into a serving dish and make a well in the center. Empty the onions into the well and serve hot.

Zucchini is available during many months of the year, but in the fall, it is both abundant and inexpensive. This vegetable freezes beautifully. Simply wash and slice the slim squash, sauté the slices in butter until transparent, then drain and freeze for use in soup, stews, and casseroles all winter long.

ZUCCHINI PANCAKES

Serves 4

BUY
3 medium zucchini
Chives
Parsley

HAVE ON HAND
2 eggs
Flour
Parmesan cheese
Salt and pepper
Sour cream (optional)

COOKWARE
Griddle *or* iron skillet

1. Wash and trim the *zucchini,* and shred with a vegetable shredder. Chop *1 tablespoon each chives and parsley.* Grate *2 tablespoons Parmesan.*

2. In mixing bowl, combine *2 eggs, 3 tablespoons flour,* the grated Parmesan, the chopped chives and parsley, and *salt and pepper* to taste. Stir in the zucchini. If the batter seems to be too thin, add *another tablespoon flour.*

3. *Grease* the griddle and heat until a drop of water on it sputters and evaporates almost immediately. Drop the batter onto it by the tablespoonful and cook until the surface of the pancakes is bubbly and the underside is lightly browned. Turn and brown the other side.

4. Serve the pancakes hot, with *a dab of sour cream* on each if desired.

RAW FOODS & SALADS

Raw Food & Salads

The value of raw fruits and vegetables in daily meals can hardly be over-estimated. Besides being power plants of vitamins and minerals, they contain the cellulose or bulk needed to support the growth of essential intestinal bacteria. Some fresh raw food should be eaten at every meal. Certainly this is about the easiest and most delectable road to good health and one that never causes you to worry about your waistline.

Fresh fruit or fruit juice is a natural way to begin the day. And since we're speaking of nutrition, let's not settle for canned or bottled juices, for these are processed and their vitamin content and flavor are appreciably reduced. There is a place for these convenience juices as refreshing between-meal beverages, but not as alternatives to raw foods. Also, let's not get brainwashed by the "orange juice for breakfast" routine. Vary your breakfast fruits with ones in season, with fresh berries, plums, apricots, grapes, sweet cherries, with fresh pineapple sticks, honeydew or cantaloupe, a thick slice of fragrant watermelon, some fresh figs, a sliced banana, and occasionally, one of the more exotic fresh fruits found in fine markets—the mangoes, papayas, persimmons, and so on.

A salad of almost any kind—fruit, vegetable, cheese, or tossed greens—makes a perfect lunch when accompanied by a slice of high-protein bread or a wheatgerm muffin or cornbread square hot from the oven and spread with dairy-fresh sweet butter.

For snacks or appetizers, you can't top something as simple and healthful as a bowl of firm red radishes, crisp stalks of celery or fennel, cucumber or carrot strips, cherry tomatoes, or almost any young vegetable served just with a bowl of coarse salt, or with a favorite dip if you prefer, or after having been marinated for a couple of hours in a light salad dressing.

When you buy vegetables to eat raw, seek out the young, tender ones. The smaller vegetables have more flavor than the larger overgrown ones, which are also apt to be tough. Try paper-thin slices of peeled young kohlrabi, small button mushrooms, finger-size strips of small firm zucchini, or tiny eggplants.

Soups

When fresh garden vegetables are at the height of their season, remember the intriguing Spanish Gazpachos, raw vegetable soups or "liquid salads," and enjoy them as luncheon dishes or as first courses before dinner. Use the reddest, vine-ripened tomatoes you can buy.

GAZPACHO

Serves 6

BUY

2 slim firm cucumbers
1 large sweet Bermuda onion
2 green peppers
8 ripe tomatoes

HAVE ON HAND

Garlic
Tarragon red wine vinegar
Olive oil
Salt
Coarsely cracked pepper
Bread

COOKWARE

Small skillet

IN ADVANCE:

1. Peel, seed, and finely dice *1 cucumber*. Peel and finely chop *half the onion*. Seed and sliver *1 green pepper*. Peel, quarter, squeeze out seeds, and chop *6 tomatoes*. Mince *2 cloves garlic*.

2. Combine all these vegetables in a bowl or pitcher, and stir in *6 tablespoons wine vinegar, ¼ cup olive oil, 1 teaspoon salt, ½ teaspoon coarsely cracked pepper,* and *1½ cups cold water.*

3. Chill in refrigerator for several hours before serving.

4. Meanwhile prepare the garnish. Peel, seed, and dice the *remaining cucumber;* chop the *remaining half onion;* seed and chop the *remaining green pepper;* and peel, seed, and chop the *remaining 2 tomatoes.* Put each vegetable in a separate bowl and refrigerate until ready to serve.

PREPARE CROUTONS:

5. Cut *3 slices bread* into cubes. Brown the cubes lightly in *2 table-spoons olive oil,* and empty onto absorbent paper to drain.

WHEN READY TO SERVE:

6. Stir soup well, and pour into soup plates. Put *1 ice cube* in the center of each serving, and pass the croutons and chopped vegetables separately.

CRAIG CLAIBORNE'S GAZPACHO

Serves 4

BUY

2 slim cucumbers
3 large ripe tomatoes
2 green peppers

HAVE ON HAND

Onions
Garlic
4 eggs
Vinegar
Olive oil
Salt
Cayenne pepper
Tomato juice
Bread

COOKWARE

Electric blender
Small skillet

1. Peel and slice *1 medium onion* and *1 clove garlic*. Peel and slice *1 cucumber* and the *3 tomatoes,* and seed and slice *1 green pepper.* Put these vegetables along with *4 eggs* into the container of an electric blender and blend to a purée.

2. Pour the blended vegetables into a bowl, and add *¼ cup vinegar, ¼ cup olive oil, ⅛ teaspoon salt, ⅛ teaspoon cayenne pepper,* and *¾ cup tomato juice.* Chill.

3. Meanwhile cut *2 slices bread* into cubes. They should measure 1 cup. Peel and mince *1 clove garlic.* Heat *2 tablespoons olive oil* with the minced garlic in a small skillet. Brown the bread lightly in this, then empty onto absorbent paper to drain.

4. Peel and dice *1 cucumber* and *1 medium onion.* Seed, peel, and chop the *remaining green pepper.*

5. When ready to serve, add the diced vegetables to the chilled soup. Pass the croutons separately, or top each serving of soup with a spoonful of croutons.

ICED CUCUMBER SOUP

Serves 4

BUY	*HAVE ON HAND*
2 cucumbers	Milk
1 pint yogurt	Garlic
Parsley *or* chives	Salt

1. Peel and seed the *cucumbers.* Chop *1½ of the cucumbers,* then combine with the *yogurt* and *½ cup milk.*

2. Peel and mince *1 clove garlic* and add to soup. Add *½ teaspoon salt.* Chop and add *1 tablespoon parsley or chives,* and correct seasoning with *salt.* Chill.

3. When ready to serve, shred the *remaining ½ cucumber.* Serve the soup with *1 ice cube* in each bowl, and garnish with the shredded cucumber.

ICED TOMATO SOUP

Serves 4. Try this in early September, when tomatoes are lush and juicy. Of course, you can substitute bottled tomato juice, but taste it just once made with the fresh. It's heaven.

BUY	*HAVE ON HAND*
3 pounds ripe tomatoes	Onion
8-ounce container heavy cream	Tabasco
Bunch green onions	Salt
Sour cream	
Parsley *or* fresh sweet basil	

1. Peel the *tomatoes;* then chop them in a large mixing bowl or pot and mash well with a potato masher. Strain through a sieve, stirring and pressing through as much of the soft pulp as possible. Discard the seeds.

2. Into 3 cups of the fresh tomato juice, stir the *heavy cream, 2 table-spoons minced green onion, 2 good dashes of tabasco,* and *salt to taste.*

3. Chill thoroughly; then pour into chilled cups, and top with *sour cream* and *a sprinkling of finely chopped parsley or sweet basil.*

Unusual & International Salads

One of the most luscious, nutritious, and satisfying fruits is the avocado. And the smallish, black, hard-shelled ones from California, known as calavos, are by far the best, being the richest in flavor and natural oils (and in calories, too!). The ways to serve avocados are many. The simplest is to cut an avocado in half lengthwise, remove the seed, and serve half to a person, with the hollow filled with lemon-juice Vinaigrette Sauce (page 127).

Guacamole is perhaps the most popular recipe for the avocado, served as a spread or dip. It also makes an excellent stuffing for small peeled tomatoes.

GUACAMOLE

Serves 4 as a dip or spread.

BUY	HAVE ON HAND
1 firm ripe California avocado	Garlic
	Lemon
	Tabasco
	Olive oil
	Salt and pepper
	Lettuce leaves
	Fritos *or* tortillas
	(*or* raw vegetables)

1. Peel the *avocado* and remove the seed. Chop the flesh coarsely into a mixing bowl.

2. Add *1 large peeled and minced clove garlic,* the *juice of ½ lemon,* about *20 drops Tabasco,* and *2 tablespoons olive oil.* Mix and mash the ingredients coarsely. It should not be a smooth spread. Mash in a *little salt and pepper* to taste.

3. Pile in a bowl lined with *lettuce leaves,* and serve with *Fritos, toasted tortillas, or raw vegetables.*

YIAOURTO SKODALIA

Makes about 1 cup. This Greek dip made with yogurt is a favorite to serve with crisp raw vegetables. Use tender hearts of romaine, strips of Belgian endive, raw cauliflowerets, carrot or cucumber sticks, scallions, small raw mushrooms, and radishes.

BUY	*HAVE ON HAND*
1 small slim cucumber	Garlic
8-ounce container unflavored	Walnut meats
yogurt	Olive oil
	Vinegar *or* lemon juice
	Salt and pepper

1. In a small mixing bowl combine *1 minced clove garlic, 3 minced walnut halves,* and *1 tablespoon olive oil.* Beat well with a fork.

2. Peel, seed, and shred the *cucumber* and add to bowl.

3. Gradually stir in the *yogurt,* and *about 1 teaspoon vinegar or lemon juice,* and *salt and pepper* to taste. Chill several hours or overnight before serving.

NOTE: See page 342 for Homemade Yogurt.

SWEDISH CUCUMBERS

Select *6 small slim, very firm cucumbers.* Peel and slice as thinly as possible into a salad bowl. Sprinkle with *1 teaspoon sugar, 1 teaspoon coarse salt,* and *some freshly ground black pepper.* Add *2 tablespoons white vinegar* and *6 ice cubes.* Refrigerate for several hours. Before serving, sprinkle lavishly with *chopped fresh dill or parsley.*

CUCUMBERS IN SOUR CREAM

Again, use *small slim, firm cucumbers.* Peel and slice thinly into a bowl. Combine to taste *sour cream, wine vinegar,* and *salt and pepper.* Pour over the cucumbers and chill for at least an hour before serving, tossing the cucumbers in the cream mixture occasionally. *Chopped fresh dill* is frequently added.

ONION SALAD

Peel and slice *several large sweet red onions* and soak in *ice water* for 2 to 3 hours. Drain well and sprinkle with *lots of chopped fresh parsley and freshly ground black pepper.* Add vinegar and salad oil in the proportion of *1 part vinegar to 3 parts salad oil,* and keep cold until ready to serve. Just before serving, sprinkle with *coarse salt.*

ONION ORANGE SALAD

Serves 3

Peel and thinly slice *1 orange* and *1 medium onion.* Sprinkle with *salt,* and add *1 tablespoon wine vinegar* and *3 tablespoons salad oil.* Chill for at least 30 minutes. Serve on *crisp lettuce leaves* with *a sprinkling of cayenne pepper* on top.

RAW MUSHROOM SALAD

Serves 4 to 6

BUY	*HAVE ON HAND*
½ pound very fresh button mushrooms	Wine vinegar
	Olive oil
	Dry mustard
	Dried tarragon
	Salt
	Coarsely ground pepper

1. Wash *mushrooms* and dry on paper towels. Cut stems off close to the caps and reserve for another use. Slice the *caps.*

2. In a mixing bowl combine *3 tablespoons wine vinegar, ½ cup olive oil, ¼ teaspoon dry mustard, ½ teaspoon dried tarragon, ¼ teaspoon salt* and *ground pepper to taste.* Add the sliced mushroom caps and toss lightly. Let marinate at room temperature for several hours before serving, tossing the mushrooms occasionally in the dressing.

MUSHROOMS IN CREAM DRESSING

Serves 4 to 6

Prepare *½ pound mushrooms* as in preceding recipe and add *1 small onion,* grated, *¼ cup heavy cream, 1 tablespoon each olive oil and lemon juice, ¼ teaspoon sugar,* and *salt and pepper to taste.* Marinate several hours or overnight before serving.

SPANISH SALAD

Serves 4

BUY	HAVE ON HAND
Head of romaine *or* lettuce	1 small onion
1 large orange	Olive oil
2 medium tomatoes	Salt and pepper
1 ripe avocado	Wine vinegar
Bunch firm radishes	
Small jar pimiento-stuffed green olives	

1. Wash and separate leaves from *head of romaine or lettuce.* Chill.

2. Peel *orange* deeply, removing all white pithy substance under the rind, right down to the fruit. Slice thinly. Peel and thinly slice *1 small onion.* Peel and quarter the *tomatoes.*

3. Put orange slices, onion, and tomatoes in a mixing bowl. Add *½ cup olive oil, ¼ teaspoon each salt and pepper,* and *3 tablespoons vinegar.* Marinate for 30 minutes, tossing ingredients once or twice.

4. Just before serving, peel the *avocado;* cut it in half and discard the seed. Slice the avocado into the bowl. Slice and add *8 radishes* and *8 olives.*

5. Toss salad and arrange it on a bed of the salad greens.

SPANISH CAULIFLOWER SALAD

Serves 6

BUY	*HAVE ON HAND*
Small jar ripe olives	Wine vinegar
1 small head cauliflower	Olive oil
1 green pepper	Salt
Jar pimientos	Freshly ground pepper
Green onions	
Romaine *or* crisp lettuce	

1. Slice *enough ripe olives to measure ½ cup* and empty into salad bowl.

2. Wash and trim the *cauliflower;* set half aside for another use and shred the other half thinly. Add shredded cauliflower to olives.

3. Add *⅓ cup finely chopped green pepper, ¼ cup chopped pimiento,* and *3 tablespoons chopped green onions.*

4. Add *1 tablespoon wine vinegar* and *3 tablespoons salad oil,* and chill for several hours.

5. When ready to serve, line individual salad plates with *crisp romaine or lettuce leaves.* Sprinkle the salad with *salt* and *freshly ground pepper,* toss again, and spoon a nest of the salad on each bed of greens.

SWISS CHEESE AND VEGETABLE SALAD

Serves 4

Dice *½ pound Swiss cheese,* and toss with *2 cucumbers,* peeled and diced,

12 radishes, thinly sliced, *1 sweet red onion,* peeled and thinly sliced, *1 cup sour cream,* and *2 tablespoons chopped fresh dill.* Mix gently, then season to taste with *salt, pepper,* and *lemon juice.* Keep cold until ready to serve. Serve on *shredded lettuce.*

CELERY ROOT RÉMOULADE

Serves 6

BUY	HAVE ON HAND
1 pound medium-size celery roots (about 3)	Mayonnaise Prepared mustard (preferably Dijon) Lemon juice Salt

1. Peel the *celery roots* with a sharp paring knife and cut them into sticks about the size of toothpicks.

2. Combine *1 cup mayonnaise, 1 tablespoon mustard,* and *lemon juice* and *salt to taste.* Add the celery root, mix well, and chill for several hours before serving.

TABOOLEY
(Parsley and Bulgur Salad)

Serves 4 to 6

BUY	HAVE ON HAND
1-pound box bulgur (cracked wheat) Large bunch fresh parsley Fresh mint leaves 1 large ripe tomato Bunch of romaine	Onions Olive oil Lemons Salt and pepper

1. Soak *1 cup bulgur* in *water to cover* for 1 hour. Drain well and press out excess water.

2. Combine soaked wheat with *1 cup chopped onions, 1½ cups finely chopped parsley, ½ cup finely chopped fresh mint leaves, ¾ cup olive oil, ½ cup lemon juice,* and *salt and pepper to taste.* Chill.

3. Wash and separate the leaves of the *romaine* and chill.

4. Peel, seed, and chop the *tomato.* Serve the salad on a bed of romaine leaves, garnished with the chopped tomato.

CHINESE CABBAGE SALAD

Serves 6

BUY	HAVE ON HAND
1 head Chinese cabbage	Salt and pepper
Bunch scallions	1 lemon
Bunch radishes	Salad oil
Bunch parsley	

1. Wash the *head of cabbage,* discarding any discolored leaves. Shred the cabbage very thinly and put into a large salad bowl.

2. Wash and mince the *scallions,* using as much as possible of the tender green stalks. Wash, trim, and thinly slice the *radishes.* Chop ¼ *cup parsley.*

3. Add scallions, radishes, and parsley to the cabbage, and sprinkle with *salt and pepper to taste.* Add *juice of ½ lemon* and *⅓ cup salad oil,* and toss lightly. Chill for about 1 hour before serving.

COTTAGE CHEESE is one of the most versatile of cheeses. It's a high-protein food and provides important calcium. Team it with fruits and vegetables for a main-dish salad. Fresh garden vegetables such as tomatoes and radishes, green peppers and cucumbers, also carrots, celery, and lettuce —and chives—all make good foils for cottage cheese.

RED CABBAGE AND COTTAGE CHEESE SALAD

Serves 4

BUY	HAVE ON HAND
1-pound can diced beets	Mayonnaise
Small bunch celery	1 lemon
Small head red cabbage	Salt and pepper
8-ounce carton creamed cottage cheese	Nutmeg

1. Drain liquid from can of *beets* and empty beets into a large mixing bowl.

2. Wash, trim, and dice the *celery* and add to beets.

3. Discard any outer wilted or discolored leaves from *cabbage* and slice enough thinly to measure 3 cups. Add cabbage to celery and beets and mix lightly.

4. In another bowl combine the *cottage cheese* with *1 cup mayonnaise, 2 tablespoons lemon juice, 2 teaspoons salt, or to taste, ½ teaspoon pepper,* and *a dash of nutmeg.* Spoon mayonnaise mixture over vegetables and toss lightly to mix. Chill for at least 1 hour before serving.

PAPAYA AND AVOCADO SALAD

Serves 6. Here's a fabulous fruit salad combination to try when papayas are in season.

BUY	HAVE ON HAND
1 head romaine	Olive oil
Limes	Salt
1 ripe papaya	Black pepper
2 ripe calavo avocados	

1. Wash and separate leaves from the *head of romaine.* Chill well.

2. Combine ¼ *cup freshly squeezed lime juice* with ½ *cup olive oil, 1 teaspoon salt,* and ¼ *teaspoon freshly ground black pepper.*

3. Arrange romaine leaves on six individual salad plates. Peel and slice the *papaya* and *avocados,* and arrange alternate slices of the fruits on each plate.

4. Whip the lime juice dressing briefly with a fork, then spoon a little over each salad. Serve immediately.

STRAWBERRY SALAD

Line a salad platter with *romaine or other crisp greens,* and spoon *a mound of cottage cheese* in the center. Surround the cheese with *large hulled strawberries.* Serve with a salad dressing made by combining ½ *cup each heavy cream and sour cream, 1 tablespoon lemon juice, 2 teaspoons sugar,* and *a dash of salt.*

DR. RISER'S PERSIMMON AND AVOCADO SALAD WITH BUTTERMILK DRESSING

Serves 4. An even more exotic fruit salad combines the sensuous persimmon with avocado.

BUY	HAVE ON HAND
1 head romaine	Mayonnaise
4 very ripe persimmons	Buttermilk
2 ripe avocados	Lemon

1. Separate leaves from the *head of romaine,* wash well, then dry and chill.

2. Combine ½ *cup mayonnaise* and ¼ *cup buttermilk* and chill.

3. Line individual salad plates with romaine leaves. Do not peel the *persimmons;* wash them, then cut them into 8 sections—slicing from the pointed end down to, but not completely through, the calyx of the fruit. Open up each persimmon like a flower and place on the romaine.

4. Peel the *avocados,* remove seeds, and slice each half avocado lengthwise into 8 thin slices. Place a slice of avocado between each two "petals" of the persimmons and sprinkle the avocado with a *little lemon juice.*

5. Serve immediately with the *buttermilk salad dressing.*

Green Salads

THE TRADITIONAL TOSSED SALAD

The first requirement is the finest of raw ingredients: crisp greens of several varieties, fully matured ripe tomatoes, crunchy cucumbers, flavorful herbs, good salad oil (part olive), and a mild vinegar, preferably wine. Then it must be seasoned just right, tossed with a light hand, and served very cold.

THE GREENS:

These are varied and abundant during a great part of the year. There are water cress, firm heads of Belgian endive, tender sprouts of field salad, oak lettuce, Bibb lettuce, romaine, escarole, curly endive or chicory, and, that wonderfully pungent green known as arugala or Italian water cress, found in most Italian vegetable markets. Buy several different varieties.

Wash your greens thoroughly, leaf by leaf, and drain just as thoroughly. If you don't have a salad basket to drain them in, spread them out on absorbent toweling and pat dry with more towels. Tear larger leaves into medium pieces, leave the small tender leaves whole. Wrap all in a dry terry-cloth towel, and place in your salad crisper. Here they will stay fresh, crisp, and cold until salad-making time.

OPTIONAL INGREDIENTS:

To these salad greens you may add an extra touch—chopped chives, chopped fresh basil or tarragon, a ripe tomato, peeled, carefully seeded and chopped, a crisp cucumber, peeled, seeded and thinly sliced, some chopped spring onions, thin slices of firm radishes, a little crumbled Roquefort-type cheese, and so on.

THE SALAD DRESSING:

Now to the dressing, which is so simple, it's unbelievable that so many poor salads are served in homes and particularly in restaurants. Alexandre Dumas gave the clue, when he wrote, "No matter what the method adopted in the preparation of salads, it is always necessary to be very restrained in the use of vinegar." Some years later, Escoffier specified the correct amount of vinegar as 1 part vinegar to 3 parts oil, but Escoffier did not take into consideration that American vinegars are higher in acidity than the French ones are, so a better proportion, unless you are using an imported wine vinegar, is 1 part vinegar to 4 parts oil. Lemon juice is a good alternative to vinegar, but some lemons are much more tart than others, so the proportion of lemon juice to oil depends on the acidity of the lemon.

Then there is the question of garlic. To many persons, a little fresh garlic is essential to a perfect salad, but never use too much as it will overpower the subtle flavor of tender greens.

The salad dressing can be made directly in the salad bowl. A large wooden bowl is best. And I do not go along with the theory that it should never be washed. Nonsense! Who wants a salad bowl with its pores filled with rancid oil? Scrub it with salt, rinse thoroughly in warm water, then dry with paper towels.

SAUCE VINAIGRETTE
(French Dressing)

Peel and cut *1 clove of garlic*. Rub the inside of the salad bowl with the cut clove. Discard the garlic. Sprinkle the bottom of the bowl with *½ tea-spoon salt* and *¼ teaspoon freshly ground black pepper*. Add *½ teaspoon dry mustard or 1 teaspoon prepared Dijon-type mustard*. Now use your salad spoon to measure the vinegar and oil. Add *1 spoonful of vinegar or lemon juice, or a combination of them both,* and blend this thoroughly with the mustard and seasonings, swirling and mixing with the back of the spoon. Then stir in *3 to 4 spoonfuls of salad oil or a mixture of oils,* always including at least 1 part olive oil. Set bowl aside until ready to serve.

To SERVE: Fill the bowl with the prepared greens, add herbs or chopped raw vegetables, and toss lightly.

CAESAR SALAD

Serves 4. This popular variation of the simple tossed salad is the creation of an imaginative chef in Tijuana, Mexico. Caesar salad depends primarily on the flavor and texture of romaine for its character. Traditionally it includes anchovy fillets but it can be enjoyed without these if one wants to be strictly "meatless."

BUY

2 heads romaine lettuce
Small can anchovy fillets (optional)

HAVE ON HAND	*COOKWARE*
Garlic	Small skillet
Olive oil	Small saucepan
Bread	
Parmesan cheese	
Salt	
Dry mustard	
Cayenne pepper *or* Tabasco	
1 large lemon	
1 egg	
Coarsely cracked pepper	

1. The day before you want to serve the salad, peel and crush *1 clove garlic* and let it soak overnight in *½ cup olive oil.*

2. Prepare *romaine leaves:* Wash and drain each leaf thoroughly; then tear them into medium-size pieces, wrap in a towel, and put into refrigerator to chill.

3. Trim crusts off *4 slices bread,* and cut the slices into cubes.

4. Heat *3 tablespoons of the garlic-olive oil* in a small skillet, and in it sauté the bread cubes over moderate heat until golden brown on all sides, tossing them frequently with a wooden spoon. Drain on paper towels and set aside.

5. If using *anchovies,* slice them into small pieces. Grate *1 tablespoon Parmesan cheese* and set aside.

6. Sprinkle the bottom of a wooden salad bowl with *½ teaspoon salt.* Add *1 teaspoon dry mustard, dash cayenne pepper or Tabasco,* and the *juice of 1 large lemon.* Stir with wooden salad spoon until the salt dissolves. Add *remaining garlic-olive oil* and stir rapidly until blended. Set aside.

7. Gently lower *1 egg* into a small saucepan of *rapidly boiling water* and boil for 1 minute. Remove to cool a little.

8. Pile the romaine leaves into the salad bowl, sprinkle with the Parmesan cheese, add the anchovies, and break the coddled egg over the greens. Sprinkle with *½ teaspoon coarsely cracked pepper* and toss everything together gently but thoroughly until each leaf is coated with the oil.

9. Sprinkle with the garlic croutons and toss again gently.

GOOD VARIATION OF A CAESAR SALAD

Serves 4

BUY

1 large firm cucumber
2 heads romaine lettuce
8-ounce container sour cream

HAVE ON HAND

Bread
Garlic
Olive oil
Parmesan cheese
1 egg
Salt
Freshly ground black pepper
1 large lemon

COOKWARE

Small skillet
Small saucepan

1. Trim crusts from *2 slices bread.* Rub the slices with *a cut clove of garlic,* then cut them into cubes. Sauté the cubes in a *little hot olive oil* until golden brown on all sides. Drain on absorbent paper.

2. Grate *enough Parmesan cheese to measure ½ cup.* Peel and dice

1 large cucumber. Boil *1 egg* for 1 minute; remove from water and set aside.

3. Wash and dry the romaine; then tear the leaves into bite-size pieces and put them into a large salad bowl rubbed with *garlic.* Add the *sour cream, 2 tablespoons olive oil, 1 teaspoon salt,* and *lots of freshly ground black pepper.*

4. Scoop the egg from the shell into the salad, and squeeze the *juice of 1 large lemon* on top of the egg. Mix gently but well. Sprinkle with the Parmesan cheese and toss again.

5. Toss in the croutons and serve.

SPINACH SALAD WITH CROUTONS

Serves 4

   BUY

1 pound fresh young spinach

HAVE ON HAND	*COOKWARE*
Bread	Small skillet
Olive oil	
Garlic	
Salt	
Dry mustard	
Peppercorns	
Wine vinegar	

1. Wash *spinach,* cut off the stems, and refrigerate the leaves.

2. Dice *enough bread to measure 1½ cups.* Sauté the cubes in a *little olive oil* until lightly browned on all sides. Drain on absorbent paper.

3. Peel and mince *2 cloves garlic,* then sprinkle them into the bottom of a salad bowl. Add *½ teaspoon salt, ¼ teaspoon each dry mustard and freshly ground pepper,* and *2 tablespoons wine vinegar.* Stir ingredients with back of spoon. Gradually stir in *½ cup olive oil.* Set bowl aside.

4. When ready to serve, pile the spinach leaves into the bowl, add the croutons, and toss briefly but well.

EGGS & CHEESE

Eggs

Eggs are nature's most perfect food. Every baby chick is evidence of the nutritional perfection packed into the egg from which it came. Out of the protective shell emerges a bird that can see, hear, walk, cheep, and eat adult food at birth. And, moreover, in its tiny furry body at the time it is hatched are stored enough nutrients for it to sustain itself for the first three days of its life.

How any food as perfect as the egg could be condemned by physicians and nutritionists is hard to understand, but until the past few years eggs were restricted in the diets of anyone suffering from high cholesterol. Today they are decidedly back in favor and are recommended in the diets of heart patients.

Adelle Davis, one of the country's leading nutritionists, states in her book *Let's Stay Well:* "Because eggs are particularly rich in methionine and lecithin, they should never be restricted in the diets of persons with atherosclerosis," and she supports this statement with convincing clinical evidence. Eggs are also high on the list of foods to help cure anemia, and the time-honored practice of serving eggnogs to the ill and elderly should be encouraged.

Eggs and cheese are perfect flavor mates, and they are combined in a number of the recipes which follow (see also Quiches & Tarts, page 48). But I begin this chapter with eggs in general and poached eggs in particular. When perfectly cooked, a poached egg is, perhaps, the epitome of egg cookery, and the egg which poaches best is the freshest that money can buy. That's not much, for, penny for penny, eggs are the best protein value in our markets today.

Poached Eggs

Poaching means to cook an egg, out of its shell, in hot liquid. The liquid may be water, milk, cream, broth, tomato juice, or wine. The important rule to remember in poaching an egg is that the liquid should NEVER BOIL. The white of an egg coagulates at 140° F.; the yolk, at 149° F. Therefore, it is obvious that boiling liquid is not necessary to poach an egg. Too high temperatures can, in fact, toughen the egg white and make the yolk less digestible.

HOW TO POACH EGGS

1. Use a shallow saucepan or skillet at least 2 inches deep. Oil the bottom lightly, unless it has a non-stick coating, and fill with water to a depth of 1½ inches. Add a little salt, bring the water to a boil, then reduce to barely a simmer.

2. Use 2 eggs per person. Break eggs one at a time into a saucer or shallow dish and slip them carefully into the water, with the edge of the dish placed as close to the water level as possible. The addition of the cold eggs will immediately lower the temperature, so increase heat until bubbles begin to rise again from bottom of the pan, or to about 185° F., the perfect simmering temperature to set a perfectly poached egg. If the temperature is allowed to remain *too* low, the egg white will not set quickly enough and will spread out into the liquid.

3. Cook the eggs for 3 to 5 minutes, or until the white is delicately firm and the yolk is set to the desired firmness.

4. Carefully remove eggs with a slotted spoon and, if the edges are jagged, trim neatly with a round cooky cutter.

5. Serve immediately on hot buttered toast or English muffin halves. If you wish to gild the lily, spoon a tablespoon of luscious Hollandaise Sauce over each egg.

TO HOLD POACHED EGGS:

If poached eggs are to be part of a more elaborate dish, or if you wish to serve poached eggs to several people at the same time, gently place each one after poaching into a pan of warm salted water; they will stay moist there but not continue to cook.

To reheat: Lift the eggs, one at a time, out of the water with a perforated or slotted spoon, lower them into a second saucepan containing hot water (140° F.), and let them warm for about 1 minute.

HOLLANDAISE SAUCE is a gorgeous egg sauce and not nearly so tricky as most people believe. If you use an electric blender, it can literally be made in seconds. I give you both the traditional and the blender recipes and methods for making it, for no good cook should have qualms about whipping up this sauce. Serve it not just on special occasions but also as a nutritious egg dish for the family. When fresh asparagus is in the markets, perch a poached egg atop a few cooked stalks and cover with Hollandaise. Heaven!

SAUCE HOLLANDAISE

Serves 6

HAVE ON HAND	*COOKWARE*
4 egg yolks	Small Pyrex bowl
Cream	8-inch skillet
Lemon	
Salt	
Cayenne pepper	
½ pound butter	

1. Into the small bowl put *4 egg yolks, 2 tablespoons cream, 1 tablespoon lemon juice, ¼ teaspoon salt,* and *a pinch of cayenne pepper.* Set bowl into a skillet containing hot water, and beat the mixture over low heat until it begins to thicken. The water should not boil, only barely

simmer. Use a wire whisk if possible, otherwise beat with two forks held in one hand.

2. Beat in ½ *pound butter,* bit by bit. When all the butter has been added, turn off the heat, and pour a little cold water into the water in the skillet to reduce the temperature and prevent further cooking of the sauce. It will stay warm while the eggs are poaching.

BLENDER HOLLANDAISE

Serves 6

HAVE ON HAND	*COOKWARE*
½ pound butter	Small saucepan
4 egg yolks	Electric blender
Lemon	
Salt	
Tabasco	

1. In saucepan heat *butter* until melted and very hot, but do not let it brown. The entire success of making blender Hollandaise is the temperature of the butter, which must be hot enough to cook the egg as it blends, but not hot enough to curdle it. Bubbling butter is no indication of temperature. It means merely that the liquid contained in the butter is evaporating. The point at which the bubbles subside and the butter is very golden is just right.

2. Into the blender container put *4 egg yolks, 1 tablespoon lemon juice, ¼ teaspoon salt,* and *¼ teaspoon Tabasco.* Cover container. Turn motor on low speed. If the blender is a multiple-speed unit, use lowest speed. As soon as the blades reach full motion, remove cover and pour in the hot butter in a steady stream. When all butter is added, turn blender off.

3. To keep the sauce hot until serving time, set the container with the sauce into a saucepan containing about 2 inches of hot but not boiling water. If the sauce becomes too thick to pour when ready to use, return container to blender. Add *1 tablespoon hot water* and blend briefly.

EGGS SARDOU

Serves 4 or 8

   BUY

2 packages frozen chopped spinach (10 ounces each)
8-ounce container heavy cream
14-ounce can imported artichoke bottoms

HAVE ON HAND	*COOKWARE*
Nutmeg	Cookware for Hollandaise
Ingredients for Hollandaise	2 small saucepans
8 eggs	1 skillet for poaching

   1. Cook *spinach* according to package directions. Drain well in a sieve and press out excess moisture with back of a wooden spoon. Return to saucepan, and stir in *a pinch of nutmeg* and *¼ cup heavy cream*. Place over very low heat.

   2. Make *Hollandaise* and keep warm.

   3. Heat *artichoke bottoms* in *liquid from can*.

   4. Poach *8 eggs* (page 133).

   5. Place 1 or 2 artichoke bottoms per serving on warm plate, hollow side up. Fill hollows with creamed spinach, and top each with a poached egg. Cover each egg with a blanket of Hollandaise.

EGGS FLORENTINE

Serves 6

   BUY

2 packages frozen chopped spinach
   (10-ounces each)
Heavy cream

<table>
<tr><td>

HAVE ON HAND

Butter
Flour
Salt
Cayenne pepper
Milk
6 eggs
Parmesan cheese, freshly grated

</td><td>

COOKWARE

2 small saucepans
6 individual baking dishes *or* 1½-
quart shallow baking dish

</td></tr>
</table>

1. In saucepan melt *⅓ cup butter*. Stir in *⅓ cup flour, ¾ teaspoon salt,* and *⅛ teaspoon cayenne*. Gradually stir in *2 cups milk* and cook, stirring constantly, until sauce is smooth and thickened. Stir in *½ cup cream* and cook over low heat until ready to use, stirring occasionally.

2. Cook *spinach* according to package directions. Drain well and stir in *½ cup of the sauce*. Spread spinach onto bottom of the baking dish, or dishes.

3. Poach *6 eggs*.

4. Stir *½ cup grated Parmesan cheese* into *remaining cream sauce*.

5. Make six depressions in the spinach and put a poached egg in each. Pour sauce over eggs and spinach, and place under broiler heat until sauce is lightly browned and bubbly.

HUEVOS RANCHEROS

Serves 6. Eggs poached in a sauce. Good with a hot corn muffin.

BUY

1 large green pepper
Mozzarella cheese
1-pound can whole tomatoes

HAVE ON HAND

Large onion
Garlic
Olive oil
Chili powder

Cumin, ground
Oregano   *COOKWARE*
Red pepper *or* cayenne   10-inch skillet
6 eggs

1. Peel and chop *1 large onion*. Seed and slice thinly the *green pepper*. Peel and mince *2 cloves garlic*. Cut 6 thin slices *mozzarella cheese*. Set aside.

2. In skillet heat *3 tablespoons olive oil* and in it sauté the onion, green pepper, and garlic until vegetables are tender and onion is golden.

3. Add *2 tablespoons chili powder*, *½ teaspoon cumin*, and *½ teaspoon oregano*. Drain and add the *tomatoes* and *¼ teaspoon red pepper or cayenne*. Bring to a simmer and cook over medium heat for 20 minutes, stirring and mashing the tomatoes occasionally.

4. Make 6 depressions in the vegetable mixture and break *1 egg* into each depression. Cover each egg with a slice of mozzarella. Cover the skillet and poach the eggs over low heat until they reach the desired degree of firmness.

Scrambled Eggs

Among the most delicious dishes in all the world are properly scrambled eggs. On the other hand, there is no dish which suffers more often from overcooking. They must be heated slowly and stirred constantly, until they are cooked through yet are still moist and creamy. All it takes is strictly fresh eggs—and enough love and care to want them to be perfect. If you don't feel you can devote the few minutes of constant stirring to assure perfection, you can resort to the use of a double saucepan. Eggs scrambled in this fashion are called Rumbled Eggs. They cook practically unattended and may be kept waiting for a short time before being served. Count on 2 to 3 eggs per serving, depending on appetites.

HOW TO SCRAMBLE EGGS FOR TWO

1. Break *6 fresh eggs* into a bowl and sprinkle with a *little salt* and *a dash of white pepper*. Beat quickly but lightly with a fork or rotary beater. Mix thoroughly if you like a uniform yellow, or slightly if you like streaks of white and yellow.

2. Melt *2 tablespoons butter* in the bottom of an 8-inch skillet over moderate heat. Swirl the pan so that the butter coats sides as well as bottom. Give one last beat to the eggs and, before the butter begins to sizzle, pour them into the pan.

3. Stir with a wooden spoon gently, constantly, scraping the bottom and sides of the skillet in order to prevent any one portion from becoming overcooked. Cook for 3 to 5 minutes, or until the eggs are thickened throughout, but are still soft, creamy, and glossy.

4. Remove pan immediately from heat and stir in *1 tablespoon butter or cream, or,* to be extra magnanimous, *1 tablespoon of each.*

5. Serve on warm plates IMMEDIATELY, since the heat of the eggs will cause them to continue to cook. If desired, sprinkle with a *little minced parsley or chives*.

RUMBLED EGGS FOR TWO

1. Put a baking dish or casserole on top of a saucepan of *boiling water*. For *4 eggs*, put *1 tablespoon butter* in the casserole to melt. Meanwhile beat eggs with *a pinch each of salt and pepper*. Pour eggs into the hot butter and stir for a moment. You can leave them over gently bubbling water while you attend to other duties, giving them an occasional stir as you pass the stove.

2. As soon as the eggs have reached a thick, creamy consistency, remove saucepan from the heat and the eggs will keep hot for a few minutes. But don't decide at this point to make muffins to go with them!

EGGS AND SPINACH HELSCHER

Serves 2

BUY

10-ounce package frozen chopped spinach
Parmesan cheese

HAVE ON HAND	*COOKWARE*
Garlic	Medium saucepan
Olive oil	10-inch skillet
Salt and pepper	
2 eggs	

1. Cook *spinach* according to package directions. Empty into a sieve to drain and, with the back of a wooden spoon, press out as much of the liquid from the spinach as possible. Set aside.

2. Grate *¼ cup Parmesan cheese*. Peel and mince *1 clove garlic*.

3. In skillet heat *3 tablespoons olive oil.* Add the garlic, and sauté until pale gold. Be careful it does not over-brown.

4. Add the spinach and spread it over the bottom of the skillet. Sprinkle spinach with *¼ teaspoon salt, some pepper,* and *2 tablespoons of the grated Parmesan.* Cook for 2 to 3 minutes, turning the spinach over with a spatula until it is very hot.

5. Break in *2 eggs,* then keep tossing and turning the spinach until the eggs are lightly scrambled into it.

6. Drain off any excess oil or liquid from skillet, turn spinach and eggs onto a warm serving plate, and sprinkle with the *remaining grated cheese.*

EGGS SOUTH OF THE BORDER

Serves 4 to 6

BUY

4 green peppers
2 large sweet onions
4 ripe tomatoes
Chives *or* green onions
8-ounce container cream

HAVE ON HAND

Garlic
Olive oil
Salt
Coarsely cracked pepper
Butter
Bread
1 dozen eggs

COOKWARE

2 medium skillets

1. Remove stems and seeds from *green peppers* and slice thinly. Peel *onions* and slice thinly. Peel and quarter the *tomatoes* and squeeze out excess seeds. Peel and mince *1 large clove garlic.*

2. In skillet heat *4 tablespoons olive oil,* and in it sauté the peppers and onions until onions are transparent. Add tomatoes, garlic, *½ teaspoon*

salt, and *a good sprinkling of pepper.* Cook, stirring, until all the vegetables are tender, but not overcooked.

3. Meanwhile *toast and butter 6 slices bread,* and cut into triangles. Chop *some chives or green onion tops* and set aside.

4. Beat *1 dozen eggs* with *½ cup of the cream.* In the second skillet melt *4 tablespoons butter.* Just as the butter begins to bubble, turn heat to low and pour in the eggs. Cook, stirring constantly, until eggs are set but not dry. Sprinkle with a *little more salt and pepper.*

5. Turn the eggs out into the center of a warm serving platter, and surround with the vegetables and pan juice. Sprinkle with the chopped chives or green onion tops and serve with the toast triangles.

EGGS SCRAMBLED WITH GREEN PEPPER AND MUSHROOMS

Serves 4

   BUY

1 green pepper
¼ pound fresh mushrooms
Parsley

HAVE ON HAND	*COOKWARE*
Onion	Medium skillet
Olive oil	
4 eggs	
Salt and pepper	

1. Seed and finely chop the *green pepper.* Trim, wash, and slice the *mushrooms.* Peel and chop *1 medium onion.* Chop *2 tablespoons parsley.*

2. In skillet heat *3 tablespoons olive oil,* and in it sauté onion, green pepper, and mushrooms for about 5 minutes, or until onion and green pepper are soft and mushrooms are tender.

3. Beat *4 eggs* with *1 tablespoon water, ½ teaspoon salt,* and *a sprinkling of pepper.* Pour egg mixture over the vegetables and cook over low heat, stirring constantly until the eggs are just set, but still soft. Sprinkle with the chopped parsley and serve with toast, muffins, or hot biscuits.

PISTO CON HUEVOS REVUELTOS
(Sautéed Vegetables with Scrambled Eggs)

Serves 4. Serve with fresh crusty bread.

BUY
1 green pepper
3 small zucchini
1 medium eggplant
4 large tomatoes

HAVE ON HAND	COOKWARE
Medium onion	10-inch skillet
Large potato	
Olive oil	
Salt	
6 eggs	

1. Halve, seed, and dice the *green pepper*. Trim the *zucchini* and cut into ½-inch thick slices. Peel and dice the *eggplant*. Peel and chop *1 medium onion* and the *tomatoes*. Peel *1 large potato* and cut into ½-inch thick rounds.

2. In heavy skillet, heat *⅓ cup olive oil*. Add the green pepper, zucchini, eggplant, onion, potato, and *1 tablespoon salt*. Sauté for 10 to 15 minutes, stirring occasionally, or until vegetables are lightly browned. Add tomatoes and cook over low heat for 15 to 20 minutes, or until all vegetables are soft.

3. Beat *6 eggs*. Pour eggs into the vegetable mixture and stir constantly until they begin to thicken. The mixture should not be allowed to set in the bottom of the skillet. Serve immediately.

Baked or Shirred Eggs

These are a delicate and beautiful dish IF they are taken from the oven before they are overcooked. And this takes care on your part. The eggs should be cooked both underneath and on top; the whites should be still creamy and soft, and the yolks barely set with just a film of transparent white over them. Baked eggs will continue to cook from the heat of the dish, so err on the undercooked side rather than on the overcooked if you must err. And if your partner likes his eggs well done, skip over to the hard-cooked egg section that follows.

Baked eggs may be cooked in a shallow baking dish large enough to accommodate the number of eggs you wish to cook, or in shallow individual baking dishes of a size to hold 2 eggs. You can use various sizes of skillets, too, if you prefer, providing the handle either is ovenproof or has been protected by a tight wrapping of aluminum foil. The oven temperature used for baking eggs is a moderate one, so a wood handle will not char. Don't forget, however, that it will be hot when you take the skillet from the oven. Use your pot holder!

HOW TO BAKE OR SHIRR EGGS
FOR ONE INDIVIDUAL DISH

1. Preheat oven to 325° F.

2. In an individual baking dish melt *1 tablespoon butter* over low heat. Don't let the butter brown. When it is melted, slip *2 eggs* into the dish and sprinkle them with a *little salt*.

3. Using a pot holder, tip the dish and spoon a little of the melted butter over the yolks.

4. Bake in the preheated oven for 15 to 20 minutes, or until the whites are milky but still creamy and the yolks are lightly set.

5. Serve from the baking dish.

EGGS SHIRRED IN CREAM

Melt *1 teaspoon butter* in bottom of a small, shallow baking dish and when butter is melted slip in *2 eggs*. Spoon a *little hot heavy cream* over the eggs, then place dish in a preheated 325° F. oven. Bake for 15 to 20 minutes, or until perfectly cooked.

SWISS EGGS

Serves 3

HAVE ON HAND	*COOKWARE*
Butter	Shallow baking dish
6 eggs	
Swiss cheese, thinly sliced	
Heavy cream	
Salt and pepper	

1. Melt *3 tablespoons butter* in a shallow heatproof baking dish large enough to accommodate *6 eggs*. Slip eggs into the melted butter, and cook over low heat for about 2 minutes.

2. Cover each egg with *a slice of cheese;* pour *½ cup cream* over the cheese slices; and sprinkle with *salt and pepper*. Bake in a preheated 325° F. oven for about 15 minutes, or until eggs are just set and cheese is melted.

HUEVOS CAMPESINOS

Serves 4

  BUY

A good cheese, such as Parmesan,
  mozzarella, Swiss, *or* Cheddar
4 slightly green tomatoes

  HAVE ON HAND   *COOKWARE*

Garlic   8- or 10-inch skillet
Parsley
Olive oil
Salt
4 eggs

1. Preheat oven to 350° F.

2. Grate or shred *½ cup cheese.*

3. Cut and discard a thin slice from both top and bottom of each
tomato, then remove the hard stem core and slice the tomatoes thickly.
Peel and chop *2 large cloves garlic.* Chop *2 tablespoons parsley.*

4. In skillet with handle that is ovenproof (or has been wrapped in
foil) heat *6 tablespoons olive oil,* and in it sauté the tomato slices for 2 to
3 minutes on each side or until fork tender.

5. Sprinkle tomato slices with the garlic and parsley and *½ teaspoon
salt.*

6. Break *4 eggs* into the skillet on top of the tomatoes, keeping each
egg separate from the other. Sprinkle eggs with the cheese.

7. Bake in preheated oven for about 20 minutes, or until eggs are set.

Hard-Cooked Eggs

The following recipe is in my last book, *Ann Seranne's Good Food & How to Cook It*. I have tried to avoid repeating recipes, but the simple technique of hard-cooking and peeling an egg is so often ignored or abused that it is worth repeating.

THE RIGHT WAY TO HARD COOK AN EGG AND PEEL IT

Put fresh eggs into a saucepan with sufficient water to cover the eggs by at least 1 inch. Bring to a rapid boil, reduce heat, and simmer the eggs for exactly 10 minutes.

Drain immediately and cover with cold water to stop further cooking and prevent the unattractive thin layer of gray which often coats the brilliant gold of the yolks.

Peel as soon as the eggs are cool enough to handle as follows: Crack the egg all over in a myriad of little cracks—easy does it—then hold the cracked egg under cold running water and the shell and thin inner membrane will come cleanly away. If you don't believe me, try it!

Hard-cooked eggs are a joy either as an appetizer or as an accompaniment to a salad luncheon. There are dozens of savory mayonnaise sauces to serve with them, and the eggs may be sliced, halved, or quartered before saucing. One of my favorite dishes featuring hard-cooked eggs is:

EGGS CRESSONNIÈRE

Hard cook *6 eggs,* then peel and cut in half lengthwise. Arrange the halves, cut side down, in a serving dish and cover generously with *Watercress Mayonnaise.* Cover dish with transparent film and refrigerate until serving time.

WATERCRESS MAYONNAISE: Combine *1 cup mayonnaise* with *¼ cup finely chopped watercress, 1 tablespoon lemon juice,* and *salt to taste.*

EGGS ANDALOUSE

Another simple favorite: Hard cook *12 eggs,* then peel, and cut in half lengthwise. Arrange the halves, cut side down, in a serving dish, and cover generously with *Sauce Andalouse.* Garnish with *strips of pimiento* and *capers.* Cover dish with transparent film and refrigerate until serving time.

SAUCE ANDALOUSE: Combine *2 cups mayonnaise* with *2 tablespoons tomato ketchup* and *2 tablespoons finely chopped pimiento.*

SPEAKING OF MAYONNAISE, why not make your own in a blender? It takes about 1 minute, and it's much cheaper and much better than any mayonnaise you can buy. For a special treat, use all fresh olive oil, or use half olive oil and half safflower oil.

BLENDER MAYONNAISE

Makes about 1½ cups. Please don't try to double this recipe—it won't work!

HAVE ON HAND

Salad oils (part olive oil, please)
1 egg

Vinegar *or* lemon juice
Dry mustard
Salt

1. Measure *1 cup of mixed salad oils* and set aside.

2. Into blender container break *1 egg.* Add *2 tablespoons vinegar or lemon juice, ½ teaspoon dry mustard, ½ teaspoon salt, and ¼ cup of the measured oil.*

3. Cover blender container and begin blending on medium or low-medium speed. IMMEDIATELY remove cover and pour in the *remaining oil* in a steady stream. All oil must be added within 18 seconds from the start.

4. Turn off blender and stir mayonnaise with a rubber spatula.

VARIATIONS:

Green Mayonnaise: Add to *egg* in container *½ small clove garlic, 1 tablespoon fresh dill, 1 tablespoon chopped chives or green onion tops.*

Aïoli Sauce (if you like garlic); try this sometime on a baked potato! Add to *egg* in container *4 cloves garlic,* peeled and sliced.

Tarragon Mayonnaise: Add to egg in container *1 tablespoon fresh tarragon leaves or 1 teaspoon dried tarragon.*

CREAMED EGGS

Serves 2 or 4. Serve on hot buttered toast or on split and buttered corn bread.

HAVE ON HAND	*COOKWARE*
Milk	Small saucepan
Butter	2-quart saucepan
Flour	
Cream	
Parsley	
Worcestershire sauce	
Tabasco	
Salt	
4 hard-cooked eggs	

1. In small saucepan measure *1 cup milk* and heat to steaming.

2. In larger saucepan melt *3 tablespoons butter*. Stir in *3 tablespoons flour,* and cook, stirring, until mixture is smooth and bubbling. Remove from heat and add hot milk, all at once. Stir vigorously until mixture is smooth. Return to medium heat and cook, stirring, for 3 minutes, or until sauce is smooth and thick. Stir in *½ cup cream.*

3. Stir in *2 tablespoons chopped parsley, ½ teaspoon Worcestershire sauce, a good dash Tabasco,* and *½ teaspoon salt, or to taste.*

4. Slice and stir in the *eggs,* and heat to serving temperature. Do not let the sauce boil after eggs are added.

CURRIED EGGS

Add *1 tablespoon good curry powder* along with the flour to the hot butter.

CURRIED EGG CAKES

Serves 6. Serve plain or with a favorite sauce such as cream, tomato or mushroom.

HAVE ON HAND	*COOKWARE*
1 dozen plus 3 eggs	Shallow baking pan
Chutney	Small saucepan
Butter	8- or 10-inch skillet
Flour	
Curry powder	
Cayenne pepper	
Salt	
Milk	
Fine bread, *or* cracker, crumbs	
Salad oil for frying	

IN ADVANCE:

1. Hard cook and peel *1 dozen eggs,* then chop coarsely. Chop *2 tablespoons chutney.*

2. In saucepan melt *4 tablespoons butter;* stir in *6 tablespoons flour, 1 tablespoon curry powder, ⅛ teaspoon cayenne,* and *1 teaspoon salt.*

Cook, stirring, for about 1 minute. Then gradually stir in *1 ¼ cups milk,* and cook over moderate heat, stirring constantly, until sauce is smooth and very thick.

3. Remove sauce from heat, and beat in *2 egg yolks.* Stir in chopped hard-cooked eggs and chutney. Spread mixture in a shallow baking pan and chill.

WHEN READY TO COOK:

4. Form the chilled mixture into 6 flat cakes.

5. Beat *1 egg with 1 tablespoon water.* Coat the egg cakes with *flour,* then with beaten egg, and finally roll in *bread crumbs,* coating the cakes well on all sides.

6. In skillet heat *enough salad oil to cover bottom of skillet by ¼ inch.* When oil is hot but not smoking, add the egg cakes and fry until golden and crisp on both sides, turning once.

7. Drain on absorbent paper and serve hot.

Omelets

An omelet can be described as scrambled eggs enclosed in their own soft blanket of coagulated egg. The actual cooking is a question of 30 seconds, and the omelet should be served golden, light, and plump while the consistency of the interior is for the most part semiliquid or, as the French would say, *baveuse.* When overcooked an omelet becomes dry and tough.

Actually there is little reason for anyone to make a poor or overcooked omelet, but anyone who tells you that it is altogether easy is an optimist. It *is* tricky, and practice is the only way to master the technique. But why not try? The worst you can end up with is scrambled eggs, and they're nothing to turn one's nose up at—unless, again, they are overcooked.

Once you have learned to make a plain omelet, you can make variations *ad infinitum* by adding chopped herbs, or vegetables (or chopped meats, fish, or seafood) to the egg mixture before cooking, by filling the omelet with a savory purée or diced mixture of your choice, or by garnishing it with sour cream or a sauce.

In addition to very fresh eggs, three things are necessary for a good omelet. These are: A correct omelet pan, brisk heat, and some courage. The relatively new non-stick omelet pans of porcelain-covered cast iron have solved the first requirement. Every cook has brisk heat, and most have courage. So let's make an omelet.

For a 3-egg omelet, use a pan with a bottom diameter of 7 to 8 inches. A smaller pan, with a bottom diameter of 5 to 6 inches, is perfect for a 2-egg omelet.

HOW TO MAKE A PLAIN OR FRENCH OMELET

1. Break *3 fresh eggs* into a bowl, add *a pinch of salt* and *1 tablespoon cold water,* and beat lightly with a fork until whites and yolks are thoroughly blended but not foamy.

2. Heat an omelet pan over brisk heat until a drop of water flicked on it sizzles and evaporates immediately. Add *a good tablespoon of sweet butter,* and when it begins to foam and give off a nutty aroma but before it browns, pour in the eggs.

3. With the left hand, shake the pan continually back and forth over the heat; at the same time, with a fork held in the right hand, stir the eggs so that you heat all the liquid evenly. (It's a little like rubbing your tummy and patting your head at the same time.)

4. When eggs are thickened but still soft and moist, continue to shake the pan, but stop stirring with the fork—instead, use the fork to smooth the egg evenly in the pan.

5. If the omelet is to be filled, now is the time to sprinkle the filling over the surface of the eggs, fold the omelet, and turn it out onto a warm serving plate. To do this neatly, grasp the handle of the omelet pan in the left hand, thumb and fingers uppermost. Then tip the pan over the plate as, with the fork in the right hand, you roll the omelet onto the plate.

If you're lucky, you have an omelet; if not, you have scrambled eggs. Don't get discouraged, try again!

CHEESE OMELET

Add *3 tablespoons grated mixed Gruyère and Parmesan cheese* to *3 beaten eggs.* Use *very little salt.*

MUSHROOM OMELET

Add *3 tablespoons minced sautéed mushrooms* to *3 beaten eggs.* Garnish omelet with *sautéed mushroom caps.*

OMELETTE FINES HERBS

Add *½ teaspoon each minced parsley, chives, tarragon, and chervil* to *3 beaten eggs.*

TOMATO OMELET

Fill omelet with *peeled, diced, and seeded ripe tomatoes* stewed in a *little butter until reduced to a thick purée.* Season to taste with *salt and pepper.*

SPANISH OMELET

Simmer *1 chopped onion, 2 peeled and chopped tomatoes or ½ cup canned tomatoes, 1 chopped sweet green pepper,* and *1 minced clove garlic,* in *2 tablespoons salad oil* for about 10 minutes, or until vegetables are tender. Fill omelet with *half the vegetable mixture,* turn out onto warm plate, and pour *remaining mixture* over and around it.

SPINACH OMELET

Sauté *1 minced small onion,* in *1 tablespoon butter* until golden. Combine onion mixture with *½ cup cooked, well-drained spinach, 2 tablespoons heavy cream,* and *a pinch of marjoram.* Season to taste with *salt and pepper.* Fill omelet with the spinach mixture, turn onto warm plate, and serve with *sour cream.*

SORREL OMELET

Sauté *a dozen or so shredded sorrel leaves* and *2 tablespoons chopped chives* in *1 tablespoon butter* until sorrel is wilted and mushy. Fill omelet with the tart sorrel mixture, turn onto warm plate, and serve with *sour cream* and lots of *chopped chives* sprinkled on top.

PRINCESS OMELET

Serves 2. The method described in step 3 is the American one for making an omelet. You may find it easier, but it is not "correct." Garnish with cooked buttered asparagus or peas.

HAVE ON HAND	*COOKWARE*
3-ounce package fresh cream cheese	8-inch skillet *or* omelet pan
Onion	
4 eggs	
Commercial dairy sour cream	
Crushed red pepper	
Salt	
Butter	

1. Cut the *cheese* into ½-inch cubes. Peel *1 small onion* and mince *enough to measure 2 teaspoons.*

2. Combine *4 eggs, ¼ cup sour cream,* the onion, *¼ teaspoon crushed red pepper,* and *½ teaspoon salt.* Beat well and fold in the cream cheese.

3. In skillet or omelet pan, heat *1 tablespoon butter* until it just begins to brown. Pour egg mixture into the hot butter. As the mixture thickens at the edges, draw these portions with a fork toward the center of the pan so that the uncooked portions flow to the bottom. Shake pan back and forth over the heat to keep the omelet from sticking.

4. When eggs are set but still moist, fold and turn onto a warm serving dish. Serve at once.

CHINESE VEGETABLE OMELET SCRAMBLE

Serves 3

BUY

Small can bean sprouts
4 medium mushrooms
1 red *or* green sweet pepper
Small can bamboo shoots
Celery

HAVE ON HAND	*COOKWARE*
Garlic	Two 8-inch skillets *or* Chinese woks
Peanut oil	One lid
Sugar	
Soy sauce	
6 eggs	
Salt	
Ground ginger	
Dry sherry	

1. Drain the *bean sprouts.* Trim, wash, and slice the *mushrooms.* Seed the *sweet pepper* and cut into ¾-inch squares. Drain and dice *½ cup bamboo shoots.* Slice *½ cup celery.* Peel and mince *1 clove garlic.*

2. In a skillet or wok, heat *2 tablespoons peanut oil* until very hot. Add bean sprouts, mushrooms, the sweet pepper, bamboo shoots, and celery, and cook over high heat for 3 to 4 minutes, stirring constantly. Remove from heat and stir in *½ teaspoon sugar* and *1 tablespoon soy sauce.*

3. In mixing bowl beat *6 eggs* lightly with *½ teaspoon salt* and *½ teaspoon ginger.*

4. In a second skillet or wok, heat *another 2 tablespoons peanut oil—* this time to medium hot. Add garlic and sauté for 1 minute. Pour in eggs, cover pan, and cook for 1 minute. Add the vegetables and give the whole mixture a gentle stir. Then flip over egg-and-vegetables with a broad spatula. When mixture is almost set, pour over it *¼ cup dry sherry;* then give the omelet another flip over, and scramble lightly. Serve immediately on warm plates.

Savory Soufflés

The basis of all savory soufflés is a thick sauce made of butter and flour and, usually, milk. The secret of a soufflé is nothing more or less than the proper beating of the eggs and the incorporation of these beaten eggs into the basic mixture.

The yolks should be beaten until light and lemon-colored and should be stirred into the sauce while the sauce is still hot; the heat of the sauce partly cooks the yolks. However, you should let the mixture cool a little before you go on to add the whites.

The egg whites should be beaten until stiff but not dry, and there should be more egg whites than egg yolks, the usual proportion being 4 whites to each 3 yolks. Even larger quantities of egg whites will not hurt, but the way the whites are beaten and the manner in which they are mixed into the egg yolk base are the most important. Also, care should be taken that the bowl and beater are absolutely clean and that the egg whites do not contain any particle of yolk, for if they do, or if either the bowl or beater is greasy, the eggs will not mound stiffly.

A round-bottomed copper bowl is the perfect bowl in which to beat egg whites, but lacking that, use porcelain, glass, stainless steel, or plastic—anything except aluminum, for that is likely to discolor the whites. Also egg whites will mound faster and to greater volume if they are hand-beaten with a large balloon whip. This large whisk can keep all the egg whites in constant motion so that they reach the right degree of stiffness in about 3 minutes, as against 8 minutes with an electric or rotary beater.

BASIC SOUFFLÉ PROCEDURES

TO BEAT EGG WHITES BY HAND:

Use a large, clean, round-bottomed bowl and a large wire whisk. Start beating with a circular motion, about 2 strokes per second until the egg whites become frothy. Then increase the strokes to 4 per second, keeping the motion in as large circles as the bowl will permit, and turning the bowl frequently. Continue to beat until a large, graceful peak will hold its shape on the end of the whip when the whisk is withdrawn. The egg whites should be glossy, not overbeaten and dry-looking.

TO BEAT WITH ELECTRIC BEATER:

Begin beating on low speed until egg whites are frothy. Gradually increase speed to moderate. If using a hand electric beater, tilt the bowl and move the beater up from the center and around the sides of the bowl until whites are stiff enough to hold a large peak. If using a stationary beater, push whites from sides of bowl into the beater with a rubber spatula while they are being beaten.

FOLDING EGG WHITES INTO EGG YOLK MIXTURE:

The way the beaten egg whites are added to the yolk mixture is an important step in a successful soufflé. They must be mixed in gently and delicately in order to retain as much of the air beaten into them as possible. First, STIR in a couple of large spoonfuls of the beaten whites (about ¼ of the total amount) to thin down the yolk mixture. Then FOLD in remaining egg whites as follows: using the palm of one hand (the best method), or a large rubber scraper, cut down from top of mixture to the bottom of the bowl, then up against the side of the bowl. Rotate the bowl frequently and continue until all the whites have been incorporated into the yolk mixture. A few unblended patches of egg whites do not matter, but there should be no visible streaks of egg yolk mixture.

PREPARING THE SOUFFLÉ DISH:

Butter bottom and sides generously; then, if desired, coat them lightly with grated Parmesan cheese or dry bread crumbs. Pour soufflé mixture into the prepared mold. The mixture should fill the mold at least ¾ full, but it should not exceed ⅞ full.

TO HOLD A PREPARED SOUFFLÉ:

Bake immediately. Or, if necessary, you can hold the soufflé for as long as 1 hour before baking if you cover it with a large soup kettle to keep drafts from dissipating the air in the mixture.

TO BAKE A SOUFFLÉ:

Preheat oven to 400° F. Place the soufflé on rack in the center of the oven, close door, and immediately turn oven temperature down to 375° F. Bake until soufflé is done to the point desired—either completely set or still creamy in the center. *To test for doneness:* Open oven door and, with a pot holder, grasp the rim of the soufflé dish and shake it gently. If the soufflé shimmies just a little in the center, it is what the French call *baveuse,* creamy in the middle. If you don't like it this way, bake for 3 or 4 minutes longer.

CHEESE SOUFFLÉ

Serves 4

BUY

2-ounces aged Parmesan cheese
4-ounces aged Cheddar *or* imported Swiss
  or Gruyère chesee

HAVE ON HAND

Milk
Butter
Flour
Cornstarch

Dry mustard *or* prepared Dijon
Salt
Cayenne pepper
6 eggs

COOKWARE

1½-quart soufflé dish
Small saucepan
1-quart saucepan

1. Grate the *Parmesan.* Shred the *Cheddar, Swiss, or Gruyère.*

2. Preheat oven to 400° F. *Butter* the soufflé dish, then sprinkle it with *1 tablespoon of the grated Parmesan.*

3. In small saucepan heat *1 cup milk* to steaming hot.

4. In larger saucepan melt *3 tablespoons butter.* Stir in *2 tablespoons flour* and cook, stirring, until mixture is bubbly. Remove saucepan from heat; add hot milk and beat vigorously until mixture is well blended and smooth. Return to moderate heat and cook, stirring, for about 1 minute, or until sauce is thickened.

5. Combine *2 teaspoons cornstarch* and *2 tablespoons water* and stir into the hot sauce. Add the shredded cheese and cook, stirring, until cheese is melted.

6. Remove from heat, and beat in *½ teaspoon dry mustard or 1 teaspoon Dijon,* and *a dash each of salt and cayenne.*

7. Separate *4 eggs,* beating the *yolks, one at a time,* into the hot sauce, and dropping the *whites* into a mixing bowl. Separate *2 more eggs;* reserve the yolks for another purpose and add the whites to the other whites in the bowl. Return sauce to low heat and cook, stirring, for 3 minutes, without letting it boil. Set aside.

8. Beat the egg whites with a rotary beater until stiff, but still glossy and BY NO MEANS DRY. Add about *¼ of the beaten whites* to the yolk mixture and stir in thoroughly. Add *remaining whites* and fold in gently.

9. Turn soufflé mixture into the prepared dish, and put into the preheated oven. IMMEDIATELY REDUCE HEAT to 375° F., and bake the soufflé for 30 to 35 minutes, or until set to taste.

VEGETABLE SOUFFLÉ

Follow preceding recipe, but in place of the cheese use *1 cup cooked, finely chopped or mashed vegetable,* such as spinach, broccoli, cauliflower, carrots, peas, eggplant, mushrooms, artichoke bottoms.

BLACK WALNUT SOUFFLÉ

Serves 4. You may substitute hazelnuts or pecans for the black walnuts if you prefer, but there is something about the flavor of black walnuts that makes this soufflé unique.

BUY

6 ounces shelled black walnuts
3 fresh medium-size mushrooms
6 very fresh eggs

HAVE ON HAND	*COOKWARE*
Onion	Mortar *or* electric blender
Garlic	Small skillet
Butter	Small saucepan
Milk	1-quart saucepan
Flour	1½-quart soufflé dish
Salt and cayenne pepper	
Dry mustard	
Brandy	

1. Crush *walnuts* to a paste in a mortar, or grind very finely in a blender. Set aside. Peel and mince *1 large onion* and *1 small clove garlic.* Wash, trim, and mince the *mushrooms.*

2. In small skillet melt *3 tablespoons butter,* and in it sauté onion, garlic, and mushrooms until onion is golden. Set aside.

3. Preheat oven to 400° F. *Butter* the soufflé dish.

4. In small saucepan heat *1 cup milk* to steaming hot. Separate the *6 eggs.*

5. In larger saucepan melt *4 tablespoons butter.* Stir in *4 tablespoons flour, a dash each of salt and cayenne,* and *½ teaspoon dry mustard.* Cook, stirring, until mixture bubbles, then remove from heat. Add hot milk all at once, and stir rapidly until mixture is blended. Return to heat and cook for about 2 minutes, stirring rapidly, until sauce is smooth and thickened.

6. Remove saucepan from heat, and beat in the *egg yolks,* onion mixture, and the crushed nuts.

7. In mixing bowl beat *egg whites* until stiff but still glossy. Add *about ¼ of the beaten whites* to the nut mixture and stir in thoroughly. Fold in *remaining whites*.

8. Turn soufflé mixture into prepared dish and put into the pre-heated oven. IMMEDIATELY REDUCE OVEN TEMPERATURE to 375° F., and bake the soufflé for 35 to 40 minutes, or until set to taste.

9. Remove from oven. Pour *1 ounce of brandy* over the soufflé, ignite the brandy, and serve the soufflé flaming.

CHEESE STRATA

Serves 6. Called a soufflé in some parts of the country because it has a similar consistency, this mixture of bread, cheese, and custard is a good, homey, inexpensive dish that can stand on its own merit without borrowing its reputation from a real soufflé.

BUY

Loaf of bread
½ pound Cheddar cheese
1 pint milk
8-ounce container light *or* heavy cream
1 large ripe tomato (optional)

HAVE ON HAND	*COOKWARE*
Butter	9 x 13 inch baking dish
Paprika	
6 eggs	
Salt	
Cayenne	
Parsley	

1. *Butter* the baking dish. Spread *12 slices bread* thinly with *butter*. Shred or thinly slice the *cheese*.

2. Line baking dish with *half the bread slices* and top with a layer of *half the cheese*. Repeat bread and cheese layers and sprinkle generously with *paprika*.

3. In mixing bowl beat *6 eggs* lightly, and stir in *2 cups milk*, the *cream, ½ teaspoon salt,* and *⅛ teaspoon cayenne pepper*.

4. Pour egg mixture over the bread and cheese, being careful that every slice of bread is thoroughly moistened. Refrigerate for at least 3 hours, or overnight.

5. When ready to bake, preheat oven to 325° F. and bake the strata for 35 minutes. Sprinkle with a *little chopped parsley*, and, if desired, arrange slices of the *tomato* on top. Return to oven and bake for 15 minutes longer. Serve hot and puffed.

SPINACH MOUSSE RING

Serves 4. Serve filled with Creamed or Curried Eggs.

BUY

2 packages frozen chopped spinach (10 ounces each)

HAVE ON HAND	*COOKWARE*
Eggs	Saucepan
Cream *or* milk	1-quart ring mold
Butter	Shallow baking pan
Salt and pepper	
Soft bread crumbs	

1. Cook *spinach* according to package directions. Drain in a sieve, pressing out as much excess liquid as possible with back of a spoon.

2. Empty spinach into a mixing bowl and add *3 eggs, ¼ cup cream or milk, ¼ cup melted butter, ¼ teaspoon pepper, 1 teaspoon salt,* and *1½ cups soft bread crumbs.*

3. *Butter* the ring mold. Preheat oven to 350° F.

4. Set mold into a shallow pan containing about *1 inch of hot water.* Fill the mold with the spinach mixture, and bake in the preheated oven for 40 minutes, or until set.

5. Remove mold from oven. Run a knife around the edges and unmold the ring onto a serving platter. Fill the center with Creamed or Curried Eggs (page 149).

There's Nothing Quite Like
Good Cheese

If I had to select one food, and one only, to live on for the rest of my life, it would be cheese. If I were allowed a second food, I would choose whole-grain breads. You can undoubtedly guess the third choice—wine, of course. Wine, bread, and cheese have been staple foods of the world since Biblical times.

Cheese is to milk what wine is to grapes: both are the end results of the preservation of the raw food. And cheese, like wine, has infinite varieties of textures, flavors, and formulae, no two cheeses or wines being identical unless made from the harvest of the same pastureland or vineyard.

To many Americans, unfortunately, cheese means those neat, convenient, relatively inexpensive, pre-packaged processed cheeses, with their unique plastic quality, so readily available in supermarkets. They come in endless flavorless flavors, colors, and shapes, and even in aerosol spray cans!

The cheese used in such products is of very little value in the first place. It is young cheese, and the very soul of cheese lies in its maturity. It is ground, along with any reject cheeses lying around, heated to stringy sterility, and homogenized with artificial flavors, colors, and other additives, until any small virtue it had in the beginning is lost forever. Finally packaged, it remains in its impotent, flavorless, waxy state for a long time in the refrigerator section of the supermarket or at home—but it will never mature.

To some Americans, however, including a rapidly growing group of rebellious truth-seekers, cheese means any one of a vast number of honest unprocessed cheeses, either properly aged or dairy fresh. They may be imported from France, Italy, Denmark, England, Switzerland, Holland, or Greece, or they may be made right here in America, for America need take no second place with the Cheddars and other carefully produced cheeses it has to offer. A fine Port-Salut is made in Wisconsin; California is famous for its Monterey Jack; our domestic Tilsit, Munster, and Brick are excellent, and our native Liederkranz can hold its own against such famous soft-ripening cheeses as Brie and Camembert.

BUYING CHEESE

Because of the growing interest in good cheeses, supermarkets are being forced to stock, among the pre-sliced packages, some respectable wedges of Cheddar (aged more than six months), Munster, and Danish Blue, boxes of Liederkranz or domestic Camembert, and real Switzerland Swiss cheese, and by popular demand new unpackaged types and flavors are added to delicatessen counters every week.

The best sources, however, of quality and variety are the speciality cheese stores and the delicacy departments of large department stores. Here the turnover is quick enough so that the cheeses are in good condition. You can be sure of the cheese you buy if you can see it being cut from bulk, and especially if you can taste a sliver before you buy. Many good cheese stores offer a sample not only to the buyer, but also to the next person waiting in line to be served. Even local grocery stores that sell cheese from bulk will seldom begrudge a sample. If the cheese you buy is good, it looks good in its own special way—moist, of typical color, and pleasantly plump, fitting its wrappings or box snugly. It is not dry (except in the case of certain aged Cheddars), or shriveled, or sunken in the middle.

WHEN TO SERVE CHEESE

Wedges of good cheese make perfect snacks or appetizers to serve with cocktails and should be part of every buffet table. In addition to these usual ways of serving cheese, many Americans are adopting the European custom of serving it as a last course, along with a bowl of ripe fruit or berries, or as the next-to-last course in a meal, with or without a tossed salad.

HOW TO SERVE CHEESE

ALL CHEESE should be served at ROOM TEMPERATURE. In warm weather, firm or semisoft cheese does not need to be out of the refrigerator for more than an hour or so, and soft cheeses like Brie and Camembert require only 30 minutes. In cooler weather, allow at least 2 hours for firm or semisoft varieties and 1 hour for the soft ones.

Bread and wine, the traditional accompaniments, should be chosen to complement the cheese. Strong cheeses, such as Cheddar, Limburger, or Liederkranz need a good rough bread such as pumpernickel and beer or a robust red wine as a beverage. A young firm cheese, such as Gruyère or the semisoft Bel Paese or Port-du-Salut, and the soft-ripening Brie and Camembert call for unsalted crackers or French or Italian bread and sweet butter. A light wine, either red or white, is appropriate. Cream-type and dairy-fresh cheeses are best with a well-chilled white wine or champagne and are often served, for dessert, with a sprinkling of sugar and fresh berries in season. Poached peaches or apricots, or preserved guavas, or even a good fruit jelly also make good accompaniments to the cream-type cheeses. The blue-veined cheeses and the soft-ripening and semisoft cheeses have a great affinity for fresh fruit, particularly apples pears, or figs, but they are also excellent with a lightly tossed salad.

HOW TO STORE CHEESES

Keep all cheese under refrigeration and return any unused portion as soon as possible to the refrigerator. Wrap it tightly in plastic film to keep it moist and to keep its flavor from penetrating other foods. Most firm and semisoft cheeses will keep well for several weeks. Fresh cheeses and soft-ripening cheese should be enjoyed as soon as possible.

Varieties of Cheese
& What Goes with Them

FRESH OR CREAM-TYPE "GREEN" CHEESES:

Usually considered dessert cheeses, these are best when served with fresh berries, stewed fruits, or fruit jellies. They deserve a well-chilled, not too dry white wine.

Boursault (France)
Boursin (France)
Brillat Savarin (France)
Cottage (U.S.)
Cream (U.S.)
Crèma Danica (Denmark)
Crème Chantilly (France)
Double Crème Gervais (France)

Fontainebleau (France)
Fromage de Monsieur (France)
Le Roi (France)
Mozzarella (Italy)
Neufchâtel (France)
Petit Suisse (France)
Ricotta (Italy, U.S.)
Une Gourmandise!!! (France)

MILD SOFT-RIPENING CHEESES:

Traditionally served after the main course and before dessert, with French or Italian bread and a dry red wine. A tossed salad may accompany them, but very little lemon juice or vinegar should be used in the dressing.

Brie (France)
Camembert (France, U.S.)
Crèma Danica (Denmark)

Crèma Royale (Denmark)
Caprice des Dieux (France)
Liederkranz (U.S.)

BLUE-VEINED CHEESES:

Beautiful served as accompaniment to a tossed salad or crumbled into the dressing; excellent as dessert with French or Italian bread and a fresh pear, apple, or peach. A dry red wine is most suitable.

Bleu d'Auvergne (France)
Bleu de Bresse (France)
Blue Cheshire (England)

Danish Blue (Denmark)
Fourme d'Ambert (France)
Gorgonzola (Italy)

Minnesota Blue (U.S.)

Norwegian Blue (Norway)

Pipo Crem' (France)

Roquefort (France)

Saingorlon (France)

Stilton (England)

STRONG CHEESES:

May be served before dessert or as a snack, with buttered dark bread. Beer is the best beverage.

Bierkase (Germany, U.S.)

Liederkranz, fully ripened (U.S.)

Limburger (Belgium, Germany, U.S.)

Livarot (France)

Maroilles (France)

Old Brick (U.S.)

Romadur (Germany)

SEMISOFT CHEESES:

Serve before dessert with French or Italian bread or as a dessert with fresh fruit. Dry red wine is the best beverage.

Beaumont (France)

Bel Paese (Italy)

Creamy Cheddars (U.S.)

Curé Nantais (France

Fontina (Italy)

Fondue de Raisin, or La Grappe (France)

Monterey Jack (U.S.)

Kernhem (Holland)

Munster (Germany, U.S.)

Pont l'Évêque (France)

Port-du-Salut (France, U.S.)

Port-Salut (Denmark)

Queijo da Serra (Portugal)

Reblochon (France)

St.-Paulin (France)

St.-Nectaire (France)

St.-Rémy (France)

Tête de Moine, or Bellelay (France)

Tilsiter (Germany, Denmark, U.S.)

White Wensleydale (England)

FIRM CHEESES:

Serve before dessert; accompany with French or Italian bread or a good dark bread, and with salad if desired. A dry red wine is the best beverage. Note, however, that in England beer is traditional with Cheddars.

Cacciocavallo (Italy)

Cheddar (England, U.S.)

Cheshire (England)

Christian IX (Denmark)

Coon Cheddar (U.S.)

Double Cream Gloucester (England)

Emmentaler (Switzerland, Austria)

Edam (Holland)

Gouda (Holland)

Grand Murols (France)

Gruyère (Switzerland, France)

Kefalotyrie (Greece)

Lancashire (England)

Leicester (England)

Provolone (Italy)

Raclette (Switzerland)   Vacherin (Switzerland)
Swiss (Switzerland, Finland, U.S.)

HARD GRATING CHEESES:

Used primarily to serve freshly grated with pasta, or sparingly in sauces, or sprinkled over the top of dishes to be gratinéed. But they can also be enjoyed as appetizers if sliced paper thin and served on buttered bread with a little freshly ground pepper.

Asiago (Italy)   Romano (Italy, U.S.)
Parmesan (Italy)   Sap Sago (Switzerland)
Pecorino Romano (Italy)   Sardo (Italy)
Pepato (Sicily)

PICKLED OR SALTED CHEESES:

Used in cooking, but excellent as appetizers served with ripe olives, hot peppers, and crisp radishes.

Feta (Greece)   Kasseri (Greece)
Bryndza de Braila (Romania)   Kash Kaval (Bulgaria)

SPICED AND FLAVORED:

Best served for dessert with fresh fruit, but they may also be presented on a buffet table or served as hors d'oeuvres on toast or crackers.

American Munster Caraway (flavored with caraway seeds)
American Pineapple (flavored with pineapple)
Dutch Leyden (spiced with clove)
French Gourmandise (flavored with cherry or kirsch)
German Kuminkase (flavored with cumin seeds)
German Kummelkase (flavored with caraway seeds)
Norwegian Gjetost (flavored with caramel or brown sugar)
Norwegian Nokkelost (flavored with cumin or caraway and clove)
Vermont Sage (flavored with sage)

MELTING CHEESES:

Cheddars   Gruyère
Emmentaler   Mozzarella
Fondue de Raisin or La Grappe   Raclette
Fontina   Switzerland Swiss
Gourmandise

Cooking with Cheese

Cheese should always be melted over low heat or simmering water. If cooked at too high temperature or for too long a time, it becomes unmanageable and stringy.

Melting cheeses should be shredded or grated before they are added to a sauce or combined with other ingredients as in a rarebit or fondue. Cheese, of course, is a prime ingredient of *quiches* and savory tarts (page 48).

Four ounces of cheese will make a generous cupful when shredded or grated.

THE FONDUE

Contrary to what most people think, fondue means "melted," not "cheese." Swiss Fondue, the original and best-known fondue, is a blend of melted cheese, white wine, and Kirschwasser. It is enjoyed as a communal dish. A large bowl containing the fondue is placed in the middle of a table and kept warm by a low-burning spirit lamp. Chunks of French bread are speared onto fondue forks and dipped into the hot cheese mixture. The fondue is stirred often to keep it smooth, and should it become too thick, a little more wine or kirsch is stirred in.

Serve the fondue with white wine, rosé wine, or beer.

In Switzerland, traditionally, anyone who loses his chunk of bread in the fondue must either drink his glass empty or kiss the person on his left. For the sake of sobriety, it's probably safest to give the kiss.

SWISS FONDUE

Serves 4 or 6

BUY

1 pound Switzerland Swiss or Gruyère cheese; DO NOT USE PROCESSED
CHEESE
Long flute of French bread
1 bottle, or more, white wine such as Neufchâtel

HAVE ON HAND	COOKWARE
Cornstarch	Fondue casserole
Garlic	
Kirschwasser	
Freshly ground black pepper	

1. Shred the *cheese* and toss it lightly with *2 teaspoons cornstarch*.
Slice the *bread* into bite-size chunks. Set aside.

2. Peel and split a *clove of garlic* and rub the casserole with the cut
pieces. Add *1 cup wine* and heat until bubbles begin to rise. Do not let
the wine boil.

3. Add cheese to the hot wine, a handful at a time, and cook over
low heat until cheese is melted and smooth, stirring constantly with a
wooden spoon. Stir in *4 tablespoons kirsch,* and sprinkle with *pepper*.

4. Keep the fondue warm over low heat, preferably by means of an
alcohol burner in a chafing dish or buffet warmer.

5. Serve with the chunks of French bread, and supply each diner
with a long-handled fork.

WELSH RABBIT

Serves 4 or 6. This is a variety of fondue in which sharp natural Cheddar
cheese is melted with beer or cream. It is usually quite highly seasoned

with mustard, cayenne, and Worcestershire. Ladle the melted mixture over hot buttered toast.

BUY

1 pound sharp natural Cheddar cheese

HAVE ON HAND	*COOKWARE*
Beer *or* ale	Heavy skillet
Worcestershire sauce	
Dry mustard	
Cayenne	
Hot buttered toast	

1. Shred the *cheese* and set aside.

2. In skillet combine *½ cup ale or beer, 2 teaspoons Worcestershire sauce, ½ teaspoon dry mustard,* and *a good dash of cayenne pepper.* Place over low heat until beer is hot but not boiling.

3. Gradually add the shredded cheese, and stir constantly until it is smooth and melted. Serve immediately on the *toast.*

In many European countries, cheese is served hot and melting without being mixed with any liquid at all. In France, slices of Swiss cheese are coated lightly with flour and pan-fried. In Italy, strips of mozzarella are dipped into a fritter batter and deep-fried. In Switzerland, a wheel of Swiss cheese known as Raclette is cut in half and then placed before an open wood fire; as the cheese melts, it is scraped off and eaten immediately. Here is an unusual Greek recipe for a melting cheese appetizer.

FLAMING KASSERI

Serves 4

BUY

½ pound wedge of Kasseri *or* mozzarella cheese
Italian *or* French bread

HAVE ON HAND	*COOKWARE*
Lemon	Ovenproof skillet *or*
Brandy (the Greeks use Metaxa)	shallow au gratin dish

1. Slice *cheese* ¼ inch thick. Slice and toast the *bread*. Cut *1 lemon* in half.

2. Arrange the cheese in an ovenproof skillet, or a shallow au gratin dish, and place 4 inches beneath broiler heat. Broil for about 6 minutes, or until cheese is soft and the surface is bubbly. Remove from oven.

3. Immediately pour *4 tablespoons brandy* over the cheese and ignite. When the flame has spread over the entire surface, extinguish it by squeezing the juice of the lemon over all.

4. Serve immediately on warm plates with the *pan juices.* Serve the hot toast on the side.

BEANS & PEAS,
GRAINS & CEREALS

Beans & Peas

Most beans and grains are incomplete protein foods, lacking some of the essential amino acids, but they gain substantially in food value when combined with complete protein foods such as eggs, milk, or cheese, or with one another. For instance, neither beans nor rice alone provides all the necessary amino acids, but what is lacking in one is present in the other, so that in combination they add up to be good nutritionally.

The poor peoples of many countries instinctively combine beans with grains or cereals, thereby providing good, low-cost protein dishes for their tables. American Indians cooked lima beans with corn in a dish known as *sauquaquatash,* which later became New England succotash. Black beans and rice is a popular dish in South American countries. Soybean curd, known as *tofu,* is frequently teamed with rice in Japan. And beans and pasta are a happy combination in *minestrone* and *pasta e fagioli* all through Italy. Knowledge of nutrition aside, beans and cereals have nourished the human race since long before Esau sold his birthright for a mess of lentil soup.

Many varieties of dried and canned beans are readily available to us today and, usually, they are interchangeable in recipes. Dried kidney beans may be substituted for dried black beans, dried pea beans or navy beans for dried pinto beans, and canned garbanzos make an excellent (often more interesting) substitute for canned kidney beans. It helps to know, however, that in making substitutions 1 pound of dried beans makes about 5 cups of cooked beans—and that 5 cups of canned cooked beans are the equivalent of the 1 pound of dried beans that is generally specified in a recipe to serve 6.

BAKED SOYBEANS

Serves 6. Here's a "quick" method of cooking dried beans which has recently been publicized. Wash *1 pound of beans* and put them into a saucepan with *1 quart water.* Bring water to a boil, and boil hard for 1 minute. Remove from heat, cover, and let stand for 1 hour. Then simmer for about 1 hour, or until tender, adding *more water* if needed. You don't save much actual cooking time, but the method is a convenience when you forget to soak your beans overnight in advance.

BUY

1 pound soybeans
Bunch green onions
1 green pepper
¼ pound fresh mushrooms

HAVE ON HAND	*COOKWARE*
Cooking oil	3-quart saucepan
Butter	Small skillet
Tomato juice	2-quart baking dish
Oregano *or* marjoram	
Brown sugar	
Salt	

1. Wash *2 cups soybeans* and soak overnight in *plenty of water* to cover.

2. Next day, bring beans to a boil, then simmer for 1 to 1½ hours or until tender, adding *additional water* if needed. Drain and set aside.

3. Meanwhile chop *½ cup green onions, ½ cup green pepper,* and *¾ cup mushrooms.* Sauté these vegetables in *2 tablespoons cooking oil* until onion is transparent. Add vegetables and pan oil to the drained beans and mix well.

4. Add *2 tablespoons butter, ¾ cup tomato juice, ½ teaspoon oregano or marjoram, ¼ cup brown sugar,* and *salt to taste.*

5. Preheat oven to 325° F. *Butter* a baking dish.

6. Empty bean mixture into the baking dish, and bake in the preheated oven for 40 to 50 minutes.

TEXAS BEANS

Serves 5 to 6. Serve over cooked rice.

BUY

1 pound dried pinto beans
4-ounce can roasted green chili peppers
8-ounce can taco sauce
1-pound can tomatoes

HAVE ON HAND

Salt
Large onion
Garlic
Black pepper
Cumin seeds

COOKWARE

4-quart saucepan with lid

1. A day in advance, soak the *pinto beans* in *water* to cover generously.

2. Next day, drain beans, and add *fresh water* to cover by 2 inches. Add *1 teaspoon salt,* bring to a boil, cover, and simmer for about 1 hour, adding *more water* if necessary.

3. Peel and chop *1 large onion* and *2 large cloves garlic.* Chop *half the chili peppers* and set aside. Refrigerate remaining chili peppers for another use.

4. To beans add *½ teaspoon black pepper, 1 teaspoon cumin seeds,* the chopped onion, garlic, and chili peppers, the *taco sauce,* and the *tomatoes.* Cook over low heat for 1 to 1½ hours longer, or until beans are tender and sauce is reduced.

FRIED BEANS WITH SOUR CREAM

Serves 6. You may use any kind of dried beans, but the small pinkish ones, known as pinto beans, are most frequently used in Mexico for this popular and simple recipe.

BUY

1 pound dry pinto beans
Container of sour cream

HAVE ON HAND

Cooking oil
Salt

COOKWARE

3- to 4-quart saucepan with lid
Large heavy skillet

1. Pick over *beans,* discarding any shriveled ones or any foreign particles which may be found among them. Wash, then cover generously with *water* in a large saucepan, and let soak overnight.

2. Drain beans, cover with *2 quarts fresh cold water,* and bring to a boil. Cover and simmer for about 1½ hours, or until beans are tender. Set aside (but do not drain) until ready to fry.

3. To fry beans, heat *½ cup cooking oil* in a heavy skillet. Use a slotted spoon to spoon some of the beans into the hot oil. Mash the beans with the back of a heavy spoon and add a *little of the bean liquor.* Continue to add beans and liquid and continue mashing until all beans are used. Add *salt to taste,* and cook until the mashed beans reach the desired consistency, dry or moist or soupy—according to your preference.

4. Serve hot with a topping of *sour cream.*

BEANS WITH RED WINE

Serves 6

BUY

1 pound dried kidney beans
8-ounce can tomato sauce

HAVE ON HAND   COOKWARE

Large onion   2-quart saucepan
Garlic   2-quart casserole with cover
Red wine
Salt and pepper
Bay leaves
Thyme
Fresh parsley
Butter

1. A day in advance, wash *beans* and soak overnight in *water* to cover generously.

2. Next day, drain beans. Preheat oven to 325° F.

3. Chop *1 large onion* and *2 cloves garlic,* and add to beans along with *1 cup red wine,* the *tomato sauce, 1 teaspoon salt, 1 teaspoon pepper, 1 bay leaf,* crumbled, *a dash of thyme,* and *2 tablespoons chopped parsley.*

4. Put bean mixture into a 2-quart casserole and add *enough water* to cover the beans by 2 inches. Cover and bake in preheated oven for 4 hours. Add *4 tablespoons butter* and, if necessary, *additional water* to keep beans moist. Continue to bake for 2 hours longer.

SPLIT PEA AND TOMATO CASSEROLE

Serves 4

BUY

Box green split peas
1-pound can stewed tomatoes

HAVE ON HAND	*COOKWARE*
Onion	2-quart saucepan
Salt	2 small skillets
Butter	2-quart baking dish
Flour	
Pepper	
Bread	
1 cup cooked *or* leftover rice	

1. Soak *1 cup green split peas* overnight in *water*. Drain the peas, and cook in *fresh water* with *2 tablespoons chopped onion* and *1 teaspoon salt* until tender. Drain, reserving *1 cup of the liquid*.

2. Melt *2 tablespoons butter* in skillet. Stir in *3 tablespoons flour*. Gradually stir in the *reserved liquid,* and cook, stirring, until sauce is smooth and thick. Stir in *salt and pepper to taste*.

3. Crumble *enough bread to make 1 cup crumbs*. In second skillet, sauté crumbs in *2 tablespoons butter* until golden.

4. *Butter* baking dish. Preheat oven to 350° F.

5. In baking dish, place alternate layers of the peas, sauce, the *stewed tomatoes,* and *1 cup cooked rice*. Sprinkle with the buttered bread crumbs and bake in the preheated oven for 30 minutes.

BLACK BEAN PURÉE

Serves 8. Black beans are difficult to buy in my section of northern New Jersey, so I have frequently substituted kidney beans in this recipe with excellent results.

BUY

1 pound dried Cuban black beans *or* kidney beans
1 green pepper
Bunch of green onions
1-pint container sour cream

HAVE ON HAND	*COOKWARE*
Large onion	4-quart saucepan
Garlic	
Olive *or* peanut oil	
Bay leaves	
Salt	
Coarsely cracked pepper	

1. A day in advance, wash *beans* and soak overnight in *6 cups cool water.*

2. Next day, DO NOT DRAIN BEANS. Peel and chop *1 large onion* and *2 cloves garlic*. Seed and chop the *green pepper*. Sauté these vegetables in *½ cup oil* until onion is transparent.

3. Add vegetables and pan oil to the beans and soaking water, and bring to a boil. Add *1 bay leaf, 1 teaspoon salt,* and *½ teaspoon cracked pepper*. Simmer for 1 to 1½ hours, or until beans are tender. Drain off any excess water, leaving the beans fairly dry.

4. Press the beans through a food mill, or, easier still, blend 2 cups of them at a time in an electric blender. Empty into a serving dish and keep warm.

5. Wash and trim the *scallions* and chop the *white part and as much of the green stalks as is tender*. Sprinkle the chopped scallions over the bean purée, and serve with *sour cream*.

LIMA BEANS IN SOUR CREAM

Serves 6. This is good whether served as a cold salad or as a hot casserole.

BUY

1 pound dried lima beans
1 pint sour cream
Bunch of fresh chives
Fresh dill, if possible
Parsley

HAVE ON HAND	*COOKWARE*
Lemons	Large saucepan
Salt and pepper	1½-quart casserole dish
Butter	

1. Wash and pick over the *beans,* and soak overnight in *water* to cover generously.

2. Next day, bring beans and soaking water to a boil and simmer for about 1 hour, or until tender, adding *more water* if necessary. Drain well.

3. Combine the cooked beans with the *sour cream, ¼ cup lemon juice, ½ cup minced chives, 1 tablespoon chopped fresh dill, ¼ cup chopped parsley, 1 teaspoon salt,* and *a good dash pepper.*

4. To serve cold, refrigerate for several hours before serving on a bed of salad greens. To serve hot, pile the bean mixture into a 1½-quart casserole, dot with *3 tablespoons butter,* and bake in a preheated 375° F. oven for 30 minutes.

KIDNEY BEAN CREOLE

Serves 2 or 4. Serve with either cooked rice or garlic bread, plus a green salad.

BUY

1 large green pepper
1-pound can kidney beans
1-pound can stewed tomatoes

HAVE ON HAND	COOKWARE
1 large onion	2-quart saucepan
Garlic	
Cooking oil	
Salt	
Cayenne pepper	

1. Peel and thinly slice the *onion,* peel and mince *1 large clove garlic.* Trim, seed, and slice the *green pepper.* In saucepan, sauté the vegetables in *2 tablespoons cooking oil* until onion is lightly browned.

2. Drain *kidney beans* and add to saucepan. Add *stewed tomatoes with liquid, 1 teaspoon salt,* and *⅛ teaspoon cayenne pepper.* Bring to a boil and simmer for 10 minutes, stirring occasionally, or until pepper slices are almost tender (they should still be slightly crisp). Correct seasoning and serve.

BLACK-EYED PEAS WITH TOMATOES

Serves 8

BUY

2 cans black-eyed peas, 1 pound each
2 cans tomatoes, 1 pound each

HAVE ON HAND	COOKWARE
Onion	2-quart saucepan with lid
Butter	
Flour	
Milk	
Salt and pepper	
Worcestershire sauce	

1. Peel and finely chop *1 medium onion.*

2. In saucepan heat *2 tablespoons butter,* and in it sauté the onion until tender.

3. Stir in *3 tablespoons flour.* Gradually stir in *1 cup milk* and cook, stirring, until sauce is smooth and thickened.

4. Drain and add the *peas* and *tomatoes,* and add *½ teaspoon salt or to taste, ½ teaspoon pepper,* and *1 teaspoon Worcestershire.* Cover and simmer over low heat for 15 minutes.

SOPA SECA

Serves 6

BUY

1 green pepper
8-ounce can Italian plum tomatoes
8-ounce can garbanzos *or* chick peas

HAVE ON HAND	COOKWARE
Onion	2-quart saucepan with lid
Garlic	
Cooking oil	
Rice	
Salt and pepper	

1. Peel and chop *1 onion* and *1 large clove garlic.* Seed and chop *half the green pepper.*

2. Heat *3 tablespoons oil* in the saucepan, and in it sauté the chopped vegetables over low heat until onion is transparent.

3. Add *1 cup rice* and continue to cook for a couple of minutes, stirring constantly, until rice is golden.

4. Add the *tomatoes with their liquid, 1 cup water,* and *½ teaspoon salt,* and bring to a rapid boil. Cover saucepan tightly, reduce heat to very low, and cook for 20 minutes.

5. Drain the *garbanzos* and add to rice mixture. Toss mixture with a fork, partially cover, and let cook over low heat for 5 minutes longer, or until rice is fluffy and all of the liquid has been absorbed.

Corn Meal & Hominy

GNOCCHI DI SEMOLINA

Serves 6. The tender dumplings known by the Italian name of *gnocchi* are a great favorite in European countries. In Germany (and sometimes in France) they are made with potatoes. In many countries, semolina, corn meal, or farina is used to make the paste. *Gnocchi* are really glorified Italian *polenta* (which bears a remarkable resemblance to our own old-fashioned corn-meal mush).

HAVE ON HAND	*COOKWARE*
Parmesan cheese	2-quart saucepan
Milk	Jelly-roll pan
Salt	˙6 individual ovenproof ramekins
Fine yellow corn meal	
Sweet butter	
1 egg	

1. Grate *enough cheese to measure 1⅓ cups.*

2. In saucepan combine *2 cups milk* and *½ cup water.* Bring to a boil. Remove from heat and stir in *1 teaspoon salt,* then slowly stir in *1*

cup corn meal, mixing well. Return to low heat and cook, stirring constantly, until thick and smooth. Cook over low heat for 20 minutes, stirring occasionally. If too thick, stir in a *little boiling water.*

3. Remove from heat and stir in *2 tablespoons butter, 1 egg,* and *⅓ cup of the grated cheese.* Mix well.

4. Moisten a jelly-roll pan with cold water and, using a rubber spatula, spread the corn-meal mixture on it in a smooth layer ½ inch thick. Cool, then cover with waxed paper and refrigerate for at least 30 minutes. Cut the chilled mixture into 1½-inch rounds with a cooky cutter.

5. *Butter* individual ramekins, and in each one place 6 or 8 rounds—they should slightly overlap. Dot each ramekin with *½ tablespoon butter* (you will use 3 tablespoons in all). Sprinkle with *remaining cheese,* and place under broiler until golden, watching carefully so they do not burn.

FARINA GNOCCHI

Serves 8

HAVE ON HAND	COOKWARE
Parmesan cheese	2-quart saucepan
Milk	1-quart loaf pan
Butter	Shallow baking dish
Salt	
Farina *or* Cream of Wheat	
2 eggs	

1. Grate and set aside *2 cups Parmesan cheese.*

2. In saucepan combine *3 cups milk, ½ cup butter,* and *1 teaspoon salt.* Bring to a simmer.

3. Gradually stir in *1 cup plus 2 tablespoons farina;* cook, continuing to stir, until mixture is thick.

4. Beat in *2 eggs,* one at a time, and beat in *1 cup of the grated cheese.*

5. Pour into *buttered* loaf pan. Cool, turn out, then slice into strips.

6. *Butter* baking dish. Preheat oven to 425° F.

7. Arrange strips in baking dish, dot with *3 tablespoons butter,* and sprinkle with *remaining grated Parmesan.*

8. Bake in the hot oven for 10 to 15 minutes, or until hot and lightly browned.

POLENTA CASSEROLE

Serves 6

HAVE ON HAND

Yellow *or* white corn meal
Salt
4 egg yolks
Swiss *or* Gruyère cheese
Cream

COOKWARE

2-quart saucepan with lid
2-quart casserole dish

1. In saucepan blend *1 cup corn meal* and *1 cup cold water.* Gradually stir in *3 cups hot water* and *1 teaspoon salt.* Bring to a boil, stirring constantly, then cover and cook over low heat for 30 minutes, stirring occasionally.

2. Meanwhile, separate *4 eggs,* reserving the whites for another use. Shred *1 cup cheese. Butter* the casserole, and preheat oven to 350° F.

3. Remove corn-meal mixture from heat, then beat in the *4 egg yolks, ½ cup cream,* and the *shredded cheese.*

4. Spoon into the casserole, and bake in the moderate oven for 25 minutes.

FRITELLE DI POLENTA

Serves 8. Serve with maple syrup for breakfast; or with melted butter and grated Parmesan cheese as a starch accompaniment for lunch or dinner.

HAVE ON HAND	*COOKWARE*
Yellow *or* white corn meal	2-quart saucepan with lid
Salt	1-quart loaf pan
2 eggs	Medium skillet
Flour	
Fine bread crumbs	
Cooking oil *or* butter	
Butter (optional)	

1. In a small bowl, mix *1 cup corn meal* with *1 teaspoon salt* and *1 cup cold water* to a smooth paste.

2. In saucepan bring *3 cups water* to a boil. Gradually stir the *corn-meal paste* into the boiling water; cook, stirring constantly, until thick. Then cover the saucepan and cook over low heat for 10 minutes, stirring occasionally.

3. Spoon mixture into the loaf pan and pack down firmly. Cool, then chill thoroughly.

4. Remove the corn-meal loaf from the pan and cut it in slices ½ inch thick.

5. Beat *2 eggs with 2 tablespoons water.* Coat the polenta slices evenly on both sides with *flour,* dip into the egg mixture, then roll in *bread crumbs.*

6. Sauté the slices in *cooking oil or butter* for about 2 minutes on each side, or until golden.

MUSHROOM POLENTA

Follow preceding recipe for Polenta Casserole, but make this addition: Wash, trim, and slice *½ pound fresh mushrooms.* Sauté them in *2 tablespoons butter* for 5 minutes, or until just tender, stirring frequently. Fold into the *corn mixture* at the same time as the *shredded cheese.*

BUTTERMILK SPOON BREAD

Serves 8

BUY

Buttermilk

HAVE ON HAND   *COOKWARE*

Milk   2-quart saucepan
Yellow corn meal   2-quart casserole
Baking soda
Salt
Butter at room temperature
2 eggs

1. In saucepan combine *2 cups each milk* and *buttermilk* and heat to steaming. Gradually stir in *1 cup corn meal,* and cook over moderate heat, stirring frequently, for 15 minutes. Cool slightly.

2. Preheat oven to 350° F. *Butter* the casserole.

3. Stir *1 teaspoon baking soda, 1 teaspoon salt,* and *3 tablespoons butter* into corn-meal mixture. Stir in *2 egg yolks,* one by one.

4. Beat the *2 egg whites* until stiff but not dry; fold into corn-meal mixture.

5. Turn batter into casserole, and bake in moderate oven for 30 minutes. Serve hot from the casserole with a large spoon.

VIRGINIA SPOON BREAD

Serves 4

HAVE ON HAND

Butter
Milk
Corn meal

3 eggs
Salt
Sugar
Baking powder
Cayenne pepper

COOKWARE

2-quart saucepan
1½-quart baking dish

1. Preheat oven to 375° F. Generously *butter* the baking dish.

2. Heat *2½ cups milk* to steaming hot. Gradually stir *1 cup corn meal* into the hot milk. Add *2 tablespoons butter* and cook, stirring, until mixture is very thick and smooth. Remove from heat and cool slightly.

3. Add *3 egg yolks,* one by one, beating well after each addition; reserve the whites.

4. Stir in *1 teaspoon salt, 1 teaspoon sugar, ½ teaspoon baking powder,* and *a dash of cayenne pepper.*

5. Beat the *3 egg whites* until stiff but not dry, and fold into yolk mixture.

6. Turn batter into prepared baking dish. Bake in preheated oven for 30 to 40 minutes. Serve hot from the dish, dipping out large spoonfuls. Serve with a *little hot melted butter* if desired.

BAKED GRITS

Serves 6

BUY

Grits (hominy grits, to Northerners)

HAVE ON HAND

Salt
1 egg
Milk
Sugar

COOKWARE

2-quart saucepan
1½-quart casserole

1. Combine *1 quart boiling water* and *¼ teaspoon salt* in saucepan. Gradually stir in *1 cup grits* and cook over moderate heat, stirring occasionally, for 1 hour. Cool.

2. Preheat oven to 400° F. *Butter* casserole.

3. Into hominy mixture, stir *1 egg, 1 cup milk,* and *½ teaspoon sugar.* Turn into the buttered casserole; bake in the hot oven for 30 minutes.

HOMINY CHEESE CASSEROLE

Serves 4 to 6

BUY

1-pound 12-ounce can whole hominy

HAVE ON HAND	*COOKWARE*
Bread	2-quart casserole
Cheddar cheese	
Parsley	
Butter	
2 eggs	
Milk	
Salt	

1. Crumb *enough bread to measure 1 cup crumbs.* Shred *1 cup cheese.* Chop *2 tablespoons parsley.* Drain the *hominy.*

2. Preheat oven to 325° F. *Butter* casserole.

3. In mixing bowl beat *2 eggs.* Stir in *1 cup milk,* the bread crumbs and cheese, *1 teaspoon salt,* the drained hominy, and the parsley.

4. Turn into casserole; bake in preheated oven for 55 to 60 minutes, or until firm.

Rice

There are several types of white rice—the long-grained; the round-grained, or Japanese; and the short-grained, or Italian. Then there is brown rice, which is more nutritious than the white ones, since it retains the coat of bran that is normally removed in the hulling and milling of white rice. "Converted" rice lies in between brown and white, as it retains some but not all of the bran.

All these rices may be cooked in the same way, with some variation in cooking time. I find I can make the best rice, tender and with each grain separate from the other, if I use the converted. It is never mushy when cooked by the classic method.

Many of the great international methods of cooking rice involve a rich broth, rather than water, for the necessary liquid. Chicken broth is the most usual, but a well-seasoned Vegetable Broth, rich in leeks and other vegetables (page 97), is something even the non-vegetarian cook will appreciate.

But first:

HOW TO COOK PLAIN RICE

Serves 4. Use a heavy 2-quart saucepan with a tightly fitting lid. In it put *1 cup rice, 1 teaspoon salt,* and *2 cups water.* Bring the water to a boil over high heat. Stir only once with a fork, and cover tightly. Turn heat to very low; without removing the lid, let the rice steep in the hot liquid for 15 to 20 minutes. Then remove the lid, add *a good chunk of butter,* and toss rice lightly with a fork. Partially cover with the lid, and let stand over the low heat to steam-dry for another 10 to 30 minutes, or until you are ready to serve it.

CHINESE RICE

Serves 6. The Chinese method of cooking rice is equally good, but no salt or butter is used.

Rinse *1½ cups rice* in a sieve under *cold running water* for 10 seconds, then empty into a heavy 3-quart saucepan with a tightly fitting lid. Add *1½ cups cold water.* Bring water to a boil, and boil hard for 1 minute. Lower heat to a minimum and let the rice simmer, uncovered, for 7 to 8 minutes, or until all water has been absorbed and the rice is quite dry. Pour in *1 cup boiling water,* cover tightly, and cook for about 6 minutes longer. Turn off heat and let the rice cook in its own heat for another 5 minutes—do not remove lid during this time. The rice is now ready to serve. Fluff it with a fork, and serve; accompany with tiny bowls of soy sauce—one for each person.

RICE SALAD

Serves 6. Combine *3 cups cold Chinese rice* with *1 sweet green pepper,* seeded and thinly sliced; *1 sweet red onion,* peeled and thinly sliced; *1 clove garlic,* minced; and *½ cup French dressing* (page 127). Refrigerate for several hours. Before serving, fold in *4 ripe tomatoes,* peeled and cut into slim wedges, and *1 cup finely chopped fresh parsley.*

PIERRE'S OVEN RICE

Serves 6 to 8. This is the method of my good friend Pierre Franey.

HAVE ON HAND

Onion
Butter
Long-grain *or* converted rice
Tabasco

Bay leaf
Broth, vegetable (page 97)
  or chicken.
Parsley
Salt

COOKWARE

Heavy 2-quart casserole with lid

1. Preheat oven to 425° F. Chop *3 tablespoons onion.*

2. In casserole melt *4 tablespoons butter.* Add the chopped onion and cook, stirring, until onion is wilted but not brown.

3. Add *2 cups rice,* and cook, stirring, for about 30 seconds.

4. Add *4 drops Tabasco, 3 cups broth (or part broth and part water), 1 bay leaf, 4 sprigs parsley,* and *a little salt* if necessary. Bring liquid to a boil over direct heat.

5. Cover casserole tightly and transfer to the hot oven. Bake for 20 minutes—no longer. The rice should now be done. When it is cooked, all the water will be absorbed and the grains tender. If not, continue baking for 1 to 10 minutes longer.

6. Remove rice from oven. It will stay hot for at least half an hour if need be, providing you leave it covered. When ready to serve, add *3 tablespoons butter,* and toss lightly with a two-pronged fork.

SAFFRON-RICE VARIATION: Cook *1 clove garlic,* peeled and minced, along with the chopped onion. Add *½ teaspoon saffron threads* along with the liquid.

RICE PILAF

Serves 3, but recipe may be doubled.

HAVE ON HAND

Butter
Onion
Garlic
Converted rice
Broth (page 97) *or* water
Salt

COOKWARE

2-quart heavy saucepan with tight-fitting lid

AN HOUR OR SO BEFORE DINNER:

1. Melt *1 stick butter (½ cup)* in saucepan, and in it sauté *1 medium onion,* minced, and *1 clove garlic,* minced, for 3 minutes or until onion is transparent.

2. Add *1 cup raw rice,* and cook, stirring, until rice grains are thoroughly coated with the butter mixture.

3. Add *1¾ cups broth or water* and *salt to taste,* and bring to a rapid boil. Cover tightly. Reduce heat to its very lowest point, and cook without raising the lid for 20 to 30 minutes.

4. Remove lid, toss rice with a fork, and partially cover. Let rice steam on very low heat until ready to serve. If it forms a golden crust on the bottom, you are lucky. No pilaf in the Near East would be worth its garlic if it didn't have that golden crust.

AT SERVING TIME:

5. Fluff the rice again with a fork, then empty into a hot serving dish. With a spoon scrape the golden crust from the bottom of the pan and pile it on top of the pilaf.

NOTE: Cooking rice this way—the perfect way—often makes the saucepan a problem to wash. If you don't want to have to soak it overnight, invest in a heavy 2-quart porcelain-coated iron saucepan. It cleans quickly and you'll use it for dozens of other dishes.

RISOTTO

Serves 6

HAVE ON HAND	*COOKWARE*
Onion	Heavy saucepan with tight-fitting
Parmesan cheese	lid
Butter	
Converted rice	
Water *or* Broth (page 97)	
Saffron	
Salt	

1. Peel and chop *1 medium onion.* Grate ½ *cup Parmesan cheese.*

2. In saucepan melt *4 tablespoons butter.* Add onion and sauté for 5 minutes, or until onion is transparent.

3. Add *2 cups rice,* then cook, stirring, for 2 minutes, or until rice is well coated with butter.

4. Add *3 cups water or broth,* ½ *teaspoon saffron,* and *1 teaspoon salt.* Bring to a rapid boil. Cover tightly. Reduce heat to very low and cook without removing cover for 20 minutes.

5. Remove cover and fluff rice with a fork. Keep warm, partially covered, until ready to serve.

6. When ready to serve, add *2 tablespoons butter* and toss rice again. Empty into serving dish and sprinkle generously with grated Parmesan.

CURRIED RICE

Serves 6

BUY

Major Grey chutney
Small can slivered toasted almonds

HAVE ON HAND	*COOKWARE*
Onion	Heavy 3-quart saucepan with
Peanut *or* cooking oil	tight-fitting lid
Good curry powder	
Converted rice	
Water *or* Broth (page 97)	
Bay leaves	
Salt	

1. Chop *1 medium onion* finely. Measure and chop ½ *cup chutney.* Set aside.

2. Heat *3 tablespoons oil,* and in it sauté the chopped onion for 3 minutes. Stir in *1 tablespoon good curry powder,* and sauté for 3 minutes longer.

3. Add *1½ cups raw rice;* cook and stir for 2 to 3 minutes, or until rice is coated with the oil.

4. Add *3 cups water or broth, 1 small bay leaf,* the chutney, and *1½ teaspoons salt.* Reduce heat to very, very low, cover saucepan tightly, and cook for 20 to 25 minutes. Toss rice, partially cover, and keep warm until ready to serve.

5. Fluff with a fork, discard bay leaf, turn into a serving dish, and sprinkle with *almonds.*

ALMOND RICE

Serves 6. In a heavy saucepan combine *1½ cups converted rice, 4 table-spoons butter, 2 tablespoons ground blanched almonds, 1 teaspoon salt,* and *3 cups water.* Bring to a boil over high heat, cover tightly, and cook, without stirring, for 20 minutes. Remove lid, toss mixture with a fork, partially cover, and keep over low heat for 10, but no more than 30, minutes.

NASI GORENG

Serves 6

HAVE ON HAND	COOKWARE
Garlic	Kettle
Salad oil	8-inch skillet
Rice	2-quart casserole with tight-fitting cover
Ground coriander	
Ground turmeric	
Ground cumin	
Salt	
3 eggs	
Pepper	
Butter	

1. Peel and mince *1 large clove garlic*. Preheat oven to 350° F. Put kettle of water on to boil.

2. In skillet heat *3 tablespoons salad oil*. Add *1½ cups rice,* and cook, stirring, until rice is golden. Empty rice and oil into casserole.

3. Add garlic, *1½ teaspoons each coriander, turmeric, and cumin,* and *1 teaspoon salt*. Pour *3 cups boiling water* over rice, stir well, cover, and bake in the preheated oven for 50 minutes.

4. Meanwhile beat *3 eggs lightly* with *½ teaspoon salt* and *¼ teaspoon pepper*. Heat *1 tablespoon butter* in the skillet, add the eggs, and cook over low heat until eggs are set like a large flat omelet. Turn omelet out onto a chopping board and cut into long strips.

5. When rice is cooked, remove from oven, uncover, and add egg strips. Toss well with two forks and serve hot.

PARSLEY RICE RING

Serves 4. Fill with creamed eggs or mushrooms or any colorful sauced vegetable. Serve with a tossed salad.

HAVE ON HAND	*COOKWARE*
Butter, at room temperature	8-inch ring mold
Rice	2-quart heavy saucepan with tight-
Salt	fitting lid
Parsley *or* water cress	

1. *Butter* ring mold.

2. In saucepan combine *1 cup rice, 1 teaspoon salt,* and *2 cups water*. Bring water to a rapid boil, cover tightly, reduce heat to low, and cook for 20 minutes, or until water is absorbed. Remove lid, add *¼ cup butter (½ stick),* and toss until butter is melted.

3. Stir in *1 cup chopped parsley or water cress*.

4. Spoon into ring mold and press down well with back of a wooden spoon. Let stand in a warm place for 5 minutes, then invert onto a serving dish.

Our American Indian rice, or wild rice, is regarded by many persons as the most delicious of all grains. Certainly it is the most expensive, for even in a good year the crop is limited by the whims of nature. So, when you do buy a box of wild rice, please make the most of it by cooking it in Indian fashion. This method transforms 1 cup wild rice into 6 cups of large tender kernels.

WILD RICE, INDIAN FASHION

Serves 6. The day before serving: wash *1 cup wild rice* thoroughly, add *8 cups boiling water,* and let soak overnight.

Next day: drain rice, pour *4 cups boiling water* over it, cover, and let stand for 20 minutes; drain. Repeat this procedure 3 times.

A few minutes before serving, again cover the rice with *boiling water,* add *1 teaspoon salt,* cover the pan, and simmer for 5 minutes. Then drain the rice and place in a hot oven for a few minutes to dry out.

Toss with *a big nugget of butter* and season to taste with *salt and pepper.*

WILD RICE WITH MUSHROOMS AND
SOUR CREAM

Serves 6. Cook *1 cup wild rice* in Indian fashion described above.

Trim, wash, and dry *1 pound whole button mushrooms,* then sauté them in *½ stick hot butter* until lightly browned on all sides. Add *1½ cups sour cream,* and heat to serving temperature. Toss into the wild rice just before serving.

Wheat & Other Cereals

BULGUR, or cracked wheat, has been around for centuries. Although underappreciated by Americans, it is well known to other peoples, particularly of the Near East and North Africa, who prize it as the staff of life. It is either soft or hard wheat that has been processed by being soaked in water, then cooked and dried.

BULGUR PILAF

Serves 6

BUY

Box or bag of cracked wheat (bulgur)

HAVE ON HAND	*COOKWARE*
Butter	Heavy 2-quart casserole with cover
Onion	
Salt	
Pepper	
Water *or* Broth (page 97)	

1. Preheat oven to 350° F.

2. In casserole melt *½ cup butter (1 stick)* and in it sauté *1 medium onion,* chopped, until golden. Add *2 teaspoons salt* and *a little pepper,* and stir in *2 cups cracked wheat.* Cover the casserole and cook over low heat for 10 minutes.

3. Add *1 quart water or vegetable broth;* cover, and bake in the preheated oven for 30 minutes. Fluff gently with a fork and bake for 15 minutes longer, or until liquid is absorbed and bulgur is moist and fluffy.

MUSHROOM BULGUR PILAF

Serves 4

BUY

½ pound mushrooms
Bunch green onions
Box or bag of cracked wheat (bulgur)

HAVE ON HAND	*COOKWARE*
Garlic	Large heavy skillet with tight-
Butter	fitting lid
Salt	
White wine *or* dry vermouth	

1. Wash, trim, and slice the *mushrooms*. Chop the *green onions* and *1 clove garlic*.

2. In saucepan or skillet melt *¼ cup butter (½ stick)*, and in it sauté the mushrooms, onions, and garlic until soft but not brown.

3. Add *1 teaspoon salt* and *1 cup cracked wheat*. Stir in *½ cup white wine or dry vermouth* and *1 cup water*. Cover tightly and cook over very low heat for about 30 minutes, or until wheat is dry and cooked.

4. Fluff with a fork, partially cover, and keep over low heat for a few minutes before serving.

BAKED BARLEY

Serves 4

BUY

½ pound fresh mushrooms
1 large sweet onion
1 box medium pearl barley
Chives *or* parsley

HAVE ON HAND	*COOKWARE*
Butter	8-inch skillet
2 cups Vegetable Broth (page 97)	2-quart casserole with cover
Salt and pepper	

1. Wash, trim, and slice the *mushrooms*. Peel and finely chop the *onion*.

2. In skillet melt *2 tablespoons butter,* and in it sauté mushrooms over moderately high heat for about 5 minutes, or until mushrooms are lightly browned; stir occasionally. Empty mushrooms into the casserole.

3. In same skillet melt *another 2 tablespoons butter;* in it sauté the onion for about 5 minutes, or until golden; stir occasionally. Empty onion into casserole.

4. In skillet melt *1 more tablespoon butter.* Add *1 cup barley;* cook for 8 to 10 minutes, or until barley becomes nut brown; stir frequently. Add barley to casserole.

5. Preheat oven to 350° F.

6. Add *2 cups broth* to skillet and bring to a boil. Empty into casserole, add ½ *cup chopped chives or parsley,* and stir well to combine all ingredients.

7. Cover casserole and bake for 30 minutes. Add *2 cups water* and *salt and pepper to taste;* then cover and cook for 1 hour longer. Serve, or reduce oven heat to very low and keep warm until ready to serve.

BAKED KASHA

Serves 6

BUY	*COOKWARE*
Buckwheat groats (kasha)	Kettle
	Large heavy skillet
	Casserole with cover

1. Preheat oven to 400° F. Boil *water* in kettle.

2. In heavy skillet melt *2 tablespoons butter.* Add *2 cups kasha,* and cook over moderate heat, stirring constantly, for 10 minutes.

3. Empty into casserole, and add *enough boiling water* to cover kasha by 1 inch. Cover, and bake in preheated oven for 30 minutes.

4. Remove cover, and add a *little more water* if kasha seems dry. Replace cover, turn temperature down to 300° F., and bake for 30 minutes longer.

Couscous is the name of *the* native dish of North Africa, a savory stew of lamb or chicken containing many vegetables and often fruit and nuts. But *couscous* is also the Arab word for the finely ground hard wheat, or semolina, which is steamed and served with the stew. It is an excellent cereal which should be more widely known. There is no reason to serve it only with North African stews! The recipe for the complete dish is given in ANN SERANNE'S GOOD FOOD & HOW TO COOK IT. Here I am repeating only the method for cooking the cereal.

COUSCOUS

Serves 4. Serve with additional butter or any savory sauce.

   BUY

1-pound box imported *couscous*

HAVE ON HAND	*COOKWARE*
Butter	Saucepan
Salt and pepper	Large kettle with lid
	Colander with handles that can sit on top of kettle without falling in

Empty *couscous* into a saucepan and moisten with *enough boiling water (about ½ cup) to make the grains swell.* Stir with a fork and let stand for 20 minutes. Break up any lumps which form with fingertips, and repeat the moistening and stirring three times at 20-minute intervals. By this time the semolina will have more than doubled in bulk. Empty it into a colander lined with cheesecloth. Sprinkle with *¼ cup melted butter* and *salt (about 1 teaspoon) and pepper to taste.* Set colander over kettle of *simmering water,* cover, and steam for 1 hour.

PASTA

A Whole World of Pasta

It's a cinch to be a vegetarian and yet eat a balanced, interesting diet if you are a pasta lover! There are so many types of pasta and so many variations of the recipes for them that one could eat pasta every day for years without repeating the same dish.

The word pasta is a generic term for a multitude of products made of semolina (a nutritious fine, hard, and pure flour milled from the heart of durum wheat) plus either water alone or water and egg.

Not so very long ago, the average supermarket carried elbow macaroni in several thicknesses, one or two types of spaghetti, and fine, medium, and wide egg noodles. Today it stocks pasta in a bewildering variety of shapes and sizes. Since the names for these products can vary not only from manufacturer to manufacturer but from location to location, the result may often be utter confusion for the cook.

But don't panic. If you understand that there are basically four different types of pasta and four basic methods of cooking them, you can vary the pasta within a recipe to please your palate and your mood.

THE TYPES OF PASTA

1. SPAGHETTI

Spaghetti, meaning "string," is a solid round rod and comes in various thicknesses from very thin *vermicelli,* to the larger *spaghettini* and *spaghetti,* to the largest form, *spaghettoni.*

2. LINGUINE

Linguine, meaning "small tongues," is a form of spaghetti, but the rods are slightly flattened or oval rather than round. They also are named according to their size, from the fine *bavettine* to the largest form, *lingue di passeri.*

3. MACARONI

Macaroni (Italian: *maccheroni*) is a general term for hollow pasta products. These, too, range from thicknesses no larger than that of spaghetti, to larger tubes like *cannelle* and the grooved tubes called *rigatoni*, to *cannelloni* or *tufoli* which are still larger tubes that are generally stuffed and baked.

4. NOODLES

These are ribbons of egg pasta ranging in size from the smallest, ⅛ inch wide, called *tagliarini;* to ¼ inch wide, *fettuccine;* ¾ inch wide, *tagliatelli;* broad noodles, or *lasagnette*, about ½ inch wide; to the extra-broad, 2-inch-wide *lasagne* or ripple-edged *mafalda.*

When noodle paste is cut into squares or rectangles it is known as *ravioli, manicotti*, or *cannelloni.*

In addition to these basic types, there is a wide range of shapes and sizes of small pasta. Some are used primarily in broths and soups; rings, threads, shells, stars, alphabets, and so on. A myriad of other shapes, like bows, snails, and shells, are boiled and sauced or they are baked in a sauce.

METHODS OF COOKING PASTA

1. Boil and serve in soups or broths: small pasta of plain or fancy shape.

2. Boil, then toss with a sauce and grated cheese: such pasta as *linguine*, spaghetti, and noodles.

3. Boil, then bake with a sauce: such pasta as macaroni, *lasagne*, and *ziti.*

4. Stuff, then boil and sauce: such pasta as *ravioli* and *agnolotti.*

5. Boil, stuff, sauce, and bake: such pasta as *manicotti, cannelloni*, and *rigatoni.*

HOW TO COOK PASTA

Generally it is best to follow the manufacturer's directions on the package, but here are some basic rules that will assure the best possible flavor.

1. Use a large, deep, heavy, pot (10- to 12-quart capacity), and *at least 6 to 7 quarts of water* for *1 pound of pasta.* The pasta needs room to swim in the water so the strands will not stick together.

2. Bring the water to a rolling boil, then add *2 tablespoons salt.* The salt should be added just before the pasta goes in. Let the water return to an active boil.

3. Add the pasta gradually so that the water continues to boil at all times, gently pushing each handful down into the boiling water until it is all submerged.

4. With a wooden fork, stir the pasta frequently as it boils, taking care to separate the strands or pieces. Stir gently.

5. Cook the minimum amount of time given in package directions, then test for doneness. Tasting the pasta is the only way to tell if it has boiled sufficiently that it has no remaining flavor of uncooked flour and yet is still *al dente,* or just firm "to the tooth." It should be a little chewy and by no means soft or mushy.

6. Drain the pasta into a large colander that has just been rinsed in hot water. Then empty immediately into a large mixing bowl to be tossed with butter or sauce and cheese. Or, fork it directly from the boiling water into individual serving dishes. In either case the mixing bowl or serving dishes should be piping hot. (By forking the pasta directly out of the boiling water, you can be certain that the pasta is as hot as it can possibly be. Also each strand is moist, so there is no chance of strands drying and sticking together. The fork-from-pot method applies only to strands of pasta. For macaroni, shells, or other broken or cut lengths, use a slotted spoon.)

When the pasta is ready, all your other ingredients—*and* your guests —must also be ready.

TO HOLD COOKED PASTA:

Drain off all but enough of the boiling water to cover the pasta, then add just enough cold water to prevent further cooking yet still keep the pasta hot until ready to serve.

HOW MUCH PASTA TO COOK?

This is a difficult question. I know a young man who can happily consume an entire pound of spaghetti bathed in a quart of sauce! But he is the exception to the general rule that: *1 pound of dry pasta will, when cooked, serve 3 to 4 persons as a main dish; 4 to 6 as an appetizer.*

NOODLES

There are many varieties of excellent commercially made noodles available, and my favorites, at the moment, are the crinkly ones, a recent addition to the vast array of pasta products in my local market. They are exceptionally tender and really sop up the sauce. But none of them can compare in texture and flavor to homemade noodles, and unless I am very pressed for time, I make them frequently and usually have a couple of bags of them in the freezer.

I have a little noodle maker which goes everywhere with me. When I sold my summer house in Saltaire, I left a fully equipped kitchen. The only pieces of equipment I took with me were my noodle maker and a very inexpensive little slicer which I use to slice potatoes for pommes Anna and cucumbers for salad.

The noodle maker is fairly expensive, around $35.00, but well worth it. If you are a noodle lover you might like to invest in one, but I'll give you methods of rolling and cutting the noodle dough both with and without mechanical aid. In either case the ingredients are the same.

HOMEMADE EGG PASTA

Makes about 1 pound. For noodles, manicotti, fettuccine, lasagne, cannelloni, tagliatelle, and tagliarini.

HAVE ON HAND

Semolina flour, *or* unbleached all-purpose flour
4 large eggs
Salt

1. In mixing bowl combine *3 cups flour* and *1 teaspoon salt*. Make a well in the center, and into the well break *4 large eggs*.

2. Using just one hand, begin to work the flour into the eggs until all of it is moistened and the the dough can be gathered together into a rough ball. If dough is too moist, add a *little flour;* if too dry, add *2 teaspoons warm water*.

TO HAND-KNEAD, ROLL, AND CUT:

3. Remove ball and place on *floured* surface. Begin kneading with both hands; knead vigorously, pulling and pressing the hard dough with the heels of the hands until it is smooth, or for about 10 minutes.

4. Return dough to the bowl, cover with a towel, and let it rest for half an hour. During this time the moisture in the dough will equalize throughout and the dough will lose its elasticity.

5. Cut dough in half, and work with one half at a time. Roll out on *floured* surface until the dough is as thin as possible, no more than ⅛ inch thick and preferably thinner, turning dough over frequently and keeping both sides lightly floured.

6. For Noodles: cut the dough into strips of the desired width. Toss the strips lightly with flour and drop lightly and loosely onto a *floured* towel to dry.

For *tagliarini:* cut ⅛ inch wide.
For *fettuccine:* cut ¼ inch wide.
For *tagliatelle:* cut ¾ inch wide.
For *lasagne:* cut 2 inches wide, then cut 4 to 6 inches in length.
For *manicotti* or *cannelloni:* cut sheet of dough into 3-inch squares for manicotti and 4-inch squares for cannelloni. Arrange squares on *floured* towel, cover lightly with another towel, and let dry for 1 hour.

TO MACHINE-KNEAD, ROLL, AND CUT:

1. The dough must be very hard. I've never found it necessary to add even a drop of warm water. Gather it together and then pull it apart into a dozen small pieces. Keep the pieces in the bowl covered with a towel and work with one piece at a time.

2. Set up the noodle maker, attaching it firmly to the edge of a table or chopping block. Set the rollers as wide apart as possible, and the handle so it turns the rollers.

3. Run *one piece of dough* through the rollers two or three times to knead it until it is a smooth rather thickish band, folding it in half crosswise between each roll. This process, too, equalizes the moisture from the eggs; however, if the dough sticks to the rollers or comes out crinkled, sprinkle each side with a little flour until the band is smooth and not sticky. Place the band on a lightly floured surface just behind the noodle maker and sprinkle with a little flour. Repeat this kneading process with the *other chunks of dough*, stacking each band, one on top of the other, with flour in between.

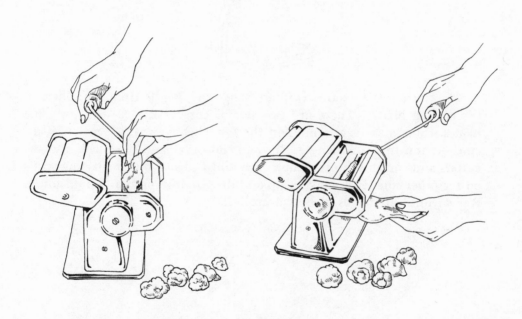

4. When all the pieces of dough have been kneaded in this way, they must be rolled thinly—in three successive runs:

Bring the rollers together a couple of notches, then run each of the bands through the rollers. Again stack the bands (which will have become a little longer) on top of each other with a little flour sprinkled between.

Reduce size of space between rollers another couple of notches, and repeat the rolling, and stacking.

Once again through the rollers, set as closely as possible, will give you very thin, very long bands of smooth dough.

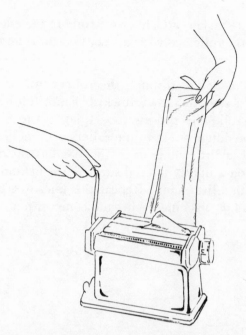

5. Cutting the noodles is fun. Change the handle from the rollers to the cutting blades. There are two sets of cutting blades: the very fine blades which make tagliarini, and the ¼-inch blades which make fettuccine. As you turn the handle, slip one end of a band of dough into the cutters and continue to turn until the dough drops out in narrow strips on the other side. Pick noodles up and drop lightly onto a floured towel. Repeat until all bands of dough are cut.

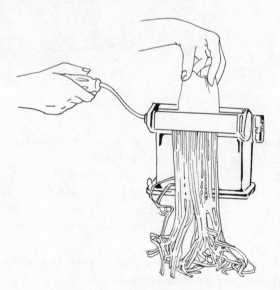

FOR FRESH NOODLES: Let dry for 1 hour, then cook or freeze.

TO FREEZE: Place noodles and towel in freezer until noodles are frozen stiff, then pack in freezer bags.

TO COOK: Fresh noodles cook very quickly. Use *a large quantity of rapidly boiling water.* Add *1 tablespoon salt,* then the *noodles.* Cook for no more than 5 minutes, testing frequently to make sure they do not become overcooked.

FOR DRY NOODLES: Let noodles dry on the floured towel for 12 hours, or overnight. Dry noodles will take from 8 to 10 minutes to cook.

GREEN PASTA
(Pasta Verde)

Makes about 1 pound green noodles or lasagne

BUY

¾ pound fresh (*or* 10-ounce package frozen chopped) spinach

HAVE ON HAND

Semolina *or* unbleached all-purpose flour
2 eggs
Salt

1. Wash *spinach* well and place in saucepan without any more water than is clinging to the leaves; cook for 5 minutes, or until tender. Or cook frozen chopped spinach according to package directions.

2. Drain spinach well, pressing out moisture with back of a spoon. Then chop FINELY.

3. Measure *3 cups flour* into mixing bowl and make a well in the center. Into the well put *2 eggs, 1 teaspoon salt,* and the finely chopped spinach. Mix center ingredients, then gradually work in the flour to make a rough dough. Turn dough out on lightly floured board and knead for 10 minutes; add a *little water* if dough is too dry, and *some flour* if dough is too soft.

4. Separate dough into 4 pieces and let rest for 30 minutes.

5. Flatten each piece, one at a time, and roll out on floured surface into very thin sheets, ⅛ inch thick or thinner. For noodles cut into strips ¼ inch wide; for lasagne into strips 2 inches wide.

212 Ann Seranne's Good Food Without Meat

6. Let pasta dry on floured towels for 1 hour.

7. Cook the pasta in large quantity of *rapidly boiling salted water* for 8 minutes or until just al dente. Drain and serve as desired.

PASTA FOR RAVIOLI AND TORTELLINI

Makes about 1½ pounds. This is a slightly softer, smoother dough, and easier to roll out.

HAVE ON HAND
Semolina *or* unbleached all-purpose flour
Salt
4 eggs
Olive oil
Ingredients for filling (see recipes on pp. 248-250)

1. Into mixing bowl measure *3 cups flour* and *1 teaspoon salt.* Make a well in the center, and into the well put *4 eggs, 1 tablespoon olive oil,* and *4 teaspoons warm water.* Mix center ingredients, then gradually work in flour to make a rough dough.

2. Turn dough out on floured board and knead for about 10 minutes, adding a few more drops of warm water if dough is too dry; a little more flour if dough is too moist.

3. Cut dough into 4 parts, cover, and let rest for 30 minutes.

4. Roll out one part at a time on floured surface, turning dough frequently and keeping both sides lightly floured, to a rectangle less than ⅛ inch thick; the thinner the better.

5. FOR RAVIOLI: Cut the rectangle lengthwise into 3-inch wide strips. Place *teaspoonfuls of the desired filling* 2½ inches apart along one strip. Cover with another strip and press the strips firmly together around each spoonful of filling. With a fluted pastry wheel or ravioli cutter, cut into 2- or 3-inch squares, depending on how large you want the ravioli. Cover with a cloth, and let dry for 1½ hours.

FOR TORTELLINI: With a floured cooky cutter or tortellini cutter, cut sheet of dough into 2-inch circles. Place *1 teaspoon of filling* on top of each circle, then fold in half to form a half circle. Press edges of dough together firmly; then bend the half circle, seam side out, to form a ring. To maintain this shape, overlap the points of the dough and press them firmly together. Cover with a towel and let the tortellini dry for half an hour.

6. For cooking directions, see individual recipes, pp 248-250.

CHEESES FOR PASTA

Several kinds of hard cheeses are popular with pasta. Top of the list, and the best to many, is Parmesan. Asiago has a nuttier flavor, while Pecorino Romano is saltier. Some pasta connoisseurs like to mix half Parmesan and half Romano; others prefer Parmesan, Romano, and Asiago in equal proportions.

Whatever you select, make sure it is well aged, for good well-aged cheese makes all the difference between a really great pasta dish and a mediocre one.

GRATE YOUR OWN CHEESE, PLEASE!

Don't ruin a good dish with commercial grated cheese! The cheese isn't very good in the first place, and secondly, grated cheese loses its flavor quickly unless frozen.

Buy your pasta cheese in big chunks and grate it in one of those efficient and inexpensive little Mouli cheese graters imported from France. You may freeze any left-over part of a chunk if you wish after wrapping it carefully in foil, but once cheese has been frozen it is never quite as fluffy when you grate it. If you have time, it's better to grate the entire chunk and then package the grated cheese in several small freezer bags. It will stay free-flowing and flavorful in the freezer for many months.

Pastas with Simple Sauces

We begin the recipes in this chapter with some of the simplest and very best dishes—perfectly cooked pastas, always *al dente,* tossed with several of the following: olive oil, garlic, butter, cheese, cream, spices, herbs, and nuts. Although each recipe specifies either a noodle or spaghetti, use your imagination and vary the pasta according to your mood. Keep on hand a wide variety of linguine, vermicelli, spaghetti, tagliolini, tagliatelle, fettuccine, and so on.

FETTUCCINE AL BURRO
(with Butter Sauce)

Serves 4 to 6 as a first course

HAVE ON HAND	COOKWARE
Parmesan cheese	Pasta pot
Fettuccine *or* spaghetti	Large skillet
Butter	
Black peppercorns	

1. Grate *½ cup Parmesan cheese* and set aside.

2. Cook *1 pound pasta* according to directions (page 206).

3. Meanwhile, put *1 stick (½ cup) butter* in a large skillet over very low heat to melt.

4. As soon as the pasta is cooked al dente, drain and empty into the skillet with the melted butter. Begin tossing, and then gradually add the grated cheese and *lots of freshly grated black pepper.*

BUTTERED FINE NOODLES

Serves 4 or 6

BUY

8-ounce package fine noodles

HAVE ON HAND   *COOKWARE*

Salt   Large saucepan
Butter, at room temperature
Freshly ground pepper

1. Bring *4 quarts water* to a rapid boil in large saucepan. Add *1 tablespoon salt* and drop in the *noodles*. When water returns to a boil, boil for 8 minutes.

2. Drain noodles in a hot colander and empty into a hot serving dish. Add *4 tablespoons butter* and toss well. Add *salt and pepper to taste*. Toss again and serve immediately.

NOODLES POLONAISE

Serves 4 as an accompaniment to other foods.

BUY

8 ounces broad egg noodles *or* curly noodles

HAVE ON HAND   *COOKWARE*

Bread   Large saucepan
Garlic   Small skillet
Butter

1. *Crumb enough bread to measure ½ cup.* Peel and mince *1 large clove garlic*.

2. Cook the *noodles* according to package directions.

3. While noodles are cooking, melt *1 stick (½ cup) butter* in a small skillet. When butter is foaming, add garlic and bread crumbs; cook, stirring constantly, until crumbs and garlic are golden brown. Set aside.

4. Drain noodles and empty into hot serving dish. Pour the crumb mixture over the noodles and toss lightly.

NOODLES FINES HERBS

Serves 4 as an accompaniment to other foods. Cook *8-ounce package egg noodles.* While noodles are cooking, melt *1 stick (½ cup) butter* with *1 tablespoon chopped chives* and *2 tablespoons chopped parsley.* Drain noodles and empty into hot serving bowl. Add butter-herb mixture and toss. Sprinkle with *salt and pepper* to taste.

FETTUCCINE ALFREDO

Serves 6 for appetizer, 4 for main course

BUY OR MAKE

½ pound aged Parmesan cheese
1 pound fettuccine *or* curly noodles
8-ounce container heavy cream

HAVE ON HAND

Butter
Salt
Black peppercorns

COOKWARE

Pasta pot
Small saucepan

1. Grate the *cheese* and set aside.

2. Cook *pasta* in *rapidly boiling salted water* until just barely tender.

3. While pasta is cooking, in small saucepan melt *1 stick (½ cup) butter* together with the *cream* over very low heat. You just want the cream hot enough to melt the butter.

4. Drain the pasta and empty into a warm bowl. Pour the butter and

cream over the noodles and start tossing. Gradually toss in *1 cup of the grated cheese.*

5. Sprinkle with a *little salt, if necessary,* and season generously with *lots of freshly ground black pepper.*

6. Serve on warm plate with *additional grated cheese* on the side.

FETTUCCINE CON TARTUFI

When you feel in an expansive mood or have a special reason to celebrate, buy *a 1-ounce can of white Italian truffles.* Make Fettuccine Alfredo (preceding recipe), but add the juice from the can of truffles to the butter-and-cream mixture. Slice the truffle (you will have 1 medium-size truffle or 2 small ones in the can) as paper-thin as possible, and toss into the noodles along with the cheese. Heaven!

NOODLES WITH BLACK PEPPER

Serves 4 or 6. This one is for pepper lovers. Cook *1 pound noodles or tagliolini* until just al dente. While noodles are cooking, melt *¼ pound sweet butter* over very low heat. Do not let it get hot. It's ready when most of the butter is melted or mushy. Empty the butter into a warm serving dish. Drain noodles, and empty them into the butter. Add *1 tablespoon coarsely cracked black pepper* and toss gently. Serve on hot plates with *grated Parmesan* on the side.

PASTA WITH OLIVE OIL AND GARLIC SAUCE

Serves 3 or 4. This is a robust sauce, good for garlic lovers. It's easy to make, yet tricky. The tricks are to use very fresh olive oil of the best quality, to slice the garlic paper thin, and to cook it very slowly until just lightly toasted in the hot oil. If the garlic is allowed to overbrown even slightly, there goes a lovely dish right down the disposal.

BUY

Chunk of Parmesan cheese
1 pound thin spaghetti, linguine, *or* vermicelli

HAVE ON HAND	COOKWARE
Large head fresh garlic	Small skillet
Olive oil	Pasta pot
Freshly ground black pepper	

1. Grate *a bowlful of cheese* and set aside.

2. Peel *10 to 12 large cloves garlic* and slice them paper thin.

3. Measure *¾ cup fresh olive oil* into a small skillet. Add the garlic and place over moderate heat. Stand by! Do not leave the stove! As soon as the oil begins to bubble around the edge of the garlic slices, turn heat to low, then cook and watch, stirring occasionally, until garlic slices become crisp and pale gold, like toasted nut flakes. Remove from heat.

4. Meanwhile cook the *pasta* in *boiling salted water* until al dente. Just before pasta is done, return garlic and oil to very low heat.

5. Drain pasta into a colander and, while it is still dripping wet, empty it immediately into a hot mixing bowl. Pour the garlic and oil over the pasta and toss with wooden spoons. Add *lots of freshly ground black pepper* and serve with grated Parmesan.

SPAGHETTI VERDE

Serves 4 to 6

BUY

Bunch fresh parsley
1 pound thin spaghetti *or* vermicelli

HAVE ON HAND

Garlic
Parmesan cheese

Butter
Olive oil
Black peppercorns

COOKWARE

Pasta pot
Small skillet

1. Peel and lightly crush *3 cloves garlic.* Mince *1 cup parsley,* and grate *1 cup cheese.* Set aside.

2. Cook the *pasta* al dente according to package directions.

3. Meanwhile in small skillet heat *12 tablespoons butter (1½ sticks)* and *2 tablespoons olive oil.* Add the cloves of garlic and sauté until lightly brown. Discard garlic, stir in parsley, and remove from heat.

4. Drain pasta and empty into hot mixing bowl. Add the butter-parsley sauce, the cheese, and *freshly ground pepper to taste.* Toss well and serve on hot plates.

PESTO ALLA GENOVESE

Serves 4. A glorious pasta sauce, if you like garlic and fresh sweet basil, is this speciality of Genoa. Dried basil cannot be substituted, so plan to make it only in the warm months when fresh sweet basil is available. If you like it as well as I do, you may want to freeze some in small plastic containers. I defrost it a few hours before needed by setting the plastic container into a small saucepan of warm water.

BUY

Large bunch fresh sweet basil
1 pound spaghetti, linguini, *or* fettuccine
Parmesan cheese
Bunch of Italian parsley
Jar pine nuts

HAVE ON HAND

Garlic
Salt
Olive oil
Butter

COOKWARE

Electric blender
Pasta pot

1. Wash the *basil* and dry on absorbent toweling; put *20 of the largest leaves* into container of an electric blender.

2. Add *3 large cloves garlic*, peeled, *¾ cup grated Parmesan, ½ cup parsley leaves, ⅓ cup pine nuts, ½ teaspoon salt,* and *½ cup olive oil.* Cover and blend on high speed until ingredients are reduced to a thick paste. Scrape paste into a large mixing bowl.

3. Cook the *pasta* according to directions. As soon as it is al dente, fork it out of the hot water directly into the mixing bowl with the cheese paste; toss well. Add *a chunk (2 tablespoons) butter* and *4 tablespoons of the hot water from the pasta pot,* and toss again. Serve hot with *additional grated Parmesan.*

FETTUCCINE WITH CREAM AND EGGS

Serves 4 to 6

BUY

Chunk of Asiago cheese
1 pound fettuccine
8-ounce container heavy cream

HAVE ON HAND	*COOKWARE*
Butter	Pasta pot
Black pepper	Large skillet
2 egg yolks	Small saucepan

1. Grate *½ cup cheese*. Set aside.

2. Cook *fettuccine* al dente according to package directions.

3. While pasta is cooking melt *1 stick (½ cup) butter* in a skillet, and warm *½ cup cream* in a small saucepan.

4. Drain fettuccine and empty into the hot butter in the skillet. Toss briefly, then gradually toss in the grated cheese, and *some freshly ground pepper.*

5. Break the *yolks of 2 eggs* into the pasta; toss again, while gradually adding the warm cream. Serve on warm plates.

PASTA WITH RICOTTA SAUCE

Serves 3 or 4

BUY

Chunk of Parmesan cheese
Fresh parsley
8 ounces noodles (curly ones are great with this), vermicelli, *or* linguine
8-ounce container ricotta cheese
8-ounce container heavy cream

HAVE ON HAND   *COOKWARE*

Butter   Pasta pot
Peppercorns   Small saucepan

1. Grate *½ cup Parmesan cheese. Chop ½ cup parsley.* Set aside.

2. Cook the *pasta* al dente according to package directions.

3. Meanwhile combine the *ricotta cheese* with *1 tablespoon butter* and the *cream,* place over low heat, and stir occasionally.

4. Drain the pasta and toss with *2 tablespoons butter.* Add the warm cheese-and-cream mixture, the Parmesan cheese, the parsley, and *freshly ground pepper to taste.* Toss well and serve on warm plates.

Hearty Tomato-Sauced Pasta Dishes

There are many good brands of tomato sauces available, but somehow they never taste as flavorful as ones made from vine-ripened tomatoes, or from canned tomatoes, when fresh ones are out of season. To me, commercial sauces are too dense and pasty. I prefer a lighter, chunkier sauce such as this first one. It's a very easy sauce to make and uses prepared marinara sauce as a base. Vegetables and spices give it character, and you may vary it according to what vegetables are the freshest in the market—mushrooms, celery, zucchini, and diced eggplant are all good.

CHUNKY TOMATO SAUCE FOR PASTA

Makes about 6 cups

BUY

2 jars marinara sauce (15½ ounces
each) *or* 4 cans tomato sauce (8
ounces each)
1-pound can stewed tomatoes
Parsley *or* sweet basil

HAVE ON HAND

Large onion
Garlic
Cooking oil
Hot red pepper flakes
Fennel seeds
Coarsely cracked pepper
Oregano

COOKWARE

Large skillet

1. Peel and chop *1 large onion* and *2 large cloves garlic.* In large skillet, heat *2 tablespoons oil,* and in it sauté onion and garlic for 5 to 10 minutes, or until transparent but not brown.

2. Add *½ teaspoon hot pepper flakes, 1 teaspoon fennel, ½ teaspoon coarsely cracked pepper, ½ teaspoon oregano, the marinara or tomato sauce,* and the *stewed tomatoes.* Stir well and bring to a simmer; continue to simmer for 20 to 30 minutes, stirring occasionally.

3. Just before serving, stir in *2 tablespoons chopped parsley or sweet basil.* Serve immediately over the hot spaghetti.

LIGHT TOMATO SAUCE

Makes about 4 cups

BUY

2-pound, 3-ounce can Italian plum tomatoes

HAVE ON HAND	*COOKWARE*
Garlic	Large heavy skillet
Olive oil	
Salt	
Black peppercorns	
Dried sweet basil	

1. Press the *tomatoes and juice* through a food mill, or blend in an electric blender and then strain to remove seeds. Set aside.

2. Mince *2 cloves garlic (or more, if desired),* and add them to a skillet containing *2 tablespoons olive oil.* Simmer over low heat until garlic is golden (DO NOT BROWN).

3. Add the *tomatoes.* Add *1 teaspoon salt, lots of freshly ground black pepper,* and *1 teaspoon dried sweet basil.* Cook over low heat, stirring frequently with a wooden spoon, until sauce is bubbling. Raise heat to medium and simmer sauce for about 30 minutes, or until excess water has evaporated and the sauce is thickened.

EGGPLANT SAUCE

For 1 pound pasta. This is a rich and hearty sauce for spaghetti or linguine.

BUY

2 pounds very ripe tomatoes *or* a 2-pound, 3-ounce can Italian plum tomatoes
1 large eggplant
Parsley
6-ounce can tomato paste

HAVE ON HAND	*COOKWARE*
Garlic	Large heavy skillet *or* saucepan
Onion	Small skillet
Olive oil	
Salt	
Crushed red pepper	
Dried basil	
Oregano	

1. If using *fresh tomatoes,* peel and chop them coarsely. Peel and chop *2 large cloves garlic* and *1 medium onion.* Peel and dice the *eggplant.* Chop ¼ *cup parsley.*

2. In large heavy skillet or saucepan sauté onion and garlic in *1 tablespoon olive oil* for about 3 minutes, or until golden brown. Add the fresh or canned tomatoes, *tomato paste, ½ cup water, 2 teaspoons salt, ¼ teaspoon crushed red pepper, 1 teaspoon basil,* and *½ teaspoon oregano.* Simmer for 20 minutes, stirring occasionally.

3. In another skillet sauté eggplant in *4 tablespoons olive oil* until lightly browned. Add to tomato sauce and cook over low heat for 30 minutes longer. Stir in *parsley,* and keep the sauce hot until ready to serve.

BASIL AND TOMATO SPAGHETTI SAUCE

Makes about 3 cups

BUY

2-pound, 3-ounce can Italian plum tomatoes
2 cans tomato purée (8 ounces each)

HAVE ON HAND

2 large onions
Garlic
Olive oil
Celery
Carrots
Fresh *or* dried basil

Oregano
Bay leaves
Salt
Coarsely ground black pepper

COOKWARE

2-quart heavy saucepan

1. Thinly slice *2 large onions.* Peel and mince *4 cloves garlic.*

2. In heavy saucepan heat *6 tablespoons olive oil,* and in it sauté onions and garlic until transparent but not brown. Add *6 stalks celery,* coarsely chopped, *2 carrots,* scraped and sliced, *1 tablespoon chopped fresh basil or 1 teaspoon dried basil, ½ teaspoon oregano, 2 bay leaves,* the *canned Italian tomatoes,* the *2 cans of tomato purée,* and *1 cup water.* Stir in *1 teaspoon salt* and *1 teaspoon coarsely ground pepper.*

3. Bring mixture to a boil; then partially cover, and simmer over low heat for 3 hours, stirring occasionally. Press sauce though a sieve, or blend it about 1 cup at a time in an electric blender.

VELVETY MARINARA SAUCE

Makes 7 cups

BUY

Two 2-pound, 3-ounce cans Italian plum tomatoes

HAVE ON HAND	*COOKWARE*
Small onions	Medium skillet
Garlic	Large saucepan
Carrots	
Olive oil	
Black peppercorns	
Salt	
Butter	
Cayenne pepper	

1. Peel and finely chop *2 small onions;* peel and mince *1 clove garlic;* scrape and chop *2 small carrots.*

2. In skillet heat *2 tablespoons olive oil,* and in it sauté onions, garlic, and carrots until onions are soft but not brown.

3. Add the *tomatoes* and *1 teaspoon freshly ground black pepper.* Stir in *salt to taste,* and cook over moderate heat for 20 minutes.

4. Rub sauce through a food mill, or blend 1 cup at a time in an electric blender. The sauce will emerge velvety.

5. Melt *3 tablespoons butter* in saucepan and add the puréed sauce. Cook, stirring frequently, for 15 minutes. Stir in *cayenne pepper to taste.*

RED-HOT TOMATO SAUCE

For 1 pound pasta

BUY

Fresh parsley
2-pound, 3-ounce can Italian plum tomatoes

HAVE ON HAND	COOKWARE
Garlic	Large heavy skillet
Olive oil	
Salt	
Crushed dried red peppers *or* 2 large fresh chili peppers	
Butter	
Grated Parmesan *or* Pecorino Romano cheese	

1. Chop *½ cup parsley.* Peel and mince *2 large cloves garlic.*

2. Sauté the garlic in *2 tablespoons olive oil* until just golden. Add the *tomatoes, 1 teaspoon salt,* the parsley, and *1 teaspoon of the crushed red peppers, or 2 large fresh chili peppers, seeded and chopped;* stir well. Simmer uncovered for 35 minutes, stirring frequently.

3. Keep hot until ready to serve. Just before serving add *2 tablespoons butter* to the sauce and swirl until butter is melted. Ladle over hot pasta, and accompany with *grated Parmesan or Pecorino Romano.*

MIXED VEGETABLE SAUCE

For 1 pound pasta

BUY

2 large green peppers
6 large ripe tomatoes
2 medium zucchini
1 small eggplant

HAVE ON HAND   COOKWARE

Celery   3-quart heavy saucepan *or* skillet
Onions
Olive oil
Salt
Coarsely cracked pepper

1. Wash, stem, and seed the *green peppers* and cut into thin strips. Peel *tomatoes* and cut each into 8 sections. Wash, trim, and slice rather thickly the *zucchini*. Peel *eggplant* and cut into 1-inch dice. Slice *3 stalks celery* thickly. Peel and dice *3 medium onions*.

2. Combine all the vegetables in the saucepan or skillet, and add *2 tablespoons olive oil, 1½ teaspoons salt,* and *1 teaspoon cracked pepper.* Cover and simmer over low heat for 1 hour, stirring frequently. Correct seasoning before serving over hot pasta.

RAW TOMATO SAUCE

For 1 pound pasta

BUY

2 pounds ripe tomatoes
Fresh parsley
Fresh sweet basil

HAVE ON HAND

Lemon
Olive oil
Garlic
Salt
Coarsely cracked pepper

1. Peel *tomatoes* and slice thinly. Put them in a bowl and add ¼ *cup chopped parsley, ¼ cup chopped fresh basil, the juice of 1 large lemon, 3 tablespoons olive oil, 1 large clove garlic,* minced, and ½ *teaspoon each of salt and pepper.* Toss well.

2. Serve over hot elbow macaroni or linguine.

Pasta with Sauces & Vegetables

It's very hard to think of any vegetable that would not combine with pasta. Some are better at this than others, certainly, but do not let the specification of one vegetable in a recipe prevent you from changing to another. Buy the freshest vegetables possible and use those which are in season.

LINGUINE WITH ZUCCHINI

Serves 2 or 4

BUY

2 medium zucchini
1 pound linguine

HAVE ON HAND	*COOKWARE*
Butter	Large heavy skillet
Olive oil	Pasta pot
Salt	
Black peppercorns	
Parmesan cheese, freshly grated	

1. Wash and slice the *zucchini;* then sauté in a large skillet in *4 table-spoons each butter and olive oil* for about 10 minutes, or until zucchini is barely tender.

2. Meanwhile cook *pasta* al dente according to package directions.

3. Drain pasta and empty into skillet with the zucchini. Sprinkle with ½ *teaspoon salt, lots of freshly ground black pepper,* and ¼ *cup grated cheese;* toss well. Serve on warm plates.

VARIATION: Substitute *two dozen small button mushrooms,* washed and trimmed, for the zucchini.

CAULIFLOWER WITH NOODLES OR SPAGHETTI

Serves 2 to 4

BUY

1 small cauliflower
Parsley *or* chives

HAVE ON HAND	*COOKWARE*
Butter	Saucepan with cover *or* vegetable steamer
Salt	
Freshly ground pepper	12-inch heavy skillet
6 ounces medium noodles, spaghetti *or* other pasta	Pasta pot
Parmesan cheese, freshly grated	

1. Trim the *cauliflower,* breaking away all leaves and cutting out and discarding the hard center core. Separate the cauliflower into bite-size flowers or pieces. Simmer in *water to cover* (or cook over steaming water) for 8 to 10 minutes, or until barely tender.

2. Meanwhile melt *1 stick (½ cup) butter* in skillet over low heat. When cauliflower is barely tender, drain, and empty into butter in the skillet. Sprinkle with *a good ½ teaspoon salt* and *lots of pepper*. Cover and set aside.

3. Chop *2 tablespoons parsley or chives* and set aside.

4. Cook the *noodles or other pasta* according to package directions until just tender. While noodles are cooking, set the skillet containing the cauliflower over low heat for 5 minutes and shake it frequently.

5. Drain noodles and empty into the skillet. Add the chopped parsley or chives and *½ cup grated cheese* and toss well.

VARIATIONS: Substitute *sliced Chinese cabbage* for the cauliflower. Substitute *2 cups fresh lima beans or peas* for the cauliflower.

BROCCOLI IN NOODLE RING

Serves 6

BUY

1 large bunch broccoli
8 ounces medium egg noodles
Pint milk

HAVE ON HAND	*COOKWARE*
Swiss *or* Cheddar cheese	1-quart saucepan
Butter	Saucepan with cover *or* vegetable steamer
Flour	
Salt and pepper	Pasta pot
Paprika	
Dry mustard	
1 egg yolk	

1. Wash and trim the *broccoli* and cut into manageable pieces. Shred *1 cup cheese*. Set aside.

2. In saucepan melt *3 tablespoons butter*. Stir in *3 tablespoons flour, ½ teaspoon salt, ⅛ teaspoon pepper, ¼ teaspoon paprika,* and *½ teaspoon dry mustard*. Gradually stir in *2 cups milk* and cook, stirring, until sauce is smooth and thickened.

3. Combine *1 egg yolk* with a *little of the hot sauce,* then stir into *remaining sauce.* Add the shredded cheese and cook over low heat, stirring constantly, for 3 minutes, or until cheese is melted. Keep warm over hot water.

4. Meanwhile steam broccoli for 10 minutes or until just fork tender.

5. Cook noodles according to package directions.

6. Drain noodles, toss with *2 tablespoons butter,* and arrange in a ring on a hot serving platter. Empty steamed broccoli into center and pour cheese sauce over all.

PASTA WITH MUSHROOMS

Serves 4. This is a delicate dish when made with fresh homemade noodles or fettuccine.

BUY

½ pound fresh mushrooms
Chunk of Parmesan cheese
1 pound noodles, fettuccine, *or* linguine

HAVE ON HAND	*COOKWARE*
Butter	Medium skillet
Coarsely cracked pepper	Pasta pot

1. Wash, trim, and slice the *mushrooms.* Grate *½ cup cheese.*

2. Sauté the mushrooms in *½ stick (¼ cup) butter* for 5 minutes, or until just tender. Set aside.

3. Cook *pasta* al dente according to package directions. If using home-made fresh noodles, do not cook them more than 5 minutes.

4. When the pasta is put into the boiling water, set mushrooms over low heat.

5. Drain cooked pasta and empty into warm serving bowl; toss with *2 tablespoons butter* and the cheese. Add the mushrooms and *cracked pepper to taste,* and toss again. Serve on warm plates.

VERMICELLI WITH GREEN PEPPERS

Serves 4 to 6

BUY

4 medium green peppers
1 pound vermicelli

HAVE ON HAND	*COOKWARE*
1 medium onion	Small skillet
Garlic	Pasta pot
Olive oil	
Butter	
Salt and pepper	
Parmesan cheese, freshly grated	

1. Remove stems from the *green peppers,* discard seeds and either dice the flesh or cut it into narrow strips. Peel and chop *1 medium onion* and *1 clove garlic.*

2. Sauté onion and garlic in *2 tablespoons olive oil* and *4 tablespoons butter* until onion is soft. Add peppers, then cover and cook for 10 minutes. Add *1 teaspoon salt* and *lots of pepper,* and keep warm over low heat.

3. Cook *vermicelli* al dente. Drain, and empty into mixing bowl.

4. Pour pepper mixture over the pasta and toss lightly. Serve hot on warm plates, sprinkling each serving generously with *grated Parmesan.*

NOODLES WITH GARDEN PEAS
AND MUSHROOMS

Serves 2 to 4

BUY

¼ pound fresh mushrooms
1 pound fresh peas in the pod
8-ounce container heavy cream
8 ounces fettuccine *or* crinkly egg noodles

HAVE ON HAND	*COOKWARE*
Butter	1-quart saucepan
Parmesan cheese, freshly grated	Small saucepan
Black peppercorns	Large skillet
	Pasta pot

1. Wash, trim, dry, and slice the *mushrooms*. Set aside.

2. Shell *peas* and cook in *a very small amount of lightly salted water* for 8 to 10 minutes, or until barely tender. Drain and set aside.

3. Warm *½ cup cream* in small saucepan over low heat.

4. In large skillet melt *1 stick (½ cup) butter* and in it sauté the mushrooms for 3 minutes, or until just tender. Keep warm.

5. Cook the *pasta* al dente.

6. Drain the pasta; empty into skillet with the mushrooms and butter; and toss. Then gradually toss in *½ cup grated Parmesan cheese* and *freshly ground pepper to taste*. Add the peas and the warm cream and toss again. Serve immediately on warm plates.

LINGUINE WITH MIXED VEGETABLES

Serves 4 to 6

BUY

2 small young carrots
2-pound, 3-ounce can Italian plum tomatoes with basil
1 small eggplant
Jar pine nuts
1 pound linguine

HAVE ON HAND

2 small white onions
Olive oil
Butter

Salt
Pepper
Parmesan cheese, freshly grated

COOKWARE

Large skillet
1 medium skillet
Pasta pot

1. Peel and chop 2 *small white onions;* scrape and chop the *2 carrots.*

2. In large skillet heat *2 tablespoons olive oil* and *2 tablespoons butter,* and in it sauté onions and carrots until onions are soft. Add *to-matoes,* breaking them with a wooden spoon. Add *1 teaspoon salt* and *lots of pepper.* Cook, uncovered, over moderate heat for 25 minutes, stir-ring frequently, until sauce is velvety and thickened.

3. Peel *eggplant* and cut into pieces. Sauté in *3 tablespoons butter,* in medium skillet, until lightly browned. Stir eggplant mixture and *2 tablespoons pine nuts* into tomato sauce, and simmer for 5 minutes longer.

4. Cook *pasta* al dente.

5. Fork pasta onto warm serving plates and spoon on the sauce. Serve *grated Parmesan* separately.

MACARONI WITH GREEN TOMATOES

Serves 4 to 6

BUY

6 green tomatos, just beginning to ripen
1 pound elbow macaroni *or* mezzani (medium-size macaroni)

HAVE ON HAND

COOKWARE

Flour
Salt
Coarsely cracked black pepper
Olive oil
Butter

Large skillet
Pasta pot

1. Discard a thin slice from both the stem end and the bottom of the *tomatoes,* then slice them about ½ inch thick. *Flour* each slice on both sides, and sprinkle with *salt and pepper.*

2. In large skillet heat *6 tablespoons olive oil,* and in it sauté the tomato slices until lightly browned on each side and just fork tender. Keep warm.

3. Cook *macaroni* al dente according to package directions.

4. Drain macaroni and toss with *3 tablespoons butter* and *more pepper if desired.* Serve on warm plates, topping each portion with several tomato slices.

Pasta Salads

MACARONI SALAD SLAW

Serves 6 to 8

BUY

8 ounces elbow macaroni
1 bunch celery
1 small cabbage
Small jar pimientos
1 green pepper
Water cress

HAVE ON HAND

Onion
Salt and pepper
1 lemon
Mayonnaise

COOKWARE

Pasta pot

1. Cook *macaroni* according to package directions; drain; and rinse with *cold water*.

2. Peel *1½ cups celery,* and shred *1½ cups cabbage.* Peel and mince *1 small onion* and mince *2 pimientos.* Wash, seed, and chop the *green pepper.*

3. Combine macaroni with prepared vegetables. Stir in *2 teaspoons salt, ¼ teaspoon pepper, 2 tablespoons lemon juice,* and *1 cup mayonnaise.* Chill thoroughly.

4. Garnish atractively with *water cress* and serve.

PATIO SALAD WITH SOUR CREAM DRESSING

Serves 6 to 8

BUY

8 ounces elbow macaroni
Celery
1 green pepper
2 large tomatoes
8-ounce container sour cream
Water cress and salad greens

HAVE ON HAND	*COOKWARE*
4 eggs	Pasta pot
Onion	Small saucepan
Salt and pepper	
Lemon	
Mayonnaise	

1. Cook *macaroni* according to package directions; drain; and rinse with *cold water.* Set aside.

2. Hard cook *4 eggs,* then cool and peel (page 147).

3. Dice *½ cup each of celery and green pepper.* Peel and chop to-matoes. Peel and mince *enough onion to measure 2 tablespoons.*

4. Combine cooked macaroni with the prepared vegetables, and stir in *2 teaspoons salt, ¼ teaspoon pepper, 2 tablespoons lemon juice, ½ cup sour cream,* and *½ cup mayonnaise.*

5. Pile the salad into a bowl lined with *crisp greens,* and garnish with the hard-cooked eggs and *water cress.*

MACARONI VINAIGRETTE

Serves 6

BUY

8 ounces elbow macaroni
1 head romaine
1 cucumber
2 large tomatoes

HAVE ON HAND	*COOKWARE*
Onion	Pasta pot
Parsley	
Salt	
Pepper	
Dry mustard	
Wine vinegar	
Salad oil	

1. Cook *macaroni* according to package directions; drain and rinse with *cold water.*

2. Peel and mince *1 small onion.* Chop *¼ cup parsley.* Peel and dice the *cucumber.* Combine cooked macaroni with the onion, parsley, and cucumber. Add *2 teaspoons salt, ¼ teaspoon pepper, ½ teaspoon dry mustard, 2 tablespoons wine vinegar,* and *6 tablespoons salad oil.* Marinate in refrigerator for 30 minutes or longer.

3. Peel and cut *tomatoes* into wedges. Separate *romaine leaves* and wash. Dry well. Line a salad bowl with the crisp romaine leaves and turn the macaroni salad into the center. Garnish with tomato wedges.

Baked Pasta Dishes

Noodles, macaroni, and other pasta products lend themselves well to being cooked in advance, sauced in a casserole, and baked when needed. There are many such dishes combining pasta, sauce, cheese, and vegetables but, in my view, it's hard to beat a really well-prepared dish of macaroni and fine, aged Cheddar cheese. Here's the best recipe for it that I know.

GOOD MACARONI AND CHEESE

Serves 4 to 6

   BUY

½ pound aged sharp Cheddar cheese
8 ounces elbow macaroni

HAVE ON HAND	COOKWARE
Milk	2 small saucepans
Butter	Pasta pot
Flour	2-quart baking dish
Salt and pepper	

1. Shred *cheese* and set aside.

2. In saucepan, heat *2 cups milk* to simmering.

3. In second saucepan, melt *2 tablespoons butter*. Stir in *2 table-spoons flour* and cook until mixture bubbles. Remove saucepan from heat and add hot milk. Return to heat and cook, stirring rapidly, for about 3 minutes or until sauce is smooth and thickened. Add cheese and cook, stirring, until cheese is melted. Season with salt and pepper.

4. Cook *macaroni* al dente according to package directions. Drain and empty into the baking dish. Pour cheese sauce over macaroni and mix well.

5. When ready to bake, place in oven preheated 375° F.

6. Bake macaroni and cheese in the moderate oven for 25 to 30 minutes, or until sauce is bubbling and lightly browned.

WITH CRUMB TOPPING:

Brown *½ cup fresh bread crumbs* in *2 tablespoons butter*. Sprinkle on top of macaroni before baking.

BAKED NOODLE DISH

Serves 4

BUY

6-ounce package medium noodles
1 pint dairy sour cream
1 container heavy cream

HAVE ON HAND

Fresh bread
Butter
Salt and pepper
Parmesan cheese, freshly grated

COOKWARE

Pasta pot
Medium skillet
1½-quart casserole

1. Crumb *enough bread to measure* ¾ *cup*. Lightly brown the crumbs in *2 tablespoons butter*. Set aside.

2. Boil *noodles* in *large quantity of salted water* for 8 minutes, or until barely tender. Drain and rinse with *hot water*. Empty into casserole.

3. Combine the *sour cream* with *½ cup heavy sweet cream, ½ cup grated Parmesan cheese, a sprinkling of salt to taste,* and *lots of freshly ground black pepper*. Add to noodles and mix well. Sprinkle bread crumbs on top.

4. When ready to bake, place in oven preheated to 350° F.

5. Bake noodles in the moderate oven for 30 minutes.

COTTAGE CHEESE AND NOODLE CASSEROLE

Serves 4 to 6

BUY

Green onions *or* chives
8-ounce package egg noodles
16 ounces cottage cheese
1 pint dairy sour cream

HAVE ON HAND

Parmesan cheese
Salt and pepper
Bread
Butter

COOKWARE

Small skillet
Pasta pot
2-quart baking dish

1. Chop *¼ cup green onions or chives*. Grate *enough Parmesan cheese to measure ½ cup*. Set aside.

2. Prepare *1 cup fresh bread crumbs*; heat *2 tablespoons butter* in small skillet; add crumbs and sauté until golden. Set aside.

3. Cook *noodles* according to package directions. Drain and empty into mixing bowl. Stir in *1½ cups cottage cheese,* the *sour cream,* the green onions or chives, *1 teaspoon salt,* and *¼ teaspoon pepper.*

4. Empty noodle mixture into baking dish, and sprinkle the crumbs and grated cheese on top.

5. When ready to bake, place in oven preheated to 350° F.

6. Bake noodles in the moderate oven for 30 minutes.

NOODLES BARBAN

Serves 3 or 4

BUY

8 ounces egg noodles
8-ounce container ricotta *or* small-curd cottage cheese
8-ounce container heavy cream

HAVE ON HAND	*COOKWARE*
Parmesan cheese	Pasta pot
Butter	Small saucepan
Black pepper	2-quart baking dish
Salt	
Flour	
Milk	

1. Grate ½ *cup Parmesan cheese* and set aside.

2. Parboil *noodles* in *boiling salted water* for just 8 minutes. They should be chewy and not quite cooked. Drain into a warm bowl and toss with *4 tablespoons butter* and ½ *teaspoon coarsely grated pepper.*

3. In smaller bowl mash the *ricotta or cottage cheese* with ¼ *cup of the cream* and ½ *teaspoon salt* to make a creamy mixture.

4. *Butter* baking dish. Cover bottom of dish with *half the cheese mixture,* then add layer of *half the noodles.* Sprinkle with *half the Parmesan.* Add *another layer of the cheese mixture* and cover it with the *remaining noodles;* do NOT add remaining Parmesan yet.

5. In a small saucepan melt *3 tablespoons butter* and stir in *3 tablespoons* flour. Slowly stir in *1½ cups milk;* cook, stirring, until sauce is smooth and thickened. Stir in *remaining cream, 1 tablespoon Parmesan cheese,* and ½ *teaspoon salt.*

6. Pour the sauce over the noodles, and sprinkle with *remaining Parmesan.* Dot with *2 tablespoons butter.*

7. When ready to bake, place in oven preheated to 400° F.

8. Bake the noodles in the hot oven for 20 to 25 minutes.

SCALLOPED SPINACH AND MACARONI

Serves 6

BUY

8-ounce package elbow macaroni
2 packages frozen chopped spinach (10 ounces each)
8-ounce container heavy cream

HAVE ON HAND	*COOKWARE*
Swiss *or* Cheddar cheese	Pasta pot
Butter	Two 1-quart saucepans
Flour	2-quart baking dish
Salt and pepper	
Nutmeg	
Milk	
Paprika	

1. Cook *macaroni* according to package directions; drain; and rinse with *hot water*. Set aside.

2. Cook *spinach* according to package directions and drain well. Set aside. Shred *1 cup cheese*.

3. In saucepan melt *4 tablespoons butter*. Stir in *4 tablespoons flour, 1 teaspoon salt, ¼ teaspoon pepper,* and *¼ teaspoon nutmeg*. Gradually stir in *2 cups milk;* continue to stir until sauce is smooth and thickened. Stir in *½ cup cream* and *half the cheese;* cook, stirring, until cheese is melted.

4. *Butter* baking dish, and in it arrange alternate layers of macaroni, sauce, and spinach, ending with sauce. Sprinkle with *remaining cheese* and a *little paprika*.

5. When ready to bake, place in oven preheated to 350° F.

6. Bake macaroni in the moderate oven for 30 minutes, or until cheese is melted and sauce is bubbling.

MACARONI BAKED WITH TOMATO SAUCE

Serves 4

BUY

Parmesan cheese
8-ounce package cut ziti, mezzani, *or* elbow macaroni
1 pint milk
1-pound can stewed tomatoes

HAVE ON HAND	*COOKWARE*
Onions	Pasta pot
Butter	1-quart saucepan
Flour	2-quart casserole
Salt	
Black peppercorns	
Thyme *or* oregano	

1. Grate and set aside *1 cup Parmesan cheese*. Chop *2 tablespoons onion*.

2. Cook the *pasta* the least amount of time given on package. Drain; then rinse with *cold water*. Set aside.

3. In saucepan melt *2 tablespoons butter,* and in it sauté the onion for 3 minutes, or until onion is transparent. Stir in *2 tablespoons flour*. Slowly stir in *1½ cups milk;* cook, stirring, until sauce is smooth and slightly thickened. Stir in *½ teaspoon salt, ½ teaspoon freshly ground black pepper, ¼ teaspoon thyme or oregano,* and *¾ cup of the cheese*.

4. Pour the cheese sauce over the macaroni and mix well.

5. In baking dish spread a layer of *half the stewed tomatoes*. Spoon the macaroni on top, then pour *remaining stewed tomatoes* over the macaroni. Sprinkle with the *remaining ¼ cup Parmesan*.

6. When ready to bake, preheat oven to 375° F.

7. Bake macaroni for 20 minutes, or until sauce is bubbling.

Stuffed Pasta Dishes

There is little reason to give you the more-or-less ordinary ways of preparing manicotti and lasagne since good recipes for them usually appear on the packages. Also there are some quite acceptable frozen manicotti and ravioli products available, especially the unsauced ones (to which you can add your own homemade sauces). So I'll give you just a few different and favorite stuffed pasta dishes, limiting my selection, of course, to ones calling for cheese and vegetables.

MANICOTTI WITH MUSHROOM CHEESE SAUCE

Serves 4. Recipe may be doubled. If you wish to take a short cut, buy 8 frozen manicotti already stuffed with cheese and keep them frozen until you are ready to sauce them. This will eliminate steps 1 and 2 except for grating some Parmesan cheese. You'll need only ½ cup.

BUY

½ pound aged Parmesan cheese
Parsley
Chives
8 ounces mozzarella
1 pound ricotta cheese
8 manicotti tubes
Ingredients for the Mushroom Cheese Sauce

HAVE ON HAND

2 eggs
Salt
Freshly ground black pepper
Olive oil
Butter

COOKWARE

Pasta pot
14 x 8½ x 2 lasagne dish

1. Grate *1½ cups Parmesan cheese.* Chop *2 tablespoons each parsley and chives.* Shred the *mozzarella.*

2. Into mixing bowl pour *1 cup of the Parmesan cheese* (reserve remaining ½ cup to sprinkle on top of the sauce). Then add the mozzarella, the *ricotta,* the chopped parsley and chives, *2 eggs, 1½ teaspoons salt, ½ teaspoon pepper.* Mix well.

3. Make Mushroom Cheese Sauce (see recipe below).

4. Put manicotti into *rapidly boiling salted water* to which *1 tablespoon olive oil* has been added; cook for the least amount of time specified in box directions. Drain, then cover with *cool water.*

5. *Butter* the lasagne dish. Fill the manicotti, one at a time, with the

cheese mixture. The best way to do this is to slit each cooked tube, lay it out flat, spread surface thickly with the cheese filling, and then roll the tube.

6. Arrange the filled manicotti side by side in the prepared dish. Spoon the Mushroom Cheese Sauce over all, and sprinkle with the *reserved ½ cup Parmesan cheese.*

7. When ready to bake, place in oven preheated to 350° F. Bake for 25 to 30 minutes, or until sauce is bubbling and hot throughout. Serve each person 2 manicotti with plenty of sauce.

MUSHROOM CHEESE SAUCE

Makes about 4 cups

BUY

¾ pound fresh mushrooms
¼ pound Gruyère *or* Swiss cheese
¼ pound aged Parmesan cheese
1 pint milk
1 pint heavy cream

HAVE ON HAND

COOKWARE

Shallots if possible; otherwise onion   2-quart saucepan
Butter
Flour
Salt
Freshly ground black pepper

1. Peel and mince *enough shallots or onion to measure ¼ cup.* Wash, trim, and slice the *mushrooms.* Shred *enough Gruyère or Swiss cheese to make 1 cup.* Grate *1 cup Parmesan.*

2. In saucepan melt *1 stick (½ cup) butter,* and in it sauté the shallots or onion for 3 to 4 minutes, or until transparent. Add mushrooms and sauté for 5 to 6 minutes longer, stirring frequently.

3. Stir in *6 tablespoons flour.* Gradually stir in *1 pint of milk;* cook, stirring constantly, until sauce is smooth and thick. Gradually stir in the *cream.* Add the cheeses, *1½ teaspoons salt,* and *pepper to taste;* cook, stirring, until cheeses are melted.

MANICOTTI WITH TOMATO SAUCE

Serves 4

BUY

Package manicotti tubes
15½-ounce jar marinara sauce
8-ounce can tomato sauce
½ pound mozzarella cheese
1-pound container ricotta cheese

HAVE ON HAND

Salt
Parsley
Oregano
Coarsely cracked pepper
Parmesan cheese
2 eggs

COOKWARE

Pasta pot
Small saucepan
11¾ x 7½ x 1¾-inch baking dish

1. *Cook 8 manicotti* in *boiling salted water* until just tender. Drain, then keep moist in a *little warm water.*

2. In saucepan combine *marinara sauce, tomato sauce, 2 tablespoons chopped parsley, ¼ teaspoon oregano, ¼ teaspoon pepper,* and *½ cup water.* Bring to a boil and simmer for 10 to 15 minutes.

3. Meanwhile grate *enough Parmesan cheese to measure ½ cup.* Shred the *mozzarella cheese.* Combine *1 cup of the shredded mozzarella* with *all of the ricotta, 2 eggs,* and *½ teaspoon salt.*

4. Drain manicotti tubes, then stuff them with cheese mixture, using about ¼ cupful for each.

5. Spread *about 1 cup of the spaghetti sauce* in bottom of baking dish. Arrange the stuffed manicotti side by side on top of the sauce. Pour *remaining sauce* over the manicotti, and sprinkle with *remaining mozzarella* and the Parmesan cheese.

6. To cook: Preheat oven to 350° F. Bake the manicotti, uncovered, for 30 minutes, or until cheese is melted and sauce is bubbling.

MEATLESS LASAGNE WITH HOMEMADE MARINARA SAUCE

Serves 8

BUY FOR THE SAUCE

4 large yellow onions
Two 2-pound, 3-ounce cans Italian plum tomatoes
1 pound mushrooms

BUY FOR THE LASAGNE

½ pound Parmesan cheese
1 pound mozzarella cheese
1 pound ricotta cheese
1-pound package of lasagne

HAVE ON HAND

Garlic
Carrots
Olive oil
Salt
Freshly ground pepper
Oregano
Basil
Butter
Parsley
3 eggs

COOKWARE

Large skillet
Pasta pot
Small saucepan
Large lasagne baking dish

MAKE MUSHROOM MARINARA SAUCE:

1. Peel and chop *enough onions to measure 4 cups*. Peel and mince *4 large cloves garlic*. Chop *2 small carrots*.

2. In large skillet heat *½ cup olive oil,* and in it sauté onion, garlic, and carrot for about 10 minutes, or until vegetables are lightly browned; stir frequently. Add *tomatoes* and *salt and pepper to taste*. Bring to a boil and simmer for 30 minutes.

3. Meanwhile wash, trim, and chop the *mushrooms*.

4. At end of half hour rub sauce through a sieve or food mill. Add

2 teaspoons oregano and *2 teaspoons basil* to strained sauce, then set it aside. Wash skillet.

5. In skillet melt *2 tablespoons butter,* and in it sauté the mushrooms for 5 minutes, or until just tender; stir frequently. Add tomato sauce, bring to a simmer, and continue to simmer for 45 minutes.

FOR THE LASAGNE:

1. Grate *enough Parmesan to measure 1½ cups.* Chop *2 tablespoons parsley.* Dice or shred the *mozzarella.*

2. Combine the *ricotta* with *3 eggs, 1 cup of the grated Parmesan,* the parsley, and *salt and pepper to taste.*

3. Cook the *lasagne* according to package directions until barely tender. Drain immediately and rinse in *cold water.*

4. Melt *6 tablespoons butter* in a small saucepan.

5. Assemble the lasagne: Spoon a layer of sauce over bottom of lasagne dish. Add a layer of lasagne. Spoon another layer of sauce over this, and add a layer of mozzarella cheese, and a sprinkling of Parmesan. Spoon *1 tablespoon melted butter* over this. Next, another layer of lasagne another of sauce, then a layer of ricotta, and a sprinkling of *1 tablespoon butter.* Repeat these two sets of layers until the lasagne dish is almost full, and end with mozzarella, Parmesan, and melted butter.

6. When ready to bake, place in oven preheated to 375° F. Bake lasagne in the moderate oven for 45 minutes, or until sauce is bubbling and mixture is piping hot throughout.

RAVIOLI WITH SPINACH AND RICOTTA

Serves 4 to 6

BUY

½ pound Parmesan cheese
½ pound fresh spinach
½ pound ricotta cheese

HAVE ON HAND | *COOKWARE*

Ingredients for Fresh Pasta for ravioli (page 212)
1 egg
Salt
Pepper
Nutmeg
Butter

1-quart saucepan with cover
Small saucepan
Large heavy pot

1. Make *fresh pasta dough.* Grate and set aside *1½ cups Parmesan cheese.*

2. Wash *spinach* thoroughly and cook in covered pan without water until tender. Drain and press out as much liquid as possible.

3. Put spinach and *ricotta* through food chopper, then mix in *1 egg,* and *1 cup of the Parmesan cheese.* Season with *salt, pepper,* and *nutmeg.*

4. Roll out dough into thin sheets. Place a teaspoon of filling on bottom sheet every 2 inches. Cover with second sheet of dough, press firmly around filling, and cut into squares with a pastry cutter.

5. Dry for 45 minutes.

6. Melt *1 stick (½ cup) butter* in small saucepan over low heat.

7. Cook ravioli a half dozen at a time in *simmering salted water.* Remove with a slotted spoon as they rise to surface of water and are cooked al dente. Drain on paper towels. Serve immediately with the hot melted butter. Pass *additional grated Parmesan.*

RAVIOLI WITH FIVE CHEESES

Serves 4 to 6

BUY

4 ounces Parmesan cheese
4 ounces Romano cheese
4 ounces mozzarella cheese
4 ounces Gruyère *or* Swiss cheese
½ pound ricotta cheese
8-ounce container heavy cream

HAVE ON HAND	*COOKWARE*
Ingredients for Fresh Pasta	Small saucepan
for ravioli (page 212)	Large heavy saucepot
1 egg	
Nutmeg	
Pepper	
Butter	

1. Make *fresh pasta dough.*

2. Grate the *Parmesan* and *Romano.* Shred the *mozzarella* and the *Swiss* or *Gruyère.*

3. In mixing bowl combine the *ricotta* with *1 cup of the Parmesan* (reserve the rest) and the other three cheeses. Stir in *1 egg,* the *cream, a dash of nutmeg,* and *freshly ground pepper to taste.* Mix well.

4. Roll out dough into thin sheets. Place a spoonful of the cheese filling on the bottom sheet of dough every 2 inches. Cover with second sheet of dough, press firmly around filling, and cut into squares with pastry cutter.

5. Let filled ravioli dry for 45 minutes.

6. Melt *1 stick (½ cup) butter* in small pan over low heat.

7. Cook a half dozen ravioli at a time in *simmering salted water* until they rise to the surface and are cooked al dente, or to taste. Remove with a slotted spoon to drain on paper towels.

8. Serve on hot plates, drenched with the melted butter and topped with *a generous sprinkling of the reserved grated Parmesan.*

BREADS

Nutritious Homemade Breads—
The Basics

Julia Child may well go down in history for her classic remark, "How can a society be great when its bread tastes like Kleenex?"

How, indeed? The spongy refined white breads found today in our markets are made of poison-sprayed, degerminated, over-bleached wheat, hydrogenated shortening, refined white sugar, and water. The initial dough is nutritionally worthless. Then chemicals are added to condition it, and more chemicals are added to prevent spoilage. You can push both ends of the baked bread together like an accordion, and when the pressure is released, the loaf bounces back to its original shape! I kept such a loaf on my kitchen counter for weeks to see how long it would remain soft until I got tired of looking at it. It didn't mold; it didn't dry out. It remained in the same spongy condition it had the day I bought it!

So, if you are not already among the many rebels who have learned to make and bake their own fresh, nutritious, whole-grain breads, it's time you started.

Making a loaf of yeast bread is easier than apple pan dowdy. It takes only a few minutes to stir up the dough and to form it into a loaf or pan rolls. It does take time for the infinitesimal living organisms known as yeast to grow and give off the carbon dioxide which raises the bread and makes it light—but the yeast does this by itself.

Once the miracle of yeast is understood, it's almost impossible to turn out a poor loaf, and there are all the satisfactions of working and kneading the living dough and feeling it respond to the touch, the unforgettable aroma of fresh yeast bread baking in the oven, the crunch of the crisp crust crumbling between the teeth, and the substantial, honest flavor of yeast mingled with the nutritious whole-grain texture beneath.

Nowadays, you don't have to go far to seek out stone-ground whole-grain flours. Country stores and health-food markets which stock a large variety of whole-grain products are multiplying. It won't be long before all the supermarkets will be forced to supply either the flours themselves or some honest bread, or both, and even then, it will be much more economical to bake your own than to buy theirs.

So promise yourself that you will bake bread at least once a week from whole grains with all their God-given goodness.

Once you learn to make a basic loaf of whole-wheat bread, you can go on to use all kinds of flour, you can alterate brown sugars, maple syrup, honey, or molasses to suit your mood, and you can add seeds, nuts, raisins, or herbs to create new and interesting flavors and textures.

WHAT MAKES A GOOD LOAF OF BREAD?

YEAST is the essential ingredient, and the fresh yeast cakes or the packets of dry active yeast are equally satisfactory. Like all living substances, yeast needs food, moisture, and warmth (75° to 85° F.) to develop, and when these three conditions are met, the yeast spores multiply rapidly.

FLOUR is the chief ingredient in all breads, and your bread is only as nutritious as the kind of flour you use. You will need to keep on hand some all-purpose flour, but buy only the unbleached kind, which is already in the supermarkets. Then seek out a variety of stone-ground or water-ground whole-grain flours: whole wheat, rye, barley, millet, soy, gluten, graham, buckwheat. Buy them in small quantities and be sure to store them in your refrigerator or freezer, for the germ of the cereal has been left in these flours and the oil contained in the germ becomes rancid quickly. Also, since no chemicals have been added, tiny insects develop and grow fat in such a happy environment, especially in warm weather. They know a good thing when they smell it!

In addition to these flours, you may want to keep on hand some oats, either quick-cooking or long-cooking, some corn meal, cracked wheat, bran flakes or 100% bran, soy grits, farina, wheat flakes, and wheat germ.

SUGAR provides quick food for the yeast, adds flavor to the bread, and is partly responsible for the golden color of the crust. Sweetening can also contribute to the nutrition of the loaf if you use brown sugars, molasses, honey, corn syrup, or maple syrup in place of refined white sugar. These may be interchanged at will.

MILK, WATER, OR POTATO WATER supplies the moisture.

SHORTENING lubricates the delicate meshwork of the dough so it can expand smoothly and easily. Our grandmothers had no such thing as hydrogenated shortening. They used butter or oil and you may do the same.

These ingredients plus a little salt and a little time are all it takes to make a loaf of bread that is vital, healthful, and utterly delicious.

Kneading the dough is guaranteed to reduce any hostility or neuroses you may be harboring.

Make two loaves, always, rather than one—a loaf to refrigerate or freeze and another one to eat hot from the oven. Slice it in good-size chunks, spread it lavishly with sweet butter, and top it occasionally with some homemade peanut butter (page 341). Heaven!

BASIC FORMULA FOR ONE LOAF

Although we are going to begin, on page 255, by making *two* loaves of bread, you might like to memorize the following very easy quantities that any single loaf of bread requires:

    1 cup liquid (usually half milk plus half water *or* potato water)
    1 cake yeast *or* 1 package active dry yeast
    1 tablespoon sugar (preferably brown)
    1 tablespoon molasses *or* dark corn syrup
    1 tablespoon shortening *or* oil
    1 teaspoon salt
    3 cups flour

While breadmaking is one of the most creative forms of culinary art —not only in its flour variations and its texture and flavor changes, but also in its shaping—if you remember these standard quantities you cannot fail. Double, triple, or quadruple them for 2, 3, or 4 loaves, but remember the formula for the single loaf.

Generally, the dough for 12 buns or rolls is equivalent to the quantity used to make one loaf.

FOUR RULES OF BREADMAKING TO REMEMBER:

1. Yeast is living! Don't kill it with too hot a liquid. For yeast cakes the liquid should be just lukewarm (80° to 85° F.). For active dry yeast the water can be slightly hot to the hand or as high as 120° F.

2. Don't knead in any more flour than necessary. The dough should be soft but not sticky.

3. Don't let the bread over-rise in the pans. If you do, it may collapse a little during baking. When the dough is just nicely rounded over sides of the pans, it is ready for the oven.

4. Don't overbake the loaves. They are done when they sound hollow when rapped with the knuckle and the crust is golden.

BASIC 100% WHOLE-WHEAT BREAD

Makes 2 loaves

BUY

2 yeast cakes *or* 2 packages active dry yeast
2-pound bag stone-ground whole-wheat flour

HAVE ON HAND	*COOKWARE*
Milk	Small saucepan
Brown sugar	Two 8½ x 4½-inch loaf pans
Molasses	(1½-quart capacity)
Salt	
Butter	
Salad oil	

1. Heat *1 cup milk* to scalding.

2. Add the *yeast* to *¼ cup lukewarm water* and let soak for 5 minutes, then stir mixture until well blended.

3. Into large mixing bowl measure *2 tablespoons each brown sugar and molasses, 2 teaspoons salt,* and *2 tablespoons butter*. Pour the hot milk over these ingredients and stir, mashing the butter against sides of bowl until melted or broken into small lumps. Stir in *¾ cup cool water*.

4. Stir in *1 cup of the flour* and beat with a wooden spoon for 1 minute. Add the yeast and *2 more cups flour* and continue to beat until batter is smooth and elastic. Stir in *another 2 cups flour*. Then, with floured fingers, work in *enough additional flour to make a dough that does not stick to the fingers yet is still soft*.

5. Turn dough out onto a floured surface and knead about 100 kneading strokes, or until dough becomes elastic.

HOW TO KNEAD:

Kneading is a three-step rhythm that quickly becomes automatic. On the floured surface, fold dough over onto itself toward you, then push dough away with heels of your hands. Give dough a quarter turn; repeat.

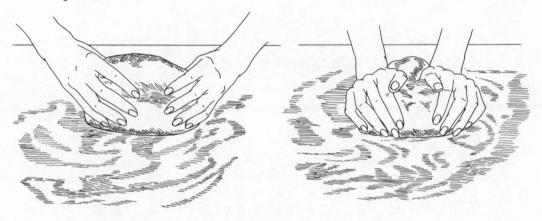

6. When you've finished kneading the dough, shape it into a ball and rub the surface with a *little salad oil.*

7. Cover lightly with a towel and let dough rise for about 1½ hours, or until double in bulk. *Oil* bread pans and set aside.

8. Plunge a floured fist into the center of the dough to deflate it and knead again briefly. Cut ball of dough in half and shape each half into a loaf.

TO SHAPE LOAF:

Flatten the ball of dough with palms of hands, fold in half lengthwise, and flatten again. Take one end of the dough in each hand, then stretch the dough gently to elongate it. Overlap ends at center and press firmly together. Now roll dough lengthwise, turn it seam side down, and seal the ends. Place each loaf, seam side down, in prepared bread pan. Cover loaves with the towel and let dough rise for about 1 hour, or until puffed and nicely rounded above sides of pans.

9. Preheat oven to 375° F. Bake the loaves for 45 to 50 minutes, or until tops are golden brown and loaves test done.

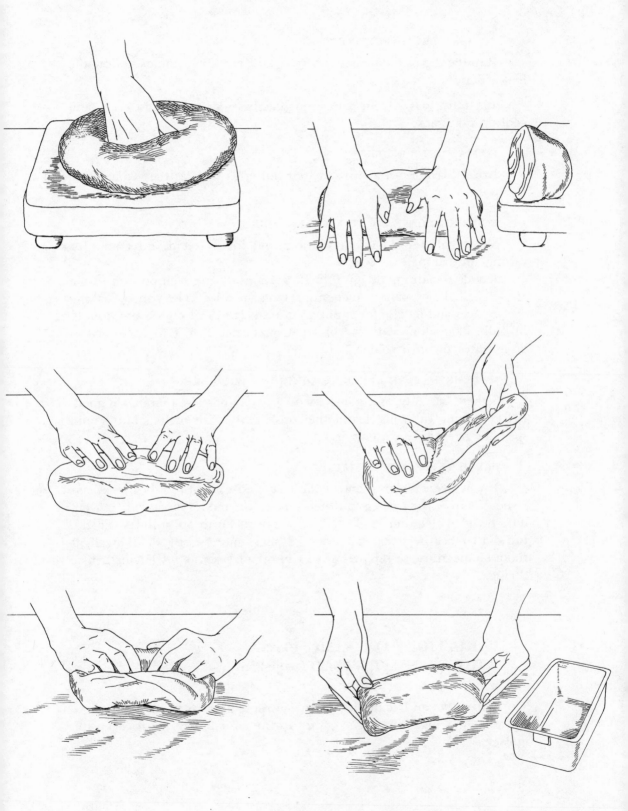

TO TEST BREAD FOR DONENESS:

Rap the top of the bread with your knuckles. If it sounds hollow the loaf is done.

10. Turn loaves from pans immediately to keep the crust crisp, and cool on cake rack.

FOR A SOFT CRUST:

Brush loaves with a little melted butter as soon as they come from the oven.

FOR ONE LOAF AND ONE DOZEN ROLLS:

Shape half the dough into a loaf and follow recipe directions for raising and baking.

Divide remaining dough into 12 portions. Shape each portion into a round ball. Place balls 2 inches apart on an oiled cake pan or baking sheet; cover and let rise for about 45 minutes, or until puffed and double in bulk. Bake along with the bread in preheated 375° F. oven for 20 to 25 minutes, or until golden.

IF DESIRED, SPRINKLE TOPS OF ROLLS WITH SEEDS

Sesame, caraway, and poppy seeds, any one of these toppings is good. Before baking the rolls, brush the tops lightly with melted butter and sprinkle generously with seeds.

BREAD FREEZES BEAUTIFULLY:

If you freeze a loaf in one of the new plastic ovenproof bags, you can remove it from the freezer and then put it, bag and all, in a 325° F. oven. The bread will be hot and ready to serve in 20 to 30 minutes. Frozen bread that has been partially thawed slices more easily than bread at room temperature, so remove a loaf from the freezer about 1 hour before slicing.

VARIATIONS ON BASIC 100% WHOLE-WHEAT BREAD (page 255)

WHITE BREAD: Use unbleached all-purpose flour in place of the whole wheat; white sugar in place of the brown; and honey in place of the molasses.

OATMEAL BREAD: Substitute 2 cups oats (quick- or long-cooking) for 2 cups of the flour.

SWEDISH RYE BREAD: Use half stone-ground rye flour and half unbleached all-purpose flour in basic recipe. Add 1 tablespoon caraway seeds to the hot milk.

BRAN BREAD: Substitute 2 cups bran flakes or 100% all bran for 2 cups of the flour.

CRACKED WHEAT BREAD: Add 2 tablespoons honey and 2 cups cracked wheat to hot-milk mixture before adding necessary flour to make a dough that does not stick to the hands.

WHEAT GERM BREAD: Add 1 cup wheat germ to hot-milk mixture before adding necessary flour to make a dough that does not stick to the hands.

SOY BREAD: Use half stone-ground soy flour and half unbleached all-purpose flour in basic recipe.

BUCKWHEAT BREAD: Substitute 1 cup buckwheat flour for 1 cup whole-wheat or all-purpose flour.

CORN BREAD: Add 1 cup stone-ground corn meal to hot-milk mixture before adding necessary flour to make a dough that does not stick to the hands. To give a nice crunch to the bread, sprinkle bottom of the bread pans with corn meal before the dough is placed in them.

GLUTEN BREAD: Like whole-wheat flour, all gluten flour (a low-starch, high-protein corn product) may be used in breadmaking and combines well with soy, rye and other specialty flours used in breadmaking.

GRAHAM BREAD: Substitute 2 cups graham flour for 2 cups whole wheat or all-purpose flour in making bread.

RYE CORNMEAL BREAD: Substitute 1 cup each rye flour and corn meal for 2 cups of the all-purpose flour.

RYE SOY BREAD: Substitute 1 cup each rye flour and soy flour for 2 cups of the all-purpose flour.

MILLET BREAD: Substitute 2 cups millet flour for 2 cups of the all-purpose flour.

WHOLE-WHEAT RYE BREAD: Substitute 2 cups rye flour for 2 cups whole-wheat flour.

Bread & Roll Recipes

HALF AND HALF BREAD

Makes 2 loaves

BUY

2 envelopes active dry yeast *or* 2 yeast cakes
1-pound bag whole-wheat flour

<table>
<tr><td>

HAVE ON HAND

Milk
Butter
Sugar
Salt
Unbleached all-purpose flour
Molasses
Salad oil
</td><td>

COOKWARE

Small saucepan
Two 8½ x 4½-inch loaf pans
</td></tr>
</table>

1. In small saucepan measure *2 cups milk*. Add *¼ cup butter (½ stick)* and heat until milk is scalding hot and butter is melted. Remove from heat and pour in *½ cup cold water*.

2. Pour *½ cup lukewarm water* into a large mixing bowl and sprinkle, or crumble, in the *yeast*. Let stand for about 5 minutes, or until yeast is softened and mixture is bubbling.

3. Stir in *⅓ cup sugar, 1 tablespoon salt,* and the milk mixture. Beat in *2 cups all-purpose flour,* then divide the dough in half.

4. Into one half stir *enough additional all-purpose flour to make a light dough.* Turn out on floured board and knead until dough is smooth and elastic.

5. Into the other half stir *4 tablespoons molasses* and *2½ to 3 cups*

whole-wheat flour. Turn out onto floured board and knead until smooth and elastic.

6. *Oil* surface of each mound of dough, cover lightly with a towel, and let rise for 1¼ to 1½ hours. Punch down and knead again briefly. Cover and let rest for 10 minutes.

7. Oil loaf pans.

8. Cut each mound of dough in half. Roll out half the white dough and half the whole-wheat dough, making two rectangles about 12 x 8 inches. Place the whole-wheat rectangle on top of the white rectangle, then roll up, starting with the short side of the dough. Repeat with remaining dough.

9. Place in 2 oiled loaf pans. Cover and let rise for 45 to 60 minutes, or until double in bulk.

10. Bake in preheated 375° F. oven for 45 to 50 minutes, or until loaves are brown and crusty and test done.

NOTE: You can adapt this recipe to make many interesting light-and-dark breads. For instance, change the plain white dough to *a rich egg dough* (page 269), and use rye, soy, or wheat-germ dough in place of the whole-wheat. To vary the flavor, add caraway, poppy, or toasted sesame seeds (page 273).

WHOLE-WHEAT BREAD WITH WHEAT GERM

Makes 2 loaves

BUY

2 packages active dry yeast *or* 2 yeast cakes
2-pound package stone-ground whole-wheat flour

HAVE ON HAND

Brown sugar
Salt
Wheat germ
Non-fat instant dry milk solids
Butter
Unbleached all-purpose flour
Salad oil

COOKWARE

Two 8½ x 4½-inch loaf pans

1. In small bowl soften the *yeast* in ½ *cup lukewarm water.*

2. In large mixing bowl combine ¼ *cup brown sugar, 2 teaspoons salt, ½ cup wheat germ, 1 cup non-fat instant dry milk powder.* Slice in *2 tablespoons butter,* and stir in *2 cups hot water.* Gradually stir in *3 cups unbleached all-purpose flour,* then stir in the yeast mixture. Gradually work in *about 4 cups whole-wheat flour,* or enough to make a dough that is stiff enough to handle.

3. Turn dough out on floured board and knead until smooth and elastic. *Oil* the top of the dough, cover lightly with a towel, and let rise for 1¼ to 1½ hours, or until doubled in bulk.

4. Oil loaf pans.

5. Punch dough and knead again briefly. Shape dough into two loaves and put each into a prepared pan. Let rise again about 45 minutes, or until well rounded above sides of pans.

6. Bake in preheated 400° F. oven for 40 minutes, or until golden brown, and hollow-sounding when tapped with the knuckles. Remove from pans to cool on racks.

OATMEAL MOLASSES BREAD

Makes 2 loaves

BUY

2 yeast cakes *or* 2 packages active dry yeast

HAVE ON HAND	*COOKWARE*
Milk	Small saucepan
Butter	Two 8½ x 4½-inch loaf pans
Molasses	
Salt	
Oats, instant *or* long-cooking	
Unbleached all-purpose flour	
Salad oil	

1. In saucepan measure *1 cup milk.* Add ¼ *cup butter (½ stick)* and heat until milk is scalding hot and butter is melted.

2. Soften the *yeast* in ½ *cup lukewarm water.*

3. In large mixing bowl put *½ cup molasses, 2 teaspoons salt,* and *2 cups oats (instant or long-cooking).* Pour the hot milk mixture over the oats and mix thoroughly. Stir in *½ cup cold water,* and gradually stir in *3 cups unbleached all-purpose flour.* Stir in yeast mixture, and gradually work in *about 2 more cups unbleached flour,* or enough to make a soft dough.

4. Turn dough out on floured board and knead until smooth and elastic. *Oil* top, cover with a towel and let rise for about 1½ hours, or until double in bulk.

5. Oil loaf pans and set aside.

6. Punch dough and knead again briefly. Divide dough in half. Shape each half into a loaf and put it into a prepared pan. Cover and let rise for 45 minutes, or until well rounded over sides of pan.

7. Bake in preheated 375° F. oven for 45 to 50 minutes, or until bread tests done. Remove loaves from pans to cool on wire racks.

RYE PUMPERNICKEL

Makes two 2-pound loaves. This is the favorite bread in our household.

BUY

3 large Idaho baking potatoes
2 yeast cakes *or* 2 packages active dry yeast
2-pound package stone-ground rye flour

HAVE ON HAND	*COOKWARE*
Salt	Two 9 x 5-inch loaf pans *or*
Molasses	9-inch round cake pans
Caraway seeds	
Unbleached all-purpose flour	
Salad oil	

1. Peel and dice *3 large Idaho potatoes;* boil in *salted water to cover* for about 20 minutes, or until potato is very tender. Drain, leaving *a couple of tablespoons of water* on the potatoes; mash thoroughly with a potato masher. Let cool.

2. In large mixing bowl, soften the *yeast* in *½ cup warm water.*

3. Stir yeast and water until well mixed, then stir in *2 cups warm water.* Stir in *3 cups rye flour, 1 teaspoon salt, 2 tablespoons molasses,* the mashed potatoes, and *2 tablespoons caraway seeds.*

4. Stir in *3 cups all-purpose flour* to make a soft dough. Turn dough out onto floured surface and knead well, kneading in *about 1 more cup of all-purpose flour,* or enough to make a dough that is smooth and elastic. The amount of flour required at this point depends on the amount of moisture in the mashed potatoes.

5. *Oil* surface of dough, cover with a towel, and let rise for about 1 hour, or until double in bulk.

6. Oil baking pans.

7. Punch dough down and divide in half. Knead each half for a few minutes, then shape it into loaf. Place dough in two prepared loaf pans, or in two round cake pans if you wish round loaves. Cover and let rise again for about 40 minutes, or until double in bulk.

8. Bake in a preheated 425° F. oven for 10 minutes; then reduce oven temperature to 375° F. and continue to bake for 40 minutes longer, or until bread tests done.

OVERNIGHT WHITE OR WHOLE-WHEAT BUNS

Makes 2 to 3 dozen. Recipe may be doubled.

BUY

1 yeast cake *or* 1 package active dry yeast

HAVE ON HAND	*COOKWARE*
Sugar	Saucepan
Butter	9 x 13-inch cake pans
Unbleached all-purpose *or*	
stone-ground whole-wheat flour	
2 eggs	
Salad oil	

1. FIRST DAY: In early afternoon combine *2 cups water* and *½ cup sugar* in saucepan. Bring to a boil and boil for 5 minutes. Remove from heat and add *1 stick (½ cup) butter*. Pour into mixing bowl and let cool to lukewarm.

2. Meanwhile soften *yeast* in *¼ cup lukewarm water*.

3. When mixture in bowl is lukewarm, stir in *2 cups flour (all-purpose or whole-wheat)*, then beat in yeast and *2 eggs*. Gradually stir in *enough additional flour (3 to 3½ cups) to make a soft dough*. Turn out on floured board and knead for about 10 minutes, or until dough is smooth and satiny. Cover dough and let rise for 3 hours.

4. Punch dough, and let rise again for about 2 hours.

5. *Oil* cake pans.

6. Punch the twice-risen dough down again and shape into rolls. Place rolls in prepared pans. Cover with a towel and refrigerate until morning.

7. NEXT MORNING: Preheat oven to 400° F. Bake the rolls for 12 to 15 minutes.

HIGH PROTEIN WHOLE-WHEAT RYE BREAD

Makes 4 loaves. A gutsy, heavy-crusted bread—marvelous!

BUY

4 yeast cakes *or* 4 packages active dry yeast
2-pound bag stone-ground whole-wheat flour
2-pound bag stone-ground rye flour

HAVE ON HAND

Milk
Butter
Salt
Non-fat instant dry milk solids
Molasses
Caraway seeds
Unbleached all-purpose flour
Salad oil

COOKWARE

Small saucepan
Four 8½ x 4½-inch baking pans *or*
8-inch round cake pans

1. In small saucepan heat *2 cups milk* and *1 stick (½ cup) butter* together until milk is scalding hot and butter is melted.

2. In large mixing bowl measure *2 teaspoons salt, 1 cup non-fat instant dry milk solids, 4 tablespoons molasses,* and *4 tablespoons caraway seeds.* Pour hot milk mixture over and stir until ingredients are well mixed. Add *1 cup cool water,* then cool to lukewarm.

3. Meanwhile soften *4 yeast cakes or packages of dry yeast* in *1 cup lukewarm water.*

4. When mixture in large bowl is lukewarm, stir in *4 cups whole-wheat flour,* then the softened yeast, and then *4 cups rye flour* to make a soft batter.

5. Stir and work in with the hands *enough all-purpose flour (from 4 to 5 cups) to make a soft dough that does not stick to the hands.*

6. Turn dough out on floured surface; knead until dough is smooth and elastic. *Grease* surface, cover with towel, and let rise for 2 hours.

7. *Oil* baking pans.

8. Punch dough down, knead again briefly, and cut into quarters. Shape each quarter into loaf and place it in prepared pan. Cover again and let rise for 45 minutes to 1 hour, or until dough is well puffed over sides of pans.

9. Preheat oven to 375° F. Bake loaves for 50 minutes, or until they are golden and test done. Remove from pans to cool on racks.

REFRIGERATOR WHOLE-WHEAT ROLLS

Makes 2 to 3 dozen. Here is a great dough if you like fresh rolls every day. It will keep in the refrigerator for at least 4 days.

BUY

2 yeast cakes *or* 2 packages active dry yeast
Package stone-ground whole-wheat flour

HAVE ON HAND	*COOKWARE*
Milk	Small saucepan
Butter	Cake pans
Brown sugar	
Salt	
Unbleached all-purpose flour	
2 eggs	
Salad oil	

1. IN ADVANCE: Soften the *yeast* in *½ cup warm water*.

2. In small saucepan measure *1 cup milk;* add *½ stick (¼ cup) butter;* heat over low heat until butter is melted and milk is scalding hot.

3. Pour hot milk mixture into large mixing bowl, preferably of an electric mixer; and add *½ cup brown sugar,* and *1 tablespoon salt.* Stir until sugar is melted. Then stir in *¾ cup cold water, 1 cup all-purpose flour,* and *1 cup whole-wheat flour.* Set mixer at medium speed and beat mixture for 2 minutes (or beat 5 minutes with a hand rotary beater), scraping the sides and bottom of bowl occasionally. Beat in yeast and *2 eggs.*

4. Now stir in *4 cups whole-wheat flour* and *enough all-purpose flour (1 to 1½ cups) to make a soft dough.* Turn the dough into an *oiled* bowl and oil surface of dough. Cover with plastic film and store in refrigerator.

5. ABOUT 2 HOURS BEFORE BAKING: Butter cake pans. Remove required quantity of dough from refrigerator; place on floured board and knead until dough is smooth and elastic. Shape into rolls, and place in prepared pans. Brush surface with *melted butter;* cover dough, and let rise for about 1½ hours.

6. Bake in preheated 400° F. oven for 20 minutes, or until brown.

RICH POTATO SWEET ROLLS

Makes 3 dozen rolls

   BUY

1 yeast cake *or* 1 package dry active yeast

HAVE ON HAND	*COOKWARE*
1 cup unseasoned mashed potatoes	Baking sheets
Sugar	
Butter (1 stick)	
4 eggs	
Salt	
Unbleached all-purpose flour	

1. FIRST DAY: In large mixing bowl soften the *yeast* in *1 cup luke-warm water*. Stir in *1 cup potatoes mashed with a little cooking water* and *1 cup sugar;* stir until sugar is dissolved. Cover with a towel and let stand in a warm place overnight. Remove *1 stick (½ cup) butter* from refrigerator and set aside.

2. NEXT DAY: beat into the potato mixture *4 eggs,* the stick of soft butter, and *1 teaspoon salt.*

3. Stir in *about 3 cups flour* to make a stiff dough that is difficult to stir. Then, with your hands, mix in another *2 to 3 cups flour* to make a soft light dough. Be careful not to add any more flour than necessary.

4. Butter baking sheets.

5. Turn dough out on floured surface and, with floured rolling pin, roll the dough out about ½ inch thick. Cut out small rounds with a floured cooky cutter. Place the rounds 1 inch apart on the buttered baking sheets.

TO BAKE WITHOUT REFRIGERATING:

Cover rolls with a towel, then let them rise at room temperature until double in bulk—about 2 hours.

Preheat oven to 400° F. Bake the rolls for just 10 minutes. Do not overbake. The rolls should be just lightly tinged with brown. Serve warm with sweet butter and honey.

TO REFRIGERATE:

The shaped rolls will keep in the refrigerator for several days before baking. Allow 3 hours rising time after removing rolls from refrigerator. Bake as above.

VARIATIONS: Substitute whole-wheat flour in place of all-purpose; or use half rye flour and half whole-wheat or all-purpose.

BRIOCHE EGG BREAD
(Rich Egg Bread)

Makes 2 loaves. This recipe is made with exactly the same ingredients as the French *brioche* but the method has been simplified and the dough is baked in conventional bread pans. It's a divine bread to slice thinly and make into watercress or onion-and-cucumber sandwiches, with lots of mayonnaise. Since it dries out quickly, store the extra loaf in the freezer. If it becomes stale, don't throw it away. Slice it paper thin (it slices easily and evenly) and make it into the best Melba toast you ever put in your mouth.

BUY

½ pound butter (2 sticks)
2 packages active dry yeast *or* 2 yeast cakes
6 large eggs

HAVE ON HAND

Sugar
Salt
Unbleached all-purpose flour
Salad oil

COOKWARE

Two 8½ x 4½-inch loaf pans

1. Soften *butter* to room temperature.

2. Soften *yeast* in *½ cup lukewarm water* with *1 teaspoon sugar.*

3. In mixing bowl measure *½ teaspoon salt,* and *¼ cup sugar.* Add *6 whole eggs* and beat with a rotary beater until eggs are fluffy and sugar and salt are dissolved.

4. Beat in *2 cups flour,* then stir in yeast.

5. Divide butter into chunks and add to yeast mixture. Add *another cup flour* and beat well. Work in *1 more cup flour,* or enough to make a soft dough that doesn't stick to the hands—be careful when adding this fourth and last cup of flour not to add more than is necessary.

6. Turn dough out onto floured board and knead until dough is smooth. Cover with towel and let rise for 1½ hours.

7. *Oil* loaf pans.

8. Punch dough down and cut into two parts. Knead each part briefly and shape into a thick loaf. Put loaves into oiled loaf pans, cover again with towel, and let rise for about 45 minutes, or until well rounded in pans. Bake in preheated 375° F. oven for 45 to 50 minutes.

SALLY LUNN EGG BREAD

Makes 2 loaves. This fine-textured bread is delicious sliced and toasted for breakfast.

BUY

1 yeast cake *or* 1 envelope active dry yeast

HAVE ON HAND	*COOKWARE*
Milk	Two 8½ x 4½-inch loaf pans
Butter	
Sugar	
Salt	
Unbleached all-purpose flour	
2 eggs	
Salad oil	

1. Scald *1 cup milk.* Add *½ cup butter, 2 tablespoons sugar,* and *2 teaspoons salt.* Stir over low heat until butter is melted. Remove from heat and cool to lukewarm.

2. Soften the *yeast* in *½ cup lukewarm water.* Add to milk mixture. Beat in *2 cups all-purpose flour.* Stir in *2 eggs,* lightly beaten. Add *3 cups flour* and beat until batter is smooth and elastic. Then work in an additional *1 cup flour* to make a dough that is soft but not sticky. Cover and let rise for 1½ hours, or until double in bulk.

3. *Oil* loaf pans.

4. Punch dough down and turn out on a lightly floured board. Knead dough until it is smooth and elastic. Cut in half. Shape each half into a loaf and put into oiled loaf pan. Cover and let rise for 1 hour, or until dough is well rounded over sides of pans.

5. Preheat oven to 425° F. Bake loaves in the hot oven for 30 minutes, or until lightly browned. Remove from pans to cool on racks. Serve warm with sweet butter and jam or jelly.

PAIN PARISIEN
(*Real French Bread*)

Makes 2 large or 3 small loaves. All unbleached flour may be used in this recipe, but the gluten flour is concentrated high protein and makes a more authentic French loaf.

BUY

2 yeast cakes *or* 2 packages active dry yeast
1-pound package gluten flour

HAVE ON HAND	*COOKWARE*
Salt	Baking sheet
Sugar	Large shallow pan
Corn *or* safflower oil	
Unbleached all-purpose flour	
Corn meal	
1 egg white	

1. Pour *2 cups lukewarm water* into a large mixing bowl. Add the *yeast* and let soak for 5 minutes. Stir to mix yeast thoroughly with water. Add *1 tablespoon salt, 2 tablespoons sugar,* and *2 tablespoons oil.*

2. Stir in *3 cups all-purpose flour* and beat well with a wooden spoon. Stir in *1 cup of the gluten flour* and beat again.

3. Turn dough out onto floured surface and knead in *1 to 1½ cups all-purpose flour* to make a soft dough that does not stick to hands. Shape into a ball; cover with a towel; and let rise for 1 hour, or until double in bulk.

4. Punch dough down, then knead for a few minutes, or until smooth and elastic. Cover and let rest for 10 minutes.

5. *Oil* baking sheet, then sprinkle it lightly with *corn meal.*

6. Cut dough either in half or in thirds. To shape each part into a long loaf, first roll the dough out into a rectangle about 16 inches long. Then roll the dough lengthwise, seal the edges, and press into shape. Place loaves, seam side down, one alongside another, on prepared baking sheet. Let rise for 20 minutes.

7. With a sharp knife score the surface of each loaf diagonally down its length, making shallow cuts at intervals of about 1 inch. Brush loaves with *lightly beaten egg white.*

8. Do NOT PREHEAT OVEN. Place a large shallow pan of boiling water on lower shelf of oven. Place bread on center shelf of oven. Set oven temperature at 400° F., and bake the loaves for 40 to 50 minutes, or until golden brown and crusty.

GARLIC BREAD

Cream *1 stick butter* until light and fluffy. Beat in *1 large clove minced garlic.* Cut long loaf of French bread diagonally into 1-inch slices, cutting well down toward the bottom but leaving bottom crust intact. Spread garlic butter generously between slices and on top. Shape heavy-duty aluminum foil around the loaf, boat-fashion, twisting ends and leaving top open. Bake in a preheated 400° F. oven for 10 to 12 minutes.

ITALIAN BREAD

Make as above but cream the *stick of butter* and *garlic* with *½ teaspoon crumbled oregano* and *1 teaspoon dry parsley flakes.* Just before baking, sprinkle top of loaf with *¼ cup grated Parmesan cheese.*

CHEESE LOAF

Split a long loaf of French bread lengthwise. Combine *2 cups shredded sharp Cheddar cheese (8 ounces)* with *⅓ cup butter, ½ cup chopped chives or green onions, ½ cup minced parsley,* and *a few drops Tabasco.* Toast the cut sides of the bread under broiler heat. Remove from boiler and spread thickly with the cheese mixture. Return to broiler and broil just long enough to melt the cheese. Slice into serving portions while bubbling hot.

PARSLEY BREAD

Trim the top and side crusts from a loaf of homemade bread and slice it very thinly down to, but not through, the bottom crust.

Chop *enough fresh parsley to measure 1 full cup*. Empty it into a towel and squeeze out excess juice, leaving the parsley dry and fluffy. Cream *1 stick butter* until soft, then beat in the parsley. If desired, also beat in *1 tablespoon chopped chives, fresh dill, or tarragon,* or *1 clove minced garlic*. Spread the parsley butter on each slice and over top and sides. Place the loaf in a baking pan and bake in a preheated 300° F. oven for 1¼ hours, or until loaf spreads open and edges are crisp and brown.

SESAME SEED BREAD

Sprinkle ½ *cup sesame seeds* thinly on botton of a baking pan and bake in a preheated 350° F. oven for 10 minutes, or until golden. Beat *1 stick butter* until light and fluffy, then beat in *2 minced cloves garlic* and the toasted sesame seeds. Split a long loaf of French bread lengthwise and toast cut sides lightly under the broiler. Remove from broiler, and while bread is hot spread it lavishly with the seed butter. Cut into serving portions and serve immediately, or keep warm in a warm oven.

MIRACLE CROISSANTS

Makes 36. Here is a miracle recipe for those wonderfully flaky *croissants* that you enjoy in France and at some of our better restaurants. Perhaps you have been sufficiently interested to look up a recipe, but have given up right there, for the technique is lengthy and difficult, or perhaps you've tried to make *croissants* and had little success. Try again. This recipe is an easy one and it's foolproof if you measure the ingredients exactly.

What's more, you can chill the dough and roll it out a day or two later; or you can roll it out, cut and form the *croissants,* and bake them, or keep them cold in the refrigerator on a baking sheet for several days until ready to bake; or you can freeze the baked rolls and reheat them when needed—a most obliging and versatile recipe for a hot bread that will make you famous.

BUY

8-ounce container light cream
1 cake yeast *or* 1 package active dry yeast

HAVE ON HAND	COOKWARE
1 egg	Baking sheets
Sugar	
Salt	
Unbleached all-purpose flour	
½ pound butter (2 sticks)	

TO MAKE THE DOUGH:

1. Measure *¾ cup cream* into a 1-cup measure. Crumble or sprinkle the *yeast* into the cream and let soak for 10 minutes.

2. Meanwhile put *1 egg, 2 tablespoons sugar,* and *1 teaspoon salt* into a mixing bowl and beat with a rotary beater until blended.

3. Stir yeast-cream mixture to blend, then stir it into egg mixture. Stir in *2* LEVEL *cups flour, 1 cup at a time,* to make a moist dough.

4. Turn dough out onto a well-floured board, sprinkle with flour, and knead gently about 12 kneading strokes.

5. With floured rolling pin, roll out dough into a square about ¼ inch thick, keeping both sides lightly floured. Unwrap *1 stick cold butter* and slice thickly. Arrange slices in center of the square. Fold all four sides of the dough over the butter, completely enclosing it. Seal edges.

6. Now begin rolling out the dough. (You'll want to do this 5 times, always keeping both sides of the dough floured.) Roll out into a band about 12 inches long and ¼ inch thick. Turn one third of the dough over center third. Fold other third on top, making three layers of dough. Turn dough ¼ turn to left. Repeat the rolling and turning four times. Don't roll too thinly.

7. Wrap dough in transparent film and store in refrigerator if croissants are not to be made until later.

TO FORM CROISSANTS:

8. Before rolling and forming dough into crescents, melt *1 stick butter.*

9. Place dough on floured board. With floured rolling pin, roll the dough into a rectangle 8 inches wide and 16 inches long and about ⅛ inch thick. Cut it lengthwise in half, then crosswise in half, making four small rectangles.

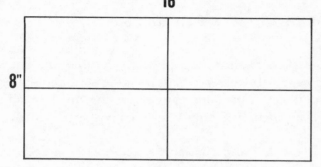

10. Work with one piece at a time. Roll it out as thinly as possible into a rectangle 6 inches wide and 12 inches long. Cut into 8 triangles with wide sides about 3 inches wide. Brush surface of each triangle with melted butter and roll, beginning at wide side and rolling to the point. Brush baking sheets with butter. Curve each roll into crescent shape and place on baking sheet. Repeat process with the three remaining pieces of dough.

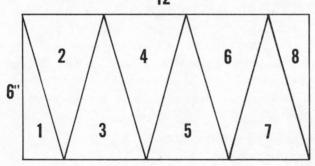

11. Brush crescents with melted butter. Cover with plastic film and refrigerate.

TO BAKE:

12. When ready to bake, preheat oven to 375° F. Bake rolls in center of the hot oven for 20 minutes and serve hot.

Quick Breads & Pancakes

No other bread offers more eating pleasure, for the amount of effort expended, than a quick bread served hot from the oven and slathered with sweet butter and honey. There are many recipes for quick breads in basic cookbooks, so I am including only a few of my special favorites in this chapter.

Recipes for quick breads in most books specify all-purpose flour. There is little reason to abide by this. Whole-wheat flour may be used in place of the all-purpose flour, and other whole-grain cereals, bran, corn meal, wheat germ and so on may be substituted for half the quantity of all-purpose flour specified in a general recipe, making these quick breads into real nutritional assets and augmenting the protein in the milk and eggs which most quick-bread recipes contain.

Also there is no need to use refined white sugar just because a recipe lists this in the ingredients. Use brown sugar, honey, maple syrup, or molasses in place of it. All of these contain B vitamins which the body needs to "burn" sugar, thereby converting it into energy.

With imagination, you can serve a variety of nutritious quick breads. They are an excellent way to begin the day, and they complement almost any soup or salad supper.

CRISP CORN DOLLARS

Makes about 36

HAVE ON HAND

Butter
White corn meal

Salt
Sugar
Boiling water

COOKWARE

Baking pan

1. Preheat oven to 450° F. *Butter* a baking pan generously.

2. In mixing bowl combine *1 cup corn meal, 1 teaspoon salt,* and *¼ teaspoon sugar.* Gradually stir into the corn-meal mixture *1¾ to 2 cups boiling water* to make a batter having the consistency of a heavy pancake batter.

3. Put baking pan in the hot oven until butter sizzles, then remove. Drop or pour batter onto the hot pan in little cakes about the size of a silver dollar. Return pan to hot oven and bake for 15 minutes, or until corn dollars are lightly browned. Serve hot.

BASIC HIGH-PROTEIN MUFFINS

Makes one dozen 2½-inch muffins

HAVE ON HAND

Vegetable oil
Butter
Unbleached all-purpose flour
Stone-ground whole-wheat *or* other
   whole-grain flour; *or* wheat germ
Baking powder
Salt
Brown sugar
Milk
1 egg

COOKWARE

Small saucepan
12-cup muffin pan

1. Preheat oven to 400° F. *Oil* muffin cups.

2. In small saucepan, put *½ stick (¼ cup) butter* over low heat to melt.

3. In mixing bowl combine (no need to sift) *1 cup all-purpose flour, 1 cup whole-grain flour or wheat germ, 3 teaspoons baking powder, 1 teaspoon salt,* and *2 tablespoons brown sugar.*

4. In small bowl combine *1 cup milk* and *1 egg;* add flour mixture

and stir gently just until dry ingredients are moistened. Stir in melted butter.

5. Fill muffin cups ⅔ full of batter. Bake in the preheated oven for 20 to 25 minutes. Serve hot with sweet butter and jam or jelly or peanut butter.

FOR SWEETER MUFFINS: Increase sugar to ¼ or ½ cup.

FOR BUTTERMILK MUFFINS: Use only 2 teaspoons baking powder, add ½ teaspoon baking soda, and substitute buttermilk for the sweet milk.

BERRY MUFFINS: Increase sugar to ¼ or ½ cup. Fold in 1 cup washed and drained blueberries or raspberries before spooning batter into pans.

CRANBERRY MUFFINS: Cut 1 cup fresh or frozen cranberries in half and sprinkle with 2 tablespoons sugar. Make muffin batter, but increase sugar to ¼ or ½ cup. Fold cranberries into batter before spooning it into the pans.

RAISIN OR DATE BRAN MUFFINS: Increase sugar to ¼ or ½ cup. Substitute 1 cup bran flakes or 100% bran for the whole-grain flour. Fold 1 cup seedless raisins (or pitted and cut dates) and ½ cup chopped nuts into the batter.

CORNMEAL MUFFINS: Substitute 1 cup stone-ground yellow corn meal for the whole-grain flour.

APPLE PECAN MUFFINS: Increase sugar to ¼ or ½ cup. Add ½ teaspoon cinnamon or nutmeg. Fold in 1 cup peeled, chopped apples and ½ cup chopped pecans.

BASIC WHOLE-WHEAT BISCUITS

Makes sixteen 2-inch biscuits

HAVE ON HAND	COOKWARE
Unbleached all-purpose flour	Baking sheet
Stone-ground whole-wheat flour	
Baking powder	
Salt	
Shortening	
Milk	

1. Preheat oven to 425° F.

2. Measure (no need to sift) *1 cup all-purpose flour* and *1 cup whole-wheat flour;* combine these in mixing bowl with *3 teaspoons baking powder* and *1 teaspoon salt.*

3. With a pastry blender or two knives, cut in *½ cup shortening* until shortening is broken into small particles.

4. Add *⅔ cup milk* and stir gently with a fork until dough holds together. Gather dough into a ball, place on a lightly floured surface, and knead gently, about 12 kneading strokes.

5. Roll dough out ½ inch thick on the floured surface, then cut into biscuits with a floured biscuit cutter.

6. Place biscuits about 1 inch apart on baking sheet. Bake in the hot oven for 12 to 15 minutes.

BUTTERMILK BISCUITS: Reduce baking powder to 2 teaspoons and add ½ teaspoon baking soda to dry ingredients. Use buttermilk in place of the milk.

WHEAT-GERM OR SOY BISCUITS: Substitute ½ cup wheat germ or soy granules for ½ cup of the all-purpose flour. Increase milk to ¾ cup.

CORN-MEAL BISCUITS: Substitute ⅔ cup corn meal for ⅔ cup of the whole-wheat flour.

PEANUT BUTTER BISCUITS: Omit salt, and substitute peanut butter for the shortening.

DUBLIN SCONES

Makes 8

BUY

Small box seedless raisins *or* currants

HAVE ON HAND

Flour
Baking soda
Cream of tartar

Salt
Vegetable shortening
Milk

COOKWARE

Baking sheet

1. Preheat oven to 400° F.

2. In a mixing bowl combine *2 cups flour, 1 teaspoon baking soda, 1 teaspoon cream of tartar,* and *½ teaspoon salt.*

3. Add *½ cup shortening;* using a pastry blender or two knives, cut in shortening until mixture looks like coarse meal. Stir in *½ cup raisins or currants.*

4. Add, all at once, *¾ cup milk* and stir gently with a fork until dough holds together.

5. With hands, gather dough into a ball, turn it out into a lightly floured board, and knead gently with floured fingers about 12 kneading strokes. Roll dough out on floured surface into a circle ½ inch thick, then cut into 8 pie-shaped wedges with a floured knife.

6. Place wedges on baking sheet about 1 inch apart. Bake in the hot oven for 15 minutes.

SCOTCH OAT SCONES

Makes 6 servings

HAVE ON HAND

All-purpose flour
Oats
Salt
Baking soda
Sugar
Butter
Buttermilk

COOKWARE

Baking sheet

1. Preheat oven to 400° F.

2. In mixing bowl combine *1 cup flour, 1 cup oats, ½ teaspoon salt, 1 teaspoon baking soda,* and *1 tablespoon sugar.* Add *1 tablespoon butter* and rub in with tips of fingers. Add *¾ cup buttermilk* and mix lightly with a fork to make a fairly soft dough that can be gathered together.

3. Turn dough out on lightly floured board and pat into a large circle about ½ inch thick. Place circle on *greased* baking sheet. Prick at frequent intervals with a fork and score into six triangles.

4. Bake in preheated oven for 15 minutes, or until lightly browned. Serve warm with butter and honey or jelly.

THE POPPINGEST POPOVERS

Makes 4. There's a lot of meaningless hokus-pokus around trying to make a mystery of how to make a popover pop. You don't need any special recipe; you don't have to preheat your oven or use special cast-iron popover pans. One basic recipe works for everyone. The trick is to use ordinary 6-ounce pyrex custard cups set wide apart on a baking sheet, and to make 4 popovers instead of 6 or 8 from the recipe. This means filling the cups three-quarters full of batter.

HAVE ON HAND	*COOKWARE*
Butter	Four 6-ounce custard cups
2 eggs	
Salt	
Milk	
All-purpose flour	

1. *Butter* custard cups lavishly.

2. If you have an electric blender, put *2 eggs, ½ teaspoon salt, 1 cup milk,* and *1 level cup all-purpose flour* (no need to sift) into container in order given; otherwise measure them into a mixing bowl. Blend or beat until batter is smooth.

3. Pour batter into prepared custard cups set wide apart on a baking sheet, filling cups ¾ full.

4. Set baking sheet in a cold oven until ready to bake—and this means until next morning, if you wish, for the batter can remain safely in the oven overnight. Turn oven to 450° F., and bake popovers for 30 minutes. Toward end of baking time, but not before, check popovers and if they are becoming too brown, turn temperature down to 400° F. and bake until popovers are crisp.

POPOVER PANCAKE

Serves 2 or 4

HAVE ON HAND

Unbleached all-purpose flour
Milk
2 eggs
Butter
Confectioners' sugar
Lemon
Honey, jam, *or* marmalade

COOKWARE

12 x 8-inch oval top-of-the stove
   au gratin dish *or* 12-inch round
   skillet with heatproof handle

1. Preheat oven to 425° F.

2. In mixing bowl combine *½ cup flour, ½ cup milk,* and *2 eggs.* Beat lightly, leaving the batter slightly lumpy.

3. In au gratin dish or skillet heat *¼ cup butter (½ stick)* until very hot. Pour in the batter. Place the dish in the hot oven and bake for 20 minutes, or until pancake is puffed all around sides of dish and golden brown. Remove from oven and sprinkle with *2 tablespoons sugar* and *juice of ½ lemon.* Return to oven for 2 to 3 minutes, or until pancake is glazed.

4. Serve immediately with honey, jam, or marmalade.

LAPLAND CAKES

Makes 12 medium cakes

BUY

8-ounce container heavy cream

HAVE ON HAND

Butter
Flour
Salt
3 eggs

COOKWARE

12-cup muffin pan

1. Preheat oven to 375° F. Generously *butter* muffin cups.

2. Combine (no need to sift) *1 cup flour* and ¼ *teaspoon salt.*

3. *Separate 3 eggs,* dropping whites into one bowl and yolks into another. Beat *egg whites* with rotary beater until stiff, but not dry. With the same beater, beat *egg yolks* thoroughly. In a third bowl, with same beater, beat *heavy cream* until stiff.

4. Fold flour mixture into egg yolks alternately with the whipped cream, then fold in egg whites.

5. Spoon batter into prepared muffin cups (about 2 rounded tablespoons per cup), and bake in preheated oven for 20 to 25 minutes, or until lightly brown. Serve hot.

BASIC WHOLE-WHEAT BREAKFAST BREAD

Makes 1 square. Homemade fruit and nut quick breads are a treat for breakfast, or for an afternoon snack. Thinly slice and toast any leftover loaf on another day.

HAVE ON HAND	*COOKWARE*
Stone-ground whole-wheat flour	Small saucepan
Baking powder	Loaf pan
Salt	
Brown sugar	
Butter	
Milk	
1 egg	

1. In small saucepan put *1 stick (½ cup) butter* over low heat to melt. *Oil* baking pan.

2. Preheat oven to 375° F.

3. In mixing bowl combine *2 cups whole-wheat flour, 3 teaspoons baking powder, 1 teaspoon salt,* and ½ *cup sugar.*

4. Combine *1 cup milk* and *1 egg* and stir gently into flour mixture to make a slightly lumpy batter. Stir in melted butter.

5. Spoon batter into prepared pan. Spread top evenly and bake in the hot oven for 25 to 30 minutes. Serve hot or remove from pan to cool on rack.

CINNAMON NUT BREAD: Before baking breakfast bread, combine ½ cup brown sugar, 1 teaspoon cinnamon, and ½ cup chopped pecans or walnuts, and sprinkle on top of batter.

STREUSEL BREAD: Before baking breakfast bread, combine and sprinkle on top ½ cup brown sugar, 1 teaspoon cinnamon, 2 tablespoons all-purpose flour, ½ cup chopped almonds, and 2 tablespoons butter.

APRICOT NUT BREAD: Fold into batter 1 cup coarsely chopped nuts and ½ cup cut, dried apricots.

POPPY SEED BREAD: Before making breakfast bread, add 1 tablespoon each grated lemon rind and poppy seeds to the milk.

ORANGE SUNFLOWER BREAD: Use ½ cup orange juice and ½ cup milk in place of all milk. Just before spooning batter into pan, fold in 1 tablespoon grated orange rind and ½ cup chopped toasted sunflower seeds.

BANANA BRAN BREAD

Makes 8½ x 4½-inch loaf

BUY

2 bananas
1 box bran flakes

HAVE ON HAND

Vegetable oil
Butter
Brown sugar
2 eggs
All-purpose flour
Baking powder
Salt
Milk
Vanilla

COOKWARE

Loaf pan

1. Preheat oven to 350° F. *Oil* loaf pan. Peel and slice *bananas*. Chop *½ cup nuts*.

2. Cream together *⅓ cup butter, ⅔ cup brown sugar,* and the sliced bananas.

3. Add *2 eggs* and beat until well blended.

4. Combine *1 cup all-purpose flour, 1 cup bran flakes, 2 teaspoons baking powder,* and *1 teaspoon salt.* Stir the dry ingredients into the banana mixture alternately with *½ cup milk.* Stir in *1 teaspoon vanilla* and the nuts. Spoon mixture into prepared pan.

5. Bake in moderate oven for 1 hour, or until done. Serve hot, or remove from baking pan to cool on rack.

DATE NUT BREAD

Makes 8½ x 4½-inch loaf

BUY

1 pound pitted dates
8-ounce can walnuts

HAVE ON HAND	*COOKWARE*
Vegetable oil	Loaf pan
Butter	
Baking soda	
Brown sugar	
Vanilla	
1 egg	
Unbleached all-purpose flour	
Baking powder	
Salt	

1. Chop or cut *dates*. Chop *walnuts.*

2. Preheat oven to 350° F. *Oil* loaf pan.

3. Put dates, nuts, and *1 cup boiling water* into large mixing bowl. Add ⅓ *cup butter* and beat until butter is broken into small pieces.

4. Add *5 tablespoons cold water* and stir in *1 teaspoon soda, ¾ cup brown sugar, 1 teaspoon vanilla, 1 egg* and *2 cups flour*. Add *1 teaspoon baking power* and *½ teaspoon salt,* beat until all ingredients are well blended.

5. Spoon batter into prepared pan and bake in the moderate oven for about 1 hour, or until loaf tests done. Remove loaf from pan to cool on rack.

BOSTON BROWN BREAD

Makes 3 small loaves or 2 large loaves

BUY

Yellow corn meal
Graham flour
Rye flour
Buttermilk
Seedless raisins

HAVE ON HAND

Baking soda
Salt
Molasses
Sugar

COOKWARE

Three 1-pound coffee cans *or*
two 1-quart pudding molds
Large kettle with rack and lid

1. In mixing bowl combine *1 cup yellow corn meal, 1 cup graham flour, 1 cup rye flour, 1 teaspoon baking soda,* and *1 teaspoon salt*. Stir in *¾ cup molasses, 1 tablespoon sugar, 2 cups buttermilk,* and *¾ cup raisins*.

2. Place rounds of greased paper in bottom of the coffee cans or pudding molds. Grease cans or molds and fill ⅔ full of batter. Place lids on the molds, or tie aluminum foil tightly over tops of cans.

3. Place containers on a rack in a large kettle and add enough warm water to reach half way up their sides. Cover kettle, bring water to a boil, and continue to boil gently for 2 hours, or until bread tests done, adding more boiling water from time to time if needed. Remove molds or cans, cool slightly, then remove bread from containers.

CORN-MEAL BUTTERMILK PANCAKES

Makes about 20

HAVE ON HAND	COOKWARE
White *or* yellow stone-ground corn meal	Griddle
All-purpose flour	
Salt	
Baking soda	
2 eggs	
Buttermilk	
Butter	
Vegetable oil	

1. In mixing bowl combine *1⅓ cups corn meal, ¼ cup flour, 1 teaspoon salt,* and *½ teaspoon baking soda.*

2. In another bowl beat *2 eggs* lightly with *2 cups buttermilk.* Stir into corn-meal mixture. Stir in *¼ cup melted butter.*

3. Heat a griddle until a drop of water on it sputters and evaporates almost immediately (350° F.).

4. Grease griddle lightly with *oil,* and spoon batter onto it to make small pancakes no larger than 2 inches in diameter. When surface of the cakes becomes bubbly and underside is lightly browned, turn cakes and brown lightly on the other side.

PINEAPPLE NUT BREAD

Makes 2 loaves

BUY

8 ounces shelled nuts (pecans, walnuts, *or* macadamia)
1 pound light brown sugar
1-pound can crushed pineapple

HAVE ON HAND	COOKWARE
Vegetable oil	Two 1-pound loaf pans
All-purpose flour	
Baking powder	
Baking soda	
Salt	
Butter, at room temperature	
2 eggs	

1. Preheat oven to 350° F. *Oil* loaf pans.

2. Chop *nuts* and set aside.

3. In mixing bowl combine *3½ cups flour, 4 teaspoons baking powder, ½ teaspoon baking soda,* and *½ teaspoon salt.* Stir in the chopped nuts.

4. In another mixing bowl cream *6 tablespoons butter* and *1½ cups brown sugar* until well blended. Beat in *2 eggs,* one at a time, and continue to beat until mixture is smooth. Stir in *half the flour mixture.* Stir in *pineapple and juice.* Stir in *remaining flour mixture.*

5. Divide batter into prepared loaf pans. Bake in the preheated oven for 50 to 60 minutes, or until bread tests done. Let loaves cool for 5 minutes, then turn out on racks to cool completely.

WHOLE-WHEAT PANCAKES

Makes about 18

HAVE ON HAND	COOKWARE
All-purpose flour	Griddle
Stone-ground whole-wheat flour	
Salt	
Sugar	
Baking powder	
Molasses	
2 eggs	
Milk	
Butter *or* vegetable oil	

1. In mixing bowl combine ¾ *cup all-purpose flour, 1 cup whole-wheat flour, 1 teaspoon salt, 2 tablespoons sugar,* and *1 teaspoon baking powder.*

2. In another mixing bowl combine *3 tablespoons molasses, 2 eggs, 1 cup milk,* and ¼ *cup melted butter or oil.*

3. Gradually stir liquid ingredients into dry ingredients, and continue to stir until batter is smooth.

4. Heat a griddle until a drop of water sputters and evaporates almost immediately (350° F.).

5. *Grease* griddle lightly. Spoon batter onto it to make cakes about 3 inches in diameter. When surface of cakes becomes bubbly and underside is nicely browned, turn cakes and cook until brown on other side.

RAISED BUCKWHEAT CAKES

Makes about 18

BUY

1 pound stone-ground buckwheat flour
1 yeast cake *or* 1 envelope active dry yeast

HAVE ON HAND

Milk
Salt
Baking soda
Molasses
1 egg
Butter *or* vegetable oil

COOKWARE

Small saucepan
Griddle

NIGHT BEFORE:

1. Scald *2 cups milk,* then cool to lukewarm.

2. In mixing bowl crumble or sprinkle the *yeast;* add the lukewarm milk; stir until yeast is softened and mixed with the milk. Stir in *2 cups buckwheat flour* and ½ *teaspoon salt.*

3. Cover bowl with a towel and let stand at room temperature overnight.

NEXT DAY:

4. Combine ½ *teaspoon baking soda* and ¼ *cup lukewarm water.* Stir the mixture into the batter. Stir in 2 *tablespoons molasses, 1 egg,* and ¼ *cup melted butter or vegetable oil.*

5. Heat griddle until a drop of water on it sputters and evaporates almost immediately (350° F.).

6. *Grease* griddle lightly, then pour or spoon the pancake mixture onto the griddle to make cakes about 3 inches in diameter. Cook until surface becomes bubbly and underside is lightly browned. Turn and brown the other side.

DESSERTS

Fruit Desserts

According to the French, there are some desserts that are interesting, some that are presumptuous, some that are memorable, and a few that are truly great. I'm going to try to give you a few of each of these in this chapter, beginning with a fresh melon—about which François de Malherbe, court poet to Henri IV, once wrote: "There are only two beautiful things in the world, roses and women; and two good morsels, women and melons."

MELON ORIENTALE

Serves 6

BUY

1 pound mixed fresh fruits in season, such as sweet cherries, peaches, apricots, strawberries, pineapple, raspberries, or blueberries
1 large cantaloupe, honeydew, *or* cassaba melon

HAVE ON HAND

Confectioners' sugar
Kirsch, Madeira, port, sherry, *or* Sauternes

1. Prepare the fresh fruits: Peel and dice the *pineapple, peaches, or apricots*. Wash and pit the *cherries*, hull the *strawberries*, or pick over the *raspberries* or *blueberries*.

2. Cut a circular piece from the stem end of the *melon*, reserving the piece, and scoop out seeds and filaments. With a French ball scoop,

carve melon balls out of the pulp, being careful not to cut through the rind.

3. Cut the thinnest possible slice from opposite end of the melon, just enough to allow it to stand upright on a serving plate. Dust the inside of the melon shell with *confectioners' sugar,* then fill the cavity with alternate layers of the mixed fruit and the melon balls.

4. Add *½ cup kirsch or wine,* and replace the top plug. Chill for 2 hours before serving. To serve, remove the plug, spoon out the fruit mélange onto serving plates, and ladle over it a little of the liquid.

Any seasonal fruit makes a perfect dessert providing it is fully ripe and at its peak. What could be better than a big bowl of fresh raspberries or strawberries in spring, a slice of red ripe watermelon in June, a juicy peach or apricot in August, a basket of fresh Concord grapes in mid-September, a shiny red apple in October, or a soft, ultrasweet persimmon during the holiday season? Fortunately, when no special fruits are available, there are always bananas.

RHUBARB STEWED IN ITS JUICE

Serves 4

BUY OR PICK
2 pounds fresh rhubarb

HAVE ON HAND	*COOKWARE*
Sugar	Double saucepan *or* baking dish; tight-fitting cover

1. Break off and discard rhubarb leaves. Wipe *rhubarb stalks* and slice into ½-inch lengths. Do not peel. Put the rhubarb and *1½ cups sugar* into the upper part of a double saucepan or into a baking dish. Stir thoroughly, then cover tightly.

2. If using a double saucepan, bring water just to simmering and cook for 30 minutes, stirring occasionally. Otherwise bake the dish in a

325° F. oven for 50 minutes, removing the cover and stirring after 20 minutes of baking.

Cherry Cobbler, Apple Pan Dowdy, Peach Brown Betty, Blueberry Grunt —all such wonderfully homespun early American names—are among my favorite desserts. A few of them are in GOOD FOOD & HOW TO COOK IT. Another is:

FRUIT SLUMP

Serves 4

BUY

2 pounds fresh rhubarb, blueberries, apples, *or* peaches
Heavy cream

HAVE ON HAND	COOKWARE
Butter	Small saucepan
Sugar	Shallow baking dish,
Ginger	8 inches in diameter
All-purpose flour	
Salt	
Baking powder	
Milk	

1. Preheat oven to 375° F. Melt *½ stick (4 tablespoons) butter* in small saucepan over low heat.

2. Prepare the *fruit*, washing and peeling if necessary; dice *enough to measure 4 cups.* Put the fruit in the baking dish and mix it with *1 cup sugar* and *½ teaspoon ground ginger.*

3. In mixing bowl combine *1 cup flour, ½ teaspoon salt, 1½ teaspoons baking powder*, and *¼ cup sugar.* Stir in *¾ cup milk* and the melted butter.

4. Pour the batter over the fruit and bake in the moderate oven for 45 minutes.

5. Serve hot or warm with *heavy cream.*

STRAWBERRY FLUMMERY

Serves 6. And how about that for a marvelous name?

BUY

2 pints fresh strawberries
8-ounce container heavy cream

HAVE ON HAND	*COOKWARE*
Light brown sugar	2-quart saucepan
Cornstarch	
Salt	
Lemon juice	

1. Wash *strawberries* in a colander placed under cool running water. Remove hulls.

2. In saucepan combine the strawberries, *1 cup light brown sugar, 2 tablespoons cornstarch, a dash of salt, ½ cup water,* and *¼ cup lemon juice.* Bring slowly to a boil, stirring constantly, then boil for 1 minute.

3. Pour into an attractive serving dish and chill thoroughly. Before serving whip the *cream* and spoon large dollops of it on top of the flummery.

BLUEBERRY COBBLER

Serves 6. And don't forget a topping of homemade ice cream.

BUY

2 pints fresh blueberries

HAVE ON HAND	*COOKWARE*
Butter	1½-quart baking dish
Flour	
Sugar	
Baking powder	
Milk	

1. Wash and pick over the *berries*, discarding any wilted or green ones.

2. Preheat oven to 425° F. Place *1 stick (½ cup) butter* in baking dish over low heat to melt.

3. In mixing bowl combine *1 cup flour* with *1 cup sugar* and *1 teaspoon baking powder*. Stir in *¾ cup milk* to make a smooth batter. Pour batter over the hot butter in the baking dish, and sprinkle the blueberries on top.

4. Bake in the preheated oven for 25 to 30 minutes, or until puffed and golden.

APPLE TART

Makes one 8-inch tart. Let's forget the American double-crust apple pie in favor of this luscious apple tart from Italy, where it is called *Crostate di Mele*. We like to serve it with a smooth sour-cream sauce that closely resembles the glorious Crème Fraîche of France.

BUY

6 fresh cooking apples (2 pounds)
4 ounces blanched slivered almonds *or* broken walnuts *or* pecans
12-ounce jar apricot preserves

HAVE ON HAND

Ingredients for Rich Dessert
　Pastry
Granulated sugar
Butter
Confectioners' sugar

COOKWARE

8-inch pie plate

1. Make *pastry* and chill as directed (page 298).

2. Meanwhile, peel, halve, and core the *apples*.

3. Preheat oven to 425° F.

4. Roll out ⅔ of the pastry thinly on a lightly floured pastry cloth, using a rolling pin with floured stocking. Transfer the pastry to the pie plate and trim off overhanging edge.

5. Slice the apples and, as you do so, arrange them in circles over the

pastry, each slice slightly overlapping the next. Sprinkle the apples with *2 tablespoons granulated sugar* and *½ cup of the almonds*. Then spread the *apricot preserves* over the apples and nuts. Dot with *2 tablespoons butter*.

6. Roll out remaining pastry thinly and cut into strips ½ inch wide. Arrange 10 strips, lattice-fashion, over filling, and trim overhanging edges. Place a strip of pastry all around edge of pie so that it covers the ends of lattice strips; flute this edge along with the bottom pastry.

6. Bake in the hot oven for 15 minutes; then reduce oven temperature to 375° F. and continue to bake for 40 to 45 minutes longer.

7. Remove from oven and, while hot, sift a little confectioners' sugar over the top. Serve with Sour-Cream Sauce.

SOUR-CREAM SAUCE
(Simulated Crème Fraîche)

Makes about 1¼ cups

Combine *1 cup dairy sour cream* with *2 tablespoons confectioners' sugar* and *¼ cup light cream, or enough to make a sauce consistency*. Flavor with *½ teaspoon vanilla, or 1 tablespoon brandy, or 2 tablespoons Grand Marnier*.

RICH DESSERT PASTRY

Makes enough pastry for a 1-crust and lattice-topped pie or tart

HAVE ON HAND

Flour
Sugar
2 egg yolks
Salt
Lemon
Butter

1. Empty *1¼ cups flour* onto a pastry board or into a mixing bowl and make a well in center. In the well put *4 tablespoons sugar, 2 egg yolks* (reserve whites for another use), *a dash of salt,* and the *grated rind of 1 lemon.* Slice *1 stick butter* on top of these ingredients.

2. Work the center ingredients to a paste with one hand, then knead in enough additional flour to make a stiff dough. Form dough into a ball, wrap in waxed paper, and refrigerate for 30 minutes.

3. See page 49 for the techniques of rolling out pastry.

HONEY RHUBARB PIE

Serves 6

BUY OR PICK

1½ pounds fresh rhubarb

HAVE ON HAND
Rich Dessert Pastry (page 297)
Sugar
Honey
Salt
Ginger, nutmeg, or cinnamon
Butter
Cornstarch

COOKWARE
9-inch pie plate

1. Line the pie plate with *pastry.*

2. Preheat oven to 425° F.

3. Wash and slice *enough rhubarb to measure 4 cups.* Combine it with *1 cup sugar, 2 tablespoons honey, ½ teaspoon salt, ½ teaspoon ginger, nutmeg, or cinnamon,* and *3 tablespoons cornstarch.* Pile fruit mixture into the prepared pie plate and dot with *1 tablespoon butter.*

4. Cover with a lattice topping, and sprinkle the topping with *2 tablespoons sugar.*

5. Bake in the preheated oven for 20 minutes; then reduce oven temperature to 350° F. and continue to bake for 20 to 25 minutes longer. Serve the pie warm.

Rich Desserts

REAL GOOEY CHOCOLATE CAKE

Serves 8. For those of you to whom dessert means chocolate cake, here is the best recipe that I know.

BUY

Box of unsweetened chocolate
1 quart buttermilk

HAVE ON HAND

Walnuts or pecans (optional)
Cooking oil
Butter, at room temperature
Sugar
3 eggs
All-purpose flour
Baking soda
Salt
Vanilla extract
Lemon
Ingredients for Chocolate Butter Cream
Ingredients for Meringue Frosting

COOKWARE

Small saucepan
Medium saucepan
3 8-inch layer cake pans *or*
a 13 x 9 x 2-inch oblong cake pan

1. Put *3 squares unsweetened chocolate* into a small saucepan and set in another saucepan of simmering water until chocolate is melted; stir occasionally. Coarsely chop *½ cup nuts, if desired.*

2. Preheat oven to 350° F. *Oil* pan or pans and line with waxed paper.

3. In mixing bowl, cream *1½ sticks butter (¾ cup)* with *2 cups sugar*

until light and fluffy. Add *3 eggs,* one at a time, beating well after each addition. Set aside.

4. Combine *3 cups flour, 1½ teaspoons baking soda,* and *1 teaspoon salt.* Add these dry ingredients alternately with *1½ cups buttermilk* to the egg mixture, stirring well after each addition until batter is smooth.

5. Stir in *1 teaspoon vanilla, 1½ teaspoons lemon juice,* and the melted chocolate. Stir in nuts, if using them.

6. Pour batter into the oblong pan, or divide it evenly among the 3 layer-cake pans.

7. Bake the layer-cake pans in the preheated oven for 30 to 35 minutes; the oblong pan for 45 minutes, or until cake is done when tested with a wooden pick or cake tester.

8. Remove cake from oven, let cool a couple of minutes, then run a knife around edge and turn cake out onto wire rack.

9. When cake is completely cool, put the layers together with Chocolate Butter Cream; frost top and sides lavishly with Meringue Frosting. Or, spread the oblong cake thickly with the butter cream.

CHOCOLATE BUTTER CREAM

In small saucepan over very low heat melt *6 ounces semi-sweet chocolate pieces* and *¼ cup hot water or coffee,* stirring occasionally until smooth. Remove from heat and beat in *3 egg yolks* (reserve the whites to make the Meringue Frosting for the 3-layer cake). Beat in *1 tablespoon vanilla or Jamaica rum,* and gradually beat in *1 stick soft butter,* bit by bit. If butter cream is too soft, chill in refrigerator for an hour.

MERINGUE FROSTING

In saucepan combine *1½ cups sugar, ½ cup water,* and *1 teaspoon lemon juice.* Bring to a boil over low heat, then boil rapidly until bubbles get thick and the syrup spins a thread when a little is dripped off the tines of a fork (236° F. on candy thermometer). Remove from heat. Beat *3 egg whites* until thick and glossy. Gradually beat in the hot syrup and continue to beat until the frosting is thick enough to hold its shape. Use an electric beater for this if you have one.

CHOCOLATE ROLL CONTAINS NO FLOUR

A favorite dessert of mine is chocolate roll, or *roulade au chocolat,* which seems as light as a breath of sweet air, literally melts in the mouth, and has never failed to bring applause whenever I have served it.

The reason for its lightness is that it is really a chocolate soufflé mixture, spread thinly on a large baking sheet, rather than a cake batter. After baking, it is allowed to deflate as a soufflé typically will do, and then is filled with whipped cream and rolled.

It's actually an easy dessert but to make it is very difficult to describe in a recipe. It would be easy to show you how, but since that is not possible, I have tried to write the technique in great detail. The drawings show what words perhaps cannot make altogether clear.

The roll may be made a day in advance and refrigerated until serving time, or it may be made several weeks in advance, wrapped loosely and carefully in aluminum foil, and frozen. Remove it from its wrappings and onto a serving board about 3 hours before you need it.

In addition to a long, narrow jelly-roll board or tray to serve it on, you will need to have on hand: waxed paper, a rimmed baking sheet or jelly-roll pan, a small covered saucepan for melting chocolate, a second and somewhat larger saucepan, 2 mixing bowls, an electric or rotary beater, and a small sieve for sifting cocoa.

ROULADE AU CHOCOLAT

Serves 8 to 10

   BUY

6-ounce package semi-sweet chocolate pieces
6 eggs
1 pint heavy cream
Small can cocoa, without sugar or powdered milk

<table>
<tr><td>

HAVE ON HAND

Cooking oil
Instant coffee
Hot water
Sugar
Vanilla
Confectioners' sugar

</td><td>

COOKWARE

Small saucepan with cover
Rimmed baking sheet or jelly-roll
pan approximately
15½ x 10½ x 1 inch

</td></tr>
</table>

1. *Oil* the baking sheet, line with waxed paper, and *oil* the paper. Use your fingertips to oil sheet and paper, for this is the only way you can be sure that all surfaces are evenly coated.

2. Put *chocolate pieces, 1 teaspoon instant coffee,* and *3 tablespoons hot water* into a small saucepan, cover tightly, and set saucepan into a larger pan or a skillet containing a couple of inches of simmering (not boiling) water. Stir occasionally until chocolate is melted and mixture is smooth, then set aside to cool. Rinse two mixing bowls with hot water and dry.

3. Preheat oven to 350° F.

4. Separate the eggs, putting yolks into one bowl and whites into another. Be careful not to let the slightest speck of yolk fall into the whites, otherwise they will not beat. If you are a novice at breaking eggs, separate one at a time, letting the white fall into a cup before transferring it to the bowl. Should you break the yolk of one egg, you haven't ruined all your egg whites.

5. Add ⅔ *cup sugar* to the *egg yolks* and begin beating. Use an electric beater for this if possible, for the egg yolks and sugar must be beaten at top speed for at least 5 minutes, or until mixture is very pale in color and as thick as cake batter. The mixture should take some time to level out when the beater is withdrawn. This is known as a "ribbon stage."

6. To this thick yolk mixture add the melted and cooled chocolate, and stir until well blended.

7. Beat the *egg whites* with a clean beater until glossy and thick enough to hold a stiff peak. Do NOT beat until they are dry. Pour the chocolate mixture on top of the egg whites, scraping out all of the chocolate mixture with a rubber spatula; then use the spatula to fold chocolate mixture into the egg whites. To FOLD: Cut down through the mixture with the side of the spatula, bring spatula along bottom of the bowl, then up and over the top. Repeat this down-across-up-and-over motion until egg whites completely disappear into the chocolate mixture.

8. Pour batter onto the prepared baking sheet, again scraping bowl well; spread evenly in a thin layer over the sheet and well into the corners of the pan. Bake in center of preheated oven for 15 minutes. Do *not* over-bake.

9. Remove baking sheet from oven, then cover top of the cake with a sheet of waxed paper. Cover the waxed paper with a damp towel and let the cake cool for 1 hour.

10. Remove towel and waxed paper. The cake will look pretty sad, but don't worry—it won't taste that way! Run a knife around edge of pan to loosen cake. Overlap two strips of waxed paper lengthwise on work table. The strips should be longer than the length of the cake and, over-lapping, they should be wider than the width of the cake. Sift enough *cocoa* over surface of the cake to coat it generously, then, with one motion, flip baking sheet and cake upside down onto the center of the waxed paper strips. The long side of the baking sheet should be horizontal to you.

11. Now remove the baking sheet. Grasp edge of waxed paper that lines the sheet on your right, and gently raise the baking sheet from right to left until it is off. Again, carefully, remove waxed paper from the bottom of the cake. If you oiled the paper well, you'll have no trouble, but if you didn't or if you left any little lumps of egg whites in the batter you may find the cake will stick a little in spots. Free these spots of cake with a knife.

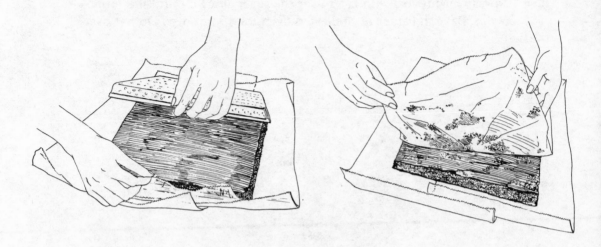

12. Beat *1½ cups of the cream until stiff*, then beat in *2 tablespoons confectioners' sugar* and *1 tablespoon vanilla*. With spatula spread the cream in an even layer over surface of the cake.

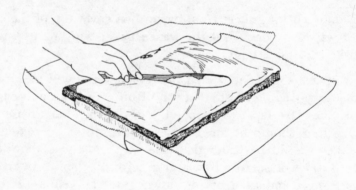

13. You're ready to roll. Using both hands, grasp the wide side of the waxed paper closest to you on the table, raise the edge of the cake, and turn about 1 inch of it over on top of the filling. Continue to lift the waxed paper and at the same time roll cake and filling, making a long roll about 4 inches in diameter and 15 inches long. Don't be upset if the cake cracks a little, especially on your first attempt. It usually does, but this doesn't hurt the flavor. The last roll of the cake should deposit the "log" well into the center of the back sheet of waxed paper. Place the serving board on the far side of the roll and parallel to it, and lift the

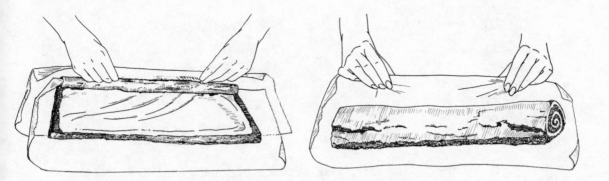

waxed paper and the roll onto the serving board. I usually leave the waxed paper under the roll until I am ready to serve the dessert. The roll will firm a little when it chills in the refrigerator.

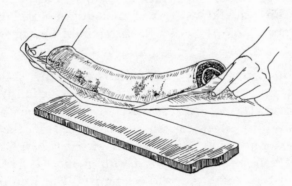

14. Now sift a *little more cocoa* over the roll to coat it generously. This helps disguise any cracks in the cake. Place in refrigerator. When ready to serve, cut away all visible waxed paper with a sharp knife, leaving a small strip under the roll. This may be discarded as the cake is served. To serve, cut into thick slices.

JELLY ROLL

Serves 8. Another cake, a favorite at the turn of the century, is a delicate jelly roll. Serve in thin slices, alone or accompanied by ice cream or fruit compote, or use it as the basis of the glorious Savoy Trifle (page 306).

HAVE ON HAND	*COOKWARE*
Cooking oil	Jelly roll pan *or* baking sheet
5 eggs	18 x 12 inches
Sugar	
All-purpose flour	
Vanilla	
Red currant jelly or raspberry jam	

1. *Oil* the baking sheet, line with waxed paper, and *oil* the paper evenly. Preheat oven to 350° F.

2. Separate *5 large eggs*. To the *egg yolks* add *4 tablespoons sugar;* beat until mixture is thick and pale in color. Carefully fold in *3 tablespoons flour*. Stir in *1 teaspoon vanilla*.

3. Beat the *egg whites* until thick and glossy, but be careful not to overbeat. The whites should be just stiff enough to hold a peak when the beater is withdrawn. Fold the egg-yolk batter into the egg whites gently but thoroughly.

4. Spread the batter evenly on the prepared baking sheet, and bake in the center of the preheated oven for 12 minutes, or until surface is a pale golden brown. Do not overbake. Remove from oven and sprinkle the surface lightly with *sugar*. Loosen waxed paper from the baking pan and turn the cake out onto a long sheet of waxed paper. Carefully peel waxed paper off bottom of cake. Spread with about *3 tablespoons of the jelly or jam,* and roll lengthwise into a long roll. Cut into thin slices to serve, or to use in the following recipe.

JUST A "LITTLE" SAVOY TRIFLE
(also known as Tipsy Pudding)

Serves 6

BUY

1 pink milk
3 containers heavy cream, 8 ounces each
1 dozen eggs

HAVE ON HAND	*COOKWARE*
Sugar	2 heavy saucepans
Flour	
Vanilla	
Jelly Roll (page 305)	
Madeira *or* port wine	
Dark rum *or* cognac	
Confectioners' sugar	

1. MAKE PASTRY CREAM: In saucepan heat *2 cups milk* and *2 of the containers of cream* to steaming hot.

2. In another saucepan beat *9 egg yolks* (reserve the whites for another use) and *¾ cup sugar*. Beat in *½ cup flour*. Gradually beat in (use a wire whisk if possible) the hot milk-cream mixture; then cook over moderate heat, stirring rapidly, for about 2 minutes, or until cream is smooth and thick. Reduce heat to low and cook for 3 minutes longer. Be careful not to let the cream boil. If it starts to simmer around the edges, remove from heat but continue to stir. Cool, stirring occasionally; then stir in *1 tablespoon vanilla*.

3. Slice the *Jelly Roll* thinly, and line a 6-cup bowl with about half of the slices. Combine *¼ cup Madeira* or *port with ¼ cup rum or cognac*, and moisten the slices of jelly roll with half of this mixture. Pour in half the pastry cream and place a layer of jelly roll slices on top. Moisten with the remaining wine mixture and cover with remaining pastry cream. Cover top with remaining slices of jelly roll.

4. Chill the trifle. Before serving, beat the *third container of heavy cream* until stiff, and fold in *2 tablespoons confectioners' sugar* and *1 teaspoon vanilla*. Garnish the top of the trifle with the whipped cream. Serve with a large spoon, dipping deeply to bottom of bowl to include some of the jelly roll slices from bottom in each serving.

CHARLOTTE RUSSE

Serves 4 to 6. Still another famous combination of cake and cream is Charlotte Russe. It may be kept for a day in the refrigerator before serving, or it may be frozen. Remove it from the freezer about 3 hours before serving.

BUY

3-ounce package ladyfingers
1 pint heavy cream
Additional heavy cream for garnish (optional)

HAVE ON HAND	*COOKWARE*
Butter	1-quart mold
Unflavored gelatin	2-quart saucepan plus
Milk	pan of larger diameter
Confectioners' sugar	
Vanilla	

1. *Butter* a 1-quart charlotte or timbale mold and line bottom with waxed paper. Split the *ladyfingers*. Place a small round of ladyfinger in center of bottom of mold; then, working outward from the center, cover bottom with close-fitting triangles of ladyfingers. Arrange remaining ladyfingers upright and close together all around inside wall of mold. Set aside.

2. *Soften 2 tablespoons gelatin in ¼ cup cold water.*

3. In saucepan heat *1 cup milk.* Add the softened gelatin and stir until gelatin is thoroughly dissolved. Remove saucepan from heat and stir into milk mixture *⅔ cup confectioners' sugar* and *1 tablespoon vanilla.* Set the saucepan into a pan of ice water and stir constantly until cream begins to set and thicken.

4. Whip the *cream* until stiff. Beat the vanilla cream until light and fluffy, then fold in the whipped cream. Turn mixture into the prepared mold and chill until set.

5. When ready to serve, unmold onto serving plate and, if desired, garnish with *rosettes of whipped cream.*

STRAWBERRY BAVARIAN CREAM

Serves 8. Rich and delicate, this is another scrumptious French favorite. For variety, it may be molded in a 2-quart charlotte or timbale mold lined with ladyfingers, as in the preceding recipe, to make a Strawberry Charlotte Russe.

BUY

1 quart fresh strawberries
1 pint heavy cream
Additional berries and cream for garnish (optional)

HAVE ON HAND	*COOKWARE*
Lemon	Small saucepan plus pan of larger
Sugar	diameter
Unflavored gelatin	2-quart mold

1. Wash and hull *berries,* then force them through a sieve, or purée them in an electric blender. To this purée, add *1 tablespoon lemon juice* and *½ cup sugar;* stir until sugar is completely dissolved.

2. Soften *2 envelopes gelatin* in *¼ cup cold water,* then stir over hot water until gelatin is clear and thoroughly dissolved. Stir dissolved gelatin into the strawberry purée. Set mixture into a pan of cracked ice, or chill in refrigerator until it begins to thicken, stirring occasionally. Do not let it set.

3. Whip the *heavy cream* and fold into the strawberry mixture. Pour the dessert into a serving dish. Chill until set. If desired, chill the cream in a decorative mold.

To mold: Rinse a 2-quart mold with cold water. Pour in the mixture and chill for at least 2 hours.

To unmold: Run a knife around the edge of the cream to loosen it from the sides of the mold. Dip the mold slowly in and out of a pan of hot-to-the-hand water three times, being careful that the water does not flow over the side of the mold into the cream. Invert on chilled serving platter.

4. Garnish with whole strawberries and whipped cream, if desired.

COEUR À LA CRÈME

Serves 6. This favorite French dessert molds cream cheese into a heart shape and sets it in a sea of fresh strawberries. When served in traditional French manner, it is accompanied by crusty French bread and a slightly sweet wine or a *vin rosé.* You should have a heart-shaped basket in which to mold the cheese mixture and to allow the excess moisture, or *petit lait,* to drain from it while it chills.

BUY

1 pint small-curd cottage cheese
1 pound cream cheese
1 pint heavy cream
1 quart fresh strawberries
Small loaf French bread

HAVE ON HAND   *COOKWARE*
Salt   Heart-shaped basket mold
Cheesecloth

1. Beat *cottage cheese* well with a rotary beater. Use an electric one if possible. Gradually add *the cream cheese,* beating constantly at high speed until all of it has been added and the mixture is smooth. Add *a dash of salt*. Reduce speed to medium and gradually beat in the *heavy cream*.

2. Line a heart-shaped basket mold with moist cheesecloth. Pour the blended cheese mixture into the lined mold. Place mold on a plate and store in the refrigerator overnight to drain.

3. To serve, unmold carefully on a chilled serving platter, and surround with *fresh strawberries*. Serve with *French bread*.

FLOATING ISLAND
(Oeufs à la Neige)

Serves 4 or 8. Here is my favorite custard dessert which should serve 8 but is so good that it serves only 4! It has a fancy French name but it is a real old-fashioned dish.

BUY

6 eggs
1 quart milk
8-ounce container heavy cream

HAVE ON HAND   *COOKWARE*
Lemon   Large skillet
Sugar   2-quart saucepan
Cornstarch
Vanilla extract

1. Separate *5 eggs,* and set the yolks aside. Beat the *egg whites* with *½ teaspoon lemon juice* until light and fluffy. Gradually beat in *⅔ cup sugar,* one tablespoon at a time, and continue to beat until you have a meringue that is glossy and holds a stiff peak when the beater is withdrawn.

2. In the skillet heat *2 cups milk,* the *heavy cream,* and *1 teaspoon vanilla* to simmering. Drop into the hot milk *heaping rounded spoonfuls of the meringue.* Let the meringues poach for 5 minutes. Turn with a slotted spoon and poach for 5 minutes longer. The milk must not boil, just barely simmer. Remove the cooked meringues with a slotted spoon to paper toweling to drain.

3. Strain the milk mixture into a quart measuring cup, then add *enough milk to make a total of 2½ cups liquid.*

4. Beat *the 5 egg yolks* with *4 tablespoons sugar, 2 teaspoons cornstarch,* and *1 teaspoon vanilla* until sugar is dissolved; then gradually beat in the hot milk mixture.

5. Pour the custard into the saucepan and cook over quite high heat, stirring vigorously, until it begins to steam. Remove from heat, but continue to stir. Repeat this cooking and stirring until custard is thick enough to coat the spoon. It will be thin, but will set a little as it cools. It should NOT be a thick custard, rather a custard sauce.

6. Pour the hot custard sauce into a serving bowl and pile the meringues on top. Cool, then chill until ready to serve.

SOUR CREAM CHEESECAKE

Serves 6

BUY

1 pound cream cheese
Box of graham crackers
1 pint dairy sour cream

HAVE ON HAND

Butter
Sugar

Cinnamon
Lemon
2 eggs

COOKWARE

Small saucepan
9-inch pie plate

1. Set *cream cheese* out at room temperature to soften. Melt *6 table-spoons butter* in small saucepan over low heat. Preheat oven to 325° F.

2. Crumb *16 graham crackers,* then mix them with *½ cup sugar, ½ teaspoon cinnamon,* and *4 tablespoons of the melted butter.* Line the pie plate with the crumbs.

3. In large mixing bowl mash the cream cheese with *½ cup sugar, 1 tablespoon lemon juice,* and *2 eggs.* Gradually beat in *1½ cups of the sour cream* and continue to beat until mixture is smooth. Beat in the *remaining 2 tablespoons melted butter.*

4. Pour mixture into the crumb-lined pan and bake in the preheated oven for 30 to 40 minutes, or until set in center. The filling will still be very soft but will firm as it cools. Chill thoroughly before serving.

CRÊPES, those delicate, paper-thin pancakes which are such fun to make, are just about perfection as a dessert. They may be served hot from the crêpe pan with a simple sprinkling of fine granulated sugar and a squeeze of lemon juice. Or they may be made well in advance (they freeze well and defrost quickly) and rolled around any number of sweet fillings. The latter process results in especially luxurious desserts.

The technique for making crêpes is included in the chapter on appetizers (see page 68). The batter is almost the same and a little sugar is added.

DESSERT CRÊPES

Makes 18 to 20 crêpes

HAVE ON HAND

All-purpose flour
Sugar
Salt
3 eggs

COOKWARE

5- *or* 6-inch crêpe pan

Milk
Butter
Cognac

1. Combine *1 cup flour, 4 tablespoons sugar,* and *a dash of salt.* In separate bowl beat *3 eggs,* then stir in *1½ cups milk.* Gradually stir egg-milk mixture into the dry ingredients, and continue to stir until batter is smooth. It should have the consistency of heavy cream and just coat the spoon.

2. Add *1 tablespoon each of melted butter and cognac.*

3. Strain the batter through a fine sieve to remove any lumps which might remain.

4. Let batter stand for 1 to 2 hours before using it. This improves the texture of the crêpes.

5. To COOK THE CRÊPES: Heat crêpe pan until very hot. Crêpes must cook quickly, otherwise they may become tough. Put *½ teaspoon butter* in pan, and swirl pan to coat bottom and sides with butter. Pour in about *2 tablespoons crêpe batter,* and again tilt pan with a circular motion to spread batter evenly and thinly to the edges. This must be done quickly before the batter has a chance to set. Cook crêpes for about 1 minute, or until set and brown on one side. Turn and brown the other side. Tip the crêpe out onto waxed paper to cool.

CRÊPES TRIUMPHANTE

Serves 4. Here is my interpretation of the ultra-rich crêpes dessert served at the Forum of the Twelve Caesars in New York City.

HAVE ON HAND	*COOKWARE*
1 orange	10-inch skillet
Butter	
Sugar	
Cognac	
2 squares (2 ounces) bitter chocolate	
Vanilla ice cream	
8 crêpes (page 312)	
Toasted slivered almonds	

1. Cut rind from ½ *orange* in one continuous piece, just as in peeling an apple.

2. In the skillet melt *4 tablespoons butter.* Add *6 tablespoons sugar* and *the spiral of orange rind,* and cook over medium heat, stirring constantly, until the mixture caramelizes to a dark brown color.

3. Immediately squeeze in about *2 tablespoons orange juice* from the half orange, and add *½ cup cognac.* Set the cognac aflame and as soon as the flame dies out, discard orange rind and add the *2 squares of bitter chocolate.* Cook, stirring, until chocolate is melted and the sauce is smooth.

4. Put a large spoonful of *vanilla ice cream* on the lower third of each crêpe, and roll the crêpes into cylinders.

5. Place two rolls side by side on each serving plate, cover with the hot chocolate sauce, and sprinkle with *almonds.*

Fruit and berries make delicious fillings for crêpes. Fresh strawberries and stewed lingonberries are especially good. Imported jars of lingonberries are sold in many food specialty shops. If you can't find them, you may substitute stewed and sweetened cranberries or cranberry preserves.

CRÊPES WITH STRAWBERRIES AND CURAÇAO

Serves 6

BUY

1 pint fresh strawberries
8-ounce container heavy cream
1 pint vanilla ice cream
4-ounce can toasted slivered almonds

HAVE ON HAND	*COOKWARE*
Butter	10-inch heavy skillet
Sugar	
Curaçao	
Maraschino, framboise, *or* kirsch	
6 crêpes (page 312)	

1. Wash, hull, and halve the *berries.* Whip the *heavy cream* and refrigerate until needed.

2. In skillet melt *½ cup butter*. Add *2 tablespoons sugar* and *3 table-spoons Curaçao*. Heat to simmering. Add the strawberries; cook, stirring, until berries and their juice are warm.

3. Add *½ cup maraschino, framboise, or kirsch* and set aflame.

4. When the flame burns out, dip a *crêpe* into the sauce, turning it to coat both sides. Roll it around a scoop of *vanilla ice cream,* place on serving dish, and top with the strawberries and their sauce. Garnish each serving with a dollop of the whipped cream and sprinkle with almonds.

CRÊPES WITH LINGONBERRIES

Sprinkle a *crêpe* thickly with *confectioners' sugar* and lightly with a little *powdered cinnamon* and *lemon juice*. Spread with *hot lingonberries* and roll into a cylinder. Place 2 crêpes on each serving plate, pour over *1 ounce warm Jamaica rum,* and serve flaming.

Homemade Ice Cream & Sherbet

In keeping with the trend toward honest, wholesome, unadulterated food is the revival of making ice cream at home. The old-fashioned hand-cranked ice-cream freezer invented sometime around 1840 by a woman named Nancy Johnson is still the most common device used for making homemade ice cream—with all members of the family or commune taking turns at the crank. Now there are also the new electric ice-cream freezers, which do an admirable job and require much less effort than the hand-crank ones.

I became an ice-cream enthusiast in the past year when a friend presented me with a recipe for Buttermilk Ice Cream. It sounded so intriguing that I invested in an electric ice-cream freezer, and since then I have made many daring combinations into frozen creams and sherbets—all delicious and all a heck of a lot better and less expensive than even the best of the commercial ones. Naturally, now I heartily recommend *everyone* getting on the homemade-ice-cream band wagon.

With a couple of basic formulas, it's almost impossible to go wrong, and the varieties of flavors and textures are innumerable, limited only by one's imagination. I'll begin the recipes with the one that captured my interest. But first, a few basic how-to's:

HOW TO MAKE ICE CREAM IN AN ELECTRIC OR HAND-CRANK FREEZER

Don't make a big production out of it unless you want to—it can all be so simple. You don't need to crack or crush ice. Just use ice cubes—but you'll need a lot of them on hand in order to keep the bucket filled at all times. You don't need rock salt, either. It's cheaper, of course, but table salt works just as well.

1. Read the instructions, in the booklet that comes with the freezer, as to assembling, cleaning, and caring for the freezer.

2. Wash ice-cream can, cover, and dasher in hot soapy water, and rinse thoroughly in hot, then cold, water.

3. Have all liquid ingredients or fruit purées cold before combining them in the freezer can.

4. Insert dasher in can.

5. Put ingredients in the can, filling it only ¾ full so that there will be room for the mixture to expand. Position the can in the freezer, and then add the cover.

6. Position the motor or hand-crank unit over the can, and lock it in place.

7. Fill the bucket with layers of ice cubes and salt, alternating each

2 inches of ice with 3 tablespoons salt until ice and salt are level with top of can. As the brine settles, add more ice and salt.

8. Allow the ice cream to churn for 30 to 60 minutes, or until either the motor slows or stops or the hand crank becomes difficult to turn. Freezing time varies according to the type of ice-cream mixture being churned, the temperature of the mix before it was put into the can, and the amount of salt used. If too much salt is used, the cream will freeze too quickly and end up with a coarse texture.

9. When ice cream is the consistency of whipped cream or mush, it's ready either to be ripened or hardened or to be spooned out onto plates and enjoyed as "soft" ice cream.

10. Clear away ice and salt from around can cover. Remove motor or crank, then wipe cover free of any salt and remove. Lift out dasher and scrape clean with a rubber spatula.

TO RIPEN OR HARDEN ICE CREAM:

The easiest way to do this is in your food freezer, if you have one. Re-cover the ice-cream can, put a cork in the hole in the cover, and put the can in the freezer. Or, you can spoon the mush into plastic containers, allowing ½ inch of space at the top for expansion, then cover with tight-fitting lids and freeze.

If you don't have a freezer, push the ice cream down into the can, cover with aluminum foil, replace cover, and put a cork in the hole. Drain the brine from the bucket, and add salt and ice to completely cover can and lid. For insulation, put a few newspapers on top of the bucket. Let the ice cream ripen for 2 to 3 hours.

HOW MUCH SALT AND ICE?

For a gallon container, you will need approximately *20 pounds of ice cubes* and a total of *3 cups table salt* (1½ cups while churning the ice cream and 1½ cups while ripening it). If you use *rock salt,* you will need a total of *5 cups.*

AD LIB ICE CREAM (General Formula)

Almost any combination is possible: The liquid can include a combination of cream plus milk, sour cream, yogurt, or buttermilk, eggs, and fruit juice and/or fruit purée. Then add sugar and flavoring. Some heavy cream should be used for a smooth texture, and the more heavy cream you use, of course, the richer and more delicious the ice cream.

For 1 gallon of ice cream you will need:

10 cups total liquid
2 cups sugar, white *or* brown
2 tablespoons vanilla extract *or* other flavoring

Try the following basic recipes, then let your imagination take over.

BUTTERMILK ICE CREAM

Makes almost 4 quarts, and costs less then 50¢ per quart!

In freezer can, churn together:

1½ quarts buttermilk
1 pint half-and-half
1 cup heavy cream
2 cups sugar
1 to 2 tablespoons vanilla extract

BASIC CUSTARD ICE CREAM

Makes 4 quarts

In freezer can, churn together:

4 eggs
2 cups sugar, white *or* light brown
5 cups milk
4 cups heavy cream
2 tablespoons vanilla extract

LIGHT-AND-EASY ICE CREAM

Makes 4 quarts

In freezer can, churn together:

10 cups light cream *or* half-and-half
2 cups sugar
2 tablespoons vanilla extract

BASIC COOKED-CUSTARD VANILLA ICE CREAM

Makes 1 gallon

In saucepan combine *2 cups sugar, 6 tablespoons flour,* and *a dash of salt.* Slowly stir in *5 cups hot milk* and cook over low heat for about 10 minutes, stirring constantly, until mixture is thickened.

Beat *6 eggs* with *a little of the hot milk mixture;* add to *remaining milk mixture* and cook for 1 minute longer, stirring rapidly. Cool; then chill in refrigerator.

In freezer can, churn together the *chilled custard* and *4 cups heavy cream.*

FRESH FRUIT ICE CREAM

In basic recipes, substitute 3 to 4 cups puréed fresh fruit, such as peaches, strawberries, or raspberries, for an equal quantity of the milk or light cream specified in the recipe.

FROZEN FRUIT ICE CREAM

Defrost three 12-ounce packages frozen peaches, strawberries, or raspberries and mash thoroughly. Substitute the mashed fruit for 4 cups of the milk or light cream, and reduce amount of sugar to 1½ cups.

CHOCOLATE SWIRL ICE CREAM

Swirl 2 cups chocolate sauce through ice cream after dasher is removed. Repack and allow to ripen.

PRUNE WALNUT ICE CREAM

Makes 3 quarts

Put *12 ounces pitted prunes* in *water to cover* and cook until soft. Purée prunes and liquid in electric blender or press them through a food mill. Chill the purée. You will have about 2 cups. In freezer can, churn together:

The chilled prune purée
4 cups half-and-half
1 cup heavy cream
2 eggs
1½ cups brown sugar
1 tablespoon vanilla
½ cup broken walnuts

APRICOT YOGURT ICE CREAM

Makes 1 gallon

Simmer *11 ounces dried apricots* in *1 quart water* for 30 minutes. Mash the apricots or purée them in a blender or a food mill. You will have about 3 cups purée. Chill. In freezer can, churn together:

The chilled apricot purée
1 pint plain yogurt
1 quart buttermilk
1 cup heavy cream

BANANA ICE CREAM

Makes 2 quarts

In freezer can, churn together:

5 bananas, sliced and slightly mashed
3 cups heavy cream
1 pint half-and-half *or* light cream
1 cup sugar
2 tablespoons vanilla

BITTER-CHOCOLATE ICE CREAM

Makes 1 gallon

In advance, heat *5 squares (ounces) unsweetened chocolate* and *5 cups milk* until scalding. In another, larger saucepan beat *4 eggs,* then stir in *2 cups sugar, 5 tablespoons flour,* and *dash of salt.* Pour the hot chocolate milk over the egg mixture, stirring constantly, and cook over low heat just until mixture thickens enough to coat the spoon. Be careful not to let it boil. Cool the chocolate custard, then chill. In freezer can, churn together:

The chilled chocolate custard
5 cups light *or* heavy cream
1 tablespoon vanilla

THREE-IN-ONE SHERBET

Makes 3 quarts

In advance, boil *1½ cups sugar* and *3 cups water or cranberry juice cocktail* for 5 minutes. Cool, then chill. In freezer can, churn together:

The chilled syrup
3 large bananas, sliced
1-pound can crushed pineapple
½ cup lemon juice
1 cup orange juice
3 egg whites beaten until stiff but still glossy

LEMON ICE

Makes 2 quarts

In advance, combine *1½ cups sugar* and *1 cup water* in saucepan. Bring to a boil and simmer for 5 minutes. Cool then chill. In freezer can, churn together:

The chilled syrup
¾ cup lemon juice
2 teaspoons grated lemon rind
4 cups water

FOR LEMON SHERBET

Add to above ingredients *2 egg whites* beaten until stiff but still glossy.

MINT SHERBET

Makes 2 quarts

In advance, combine *1½ cups sugar* and *2 cups water* in saucepan. Bring slowly to a boil and simmer for 5 minutes. Shred *2 cups fresh mint leaves*. Add to the boiling hot syrup, cover and cool, then chill. In freezer can, churn together:

The chilled mint syrup
1 cup lemon juice
2 cups water
A couple of drops of green food coloring
4 egg whites beaten until stiff but still glossy

PARFAIT AU CAFÉ

Makes 2 quarts

In freezer can, churn together:

1 cup sugar
1 cup strong black coffee
8 egg yolks, beaten
3 cups heavy cream, whipped

With homemade ice cream in your freezer and a few good dessert sauces in the refrigerator, you can make any number of fancy coupes, parfaits, and other yummy ice-cream desserts for gala occasions—or simply to please the family. By the way, those big brandy snifters that you use so rarely make elegant containers for these fun and fancy desserts.

RASPBERRY SAUCE

Makes 1 cup

Defrost a *10-ounce package frozen raspberries.* Purée in an electric blender, and strain to remove the seeds; or press the defrosted berries through a food mill. Stir *¼ cup sugar or sugar to taste* into the purée.

RICH CHOCOLATE SAUCE FOR ICE CREAM

Makes 2 cups

This sauce will keep in the refrigerator for several weeks. Into a small saucepan empty *6 ounces semi-sweet chocolate pieces.* Add *1 cup cream, 1 cup light brown sugar,* and *4 tablespoons grated orange rind,* and stir over low heat until chocolate is melted and sauce is smooth. Remove from heat and, if desired, stir in *4 tablespoons Jamaica rum.*

CHERRIES JUBILEE

Serves 4 to 6

BUY

1 pound dark sweet cherries

HAVE ON HAND

Sugar
Cornstarch
Kirsch *or* cognac
Vanilla ice cream

1. Wash stem, and pit the *cherries.*

2. In saucepan combine *1 cup sugar* and *½ cup water.* Bring to a boil and boil rapidly for 5 minutes. Add cherries and simmer for 5 minutes.

3. Combine *2 teaspoons cornstarch* and *1 tablespoon water;* add to cherries. Cook, stirring constantly, for 1 minute longer, or until syrup is clear and slightly thickened.

4. Just before serving, add *2 ounces kirsch or cognac,* ignite the liquor, and serve the flaming cherries over vanilla ice cream.

CARAMEL PECAN DESSERT

Cook *an unopened can of sweetened condensed milk* in *boiling water to cover* for 2 hours. Cool before opening. The milk will have turned to a rich caramel sauce which will keep for several weeks in the refrigerator. Break *ladyfingers* into a serving dish, add *a scoop of vanilla ice cream,* cover with the *caramel sauce,* sprinkle with *pecan halves,* and top with *whipped cream!*

APPENDIX

Everyone Should Know
a Little About Nutrition

Good health is the greatest asset anyone can have. Without it we cannot go about our daily work or play with enthusiasm and pleasure, and no single factor is more important to the achievement and maintenance of good health than nutrition. Therefore it is important that everyone know a little about the subject, for the kinds of food we eat can make the difference between feeling just all right and radiant good health, true *joie de vivre*.

Generally speaking, as I have said before, good food is nutritious food, and the more flavorful it is, the more nutritious it is. Yet, a knowledge of the essentials of nutrition, and an understanding of how they work, can bring about a revolutionary improvement in health and vitality and can do much to alleviate the stresses and strains of modern-day living.

So whether you bought this book for economy reasons, because you are a vegetarian, or just because you enjoy good food, you should have a nutritional blueprint from which you can build your daily menus, and I'm going to try to give it to you. This does not mean that you cannot eat the dishes you enjoy most; it simply means that you should combine these favorite dishes in balanced meals that contain all the essential nutrients that your body requires.

The subject of nutrition today is especially important, for our vegetables are grown on exhausted soil, chemically fertilized, sprayed with pesticides, then travel long exhausting miles from processor to warehouse, from warehouse to market. Our grains are processed to remove the germ and along with it a dozen or more essential nutrients contained in the germ, then bleached to further rob them of more valuable properties. Stabilizers, dyes, emulsifiers, and other chemicals are added to our foods, some containing as much as twenty or more different chemical additives. Our bean and seed oils and our nut butters are hydrogenated, and our frozen products are mishandled in transportation and at their destination, so that serious thawing can and does take place.

Therefore we must work intelligently at supplying our bodies each day with the nutrients they require. Forty such nutrients are known.

Supplementing our meals with vitamin pills can assure us of an adequate supply of these, BUT it is more than possible that forty or more additional essential nutrients are still undiscovered, and these can be supplied only by natural, unrefined foods. Nature has a way of putting all living substances together in pretty perfect packages, with all the nutrients in the correct proportion one to the other to nurture and sustain life. A lack of any one of the essential nutrients can result in the underproduction of an estimated ten thousand compounds that work together in perfect harmony to give us good health, vitality, and longevity.

OUR DAILY MEALS SHOULD INCLUDE THE BIG FIVE

These are complete proteins, carbohydrates (starches and sugars), fats (essential fatty acids), vitamins, and minerals. Let's deal with each of these individually.

PROTEINS PROVIDE THE MATERIAL NEEDED FOR OUR BODIES TO BUILD AND REPAIR LIVING TISSUE

All living tissue—nails, hair, skin, muscles—are made of proteins, and without them our bodies cannot replace the cells which are constantly dying.

There are two types of proteins: complete proteins, such as eggs, milk and milk products, and liver and other organ foods, such as muscle meats, fish, seafood, fowl, wheat germ, soy beans or soy flour, and natural cheeses. These contain all the essential amino acids, of which there are twenty-two known. Digestion breaks protein foods down into these acids, so the body can use what it needs.

Other grains, beans, and most nuts are incomplete protein, lacking some of the amino acids, and are of food value only when combined with a complete protein food.

Half as many grams of complete protein as our ideal weight are needed daily. If your normal weight is one hundred twenty pounds, you need sixty grams of protein; if your normal weight is one hundred eighty pounds, then you need ninety grams of protein. So it is just is important that you learn to count grams of proteins as it is calories.

If you are not a big meat eater, or do not eat meat at all, a good way to ensure adequate protein is to eat wheat germ or soy granules in preference to other breakfast cereals, and to add these highly nutritious natural grains to muffins, breads, pancakes, waffles, omelets, scrambled eggs, and vegetable croquettes and loaves. One-half cup of wheat germ contains twenty-four grams of complete proteins, and a half cup of soy granules contains thirty grams. Another easy way is to add natural desiccated liver tablets to your diet, along with natural grains, legumes, and nuts, combined with eggs and milk products.

CARBOHYDRATES SUPPLY BODY ENERGY

These are the sugars and starches, which are converted into sugar in in our intestines and supply very necessary body energy. They are normally associated with problems of overweight, and rightly so if we are thinking of the refined flours that go into commercial baked goods, cookies, pastries, and packaged mixes, or the refined white sugars used in candy, soft drinks, and in tea and coffee. These are "empty" carbohydrates that have been robbed of their natural vitamins and minerals. When such carbohydrates are eaten, the blood-sugar level rises quickly, but the body cannot assimilate them, so they are stored as fat and the blood-sugar level drops quickly, leaving fatigue in its path.

On the other hand there are GOOD carbohydrates, the natural ones containing B vitamins, which the body needs to "burn" or metabolize them into body energy. These are found in whole grains and whole-grain cereals, potatoes, fresh fruits and juices, dried fruits, honey, molasses, and brown sugars. Some of these natural carbohydrates should be included at each meal for balanced diet, even if only in small amounts. When proteins and some fat are included in a meal with some natural carbohydrates, the blood-sugar level rises slowly and the level of energy is properly maintained.

Is it so very difficult to substitute good starches and sugars in place of empty ones? It really isn't, and if weight is a serious problem, learn moderation not only in your intake of carbohydrates, but of all foods.

GOOD CARBOHYDRATES	EMPTY CARBOHYDRATES
Whole grains and cereals	"Enriched" cereals
Breads made from whole grains	Commercial white bread
Root vegetables, such as yams	Canned fruits
Potatoes	Soft drinks
Fresh fruits and juices	Instant puddings and desserts
Dried fruits	Commercial candy
Pure maple syrup and maple sugar	Refined white sugar
Honey	Packaged mixes
Dark molasses	Ready-whipped toppings
Brown sugars	
Unrefined crystallized sugars	
Malted-milk tablets	

FATS COMBINE WITH PHOSPHORUS TO FORM EVERY CELL

Just as there are good and bad carbohydrates, there are good and bad fats, and the right kinds are essential to stimulate the flow of bile and promote good health.

The bad fats are the saturated ones such as the hard or solid fats on meats and margarines, lards, and hydrogenated cooking fats, which cannot dissolve in the blood at body temperature. These are the fats that turn into a fatty substance known as cholesterol which is deposited on the walls of the arteries, narrowing the channels through which the blood passes and decreasing circulation. When such a condition exists in the body it is known as atherosclerosis and, if not corrected, can result in premature senility, strokes, or death by heart attack.

The good fats are the unsaturated liquid fats from vegetables. In these clear liquid oils are essential fatty acids which are necessary to utilize cholesterol and the saturated fats. According to the noted nutritionist, Adelle Davis, the most essential of fatty acid is linoleic acid—contained in safflower seeds and oil—which if sufficient, and with the help of many vitamins and minerals, can synthesize the two other essential fatty acids and increase a substance in the blood known as lecithin, an agent which emulsifies cholesterol and breaks it down into minute particles. These particles are small enough to be held in suspension in the blood and can then pass through the walls of the arteries and be utilized in the tissues.

Lecithin is naturally available in such food products as egg yolks, liver, some nuts, soy oil, and wheat germ oil and 'is available in capsule form. However, it can also be manufactured in our bodies from the essential fatty acids, the B vitamins known as choline and inositol vitamin B 6 (pyridoxine), plus magnesium and other nutrients found in a balanced diet.

GOOD FATS	BAD FATS
Safflower oil	Hard animal fats on roasts and chops
Poppy-seed and sesame-seed oils	Hydrogenated fats
Sunflower seed oil	Hard oil margarines or peanut butters
Soybean and corn oil	Processed cheeses
Peanut oil	
Wheat germ oil	
Peanut butter (natural)	
Mayonnaise (made of the above oils)	
Fresh butter and cream	

A most enjoyable way to include essential fatty acids in the daily diet is by tossing salads with your own dressing made of wine vinegar or lemon juice and a mixture of fresh vegetable oils. They must be fresh, for even a slight rancidity in oils can destroy many of the nutrients. Buy the oils in small quantities and combine in one jar equal parts of safflower, soy, peanut, and olive oil (for flavor). Use the mixture for both salads and cooking.

To dress vegetables and for a spread on breads and biscuits, fresh butter should be used in preference to margarine. With an adequate supply of linoleic acid, there is no need whatsoever to hold back on butter and rich cream sauces. Again, if you are a weight watcher, just use in moderation.

VITAMINS AND MINERALS REGULATE BODY PROCESSES AND ARE ESSENTIAL FOR HEALTH AND GROWTH

VITAMIN A

This important vitamin is needed to prevent certain infections, to promote appetite, digestion, and longevity and to maintain vigor. It aids in the development of body cells, prevents night blindness, and keeps the skin healthy. The best natural sources of vitamin A are: liver, fish-liver oils, eggs, butter, cream, whole milk, dark-green leafy vegetables, carrots, apricots, cantaloupe, papaya, prunes, sweet potatoes, winter squash, and Swiss or Roquefort-type cheeses.

Nobody really knows how many units of vitamin A a person should consume each day, but it's possible that as many as fifty thousand units are not too many. In order to supply this amount in natural foods, a person would have to consume four and one-half pounds of butter or three and one-half quarts of heavy cream, four dozen eggs, three cups of cooked diced carrots or dried apricots, or one quart of steamed spinach! It's obviously easier to depend on a single vitamin A capsule each day.

VITAMIN C

This is another very important vitamin that is difficult to consume in adequate amounts via the table. One hundred mgs. daily are adequate, but more—even a great deal more—cannot do any harm, for it is a water-soluble vitamin and is expelled in the urine. It is generally believed that the body is unable to store it and therefore it is better taken several times daily in small doses.

Vitamin C is necessary for the health of the tissues which surround and cushion bones and joints and for healthy bones, gums, teeth, and capillary walls. It speeds up the production of natural cortisones in the body, and guards against infections of the head and chest and some allergies, especially those produced by insect bites. It is especially important in the detoxification of dangerous substances formed in the body during times of stress.

The best natural sources of vitamin C are citrus juices, strawberries, raw green peppers, dark-green leafy vegetables, avocados, tomatoes, pineapple, cantaloupe, bean sprouts, and rose hips, and it is available as ascorbic acid in tablets ranging from fifty to five hundred mgs. each.

Vitamin D

The "sunshine" vitamin regulates the metabolism of calcium and phosphorus, the elements that form strong bones and teeth. The body manufactures its own vitamin D in the skin from the direct rays of the sun. Twenty-five hundred units of vitamin D daily are not too much. This is more than the amount recommended by the Food and Nutrition Board, but the daily allowances suggested by various government agencies are based on simply staying alive and not necessarily on promoting vigorous health. If your body cannot absorb or use twenty-five hundred units, any excess is detoxified by vitamin C.

The best sources of vitamin D are: fish-liver oils, irradiated vegetable oils, yeast, canned salmon, moderate sun tanning in summer, and careful use of a sun lamp in winter months.

Vitamin E

After forty years of intensive research, this vitamin is the last to be officially recognized as nutritionally necessary, and may turn out to be one of the most important of all vitamins to children and adults for reproduction and longevity. It is known to supply vascular muscle tone, and recent experiments indicate that it may be a possible cure for gout and for muscular distrophy. Although no minimum daily requirement has yet been set for vitamin E, most doctors recommend at least one hundred units of water-soluble vitamin E per day for adults. It is found naturally in eggs and wheat germ.

Vitamin K

This is the vitamin responsible for the clotting of blood and is normally manufactured in the body by intestinal bacteria. In synthetic form it should only be taken on the advice of a doctor. The best food sources of vitamin K are all green leafy vegetables and vegetables belonging to the cabbage family.

The vitamin B complex

And complex it is indeed, so I have left it until the last of the vitamins to explain. More than fifteen different nutrients make up the B complex, which is necessary to convert sugar to energy, and a lack of it can produce great fatigue and accompanying irritability.

No complete B complex is available in tablet form, so supplements of any of the B vitamins should be taken only if accompanied by natural foods which are a source of the complete complex. These are liver, wheat germ, yeast, whole grains, and soy beans.

However, by the simple expedient of developing sound eating habits, the B complex can be quite easily supplied via our daily meals. And these sound eating habits include fortifying breads, pancakes, waffles, and muffins with wheat germ and powdered milk, AND it means including the occasional cup of yogurt for a snack or as a dessert.

Why yogurt?

All the B vitamins can be synthesized in the intestines by means of the bacteria found in yogurt. These are lactic acid organisms which destroy the harmful bacteria that produce gas and odor. Once you supply your system with these organisms, in much the same way as you seed your garden, they will grow and thrive for a long time providing they are well fed. They are nurtured by the cellulose found in whole-grain cereals and raw vegetables and on the milk sugars readily available in powdered or malted milk, in buttermilk, or in yogurt itself. They provide your body with the ability to manufacture the B complex, including the essential vitamin, pantothenic acid, or calcium pantothenate.

So stock your system with the valuable organisms found in yogurt and maintain these organisms and keep them vigorous with the cellulose in raw vegetables and natural grains and with milk sugars.

THE MOST IMPORTANT VITAMINS IN THE B COMPLEX
AND THEIR FUNCTIONS AND SOURCES

Vitamin	Function	Best Natural Sources
VITAMIN B 1 (thiamin)	For the relief of fatigue and depression	Salad greens, eggs, meats, nuts, seeds, soybeans, and brewer's yeast
VITAMIN B 2 (riboflavin)	For healthy nerves and skin, good blood, and normal functions	Nuts, eggs, milk, molasses, green vegetables, liver, poultry, and fish

VITAMIN B 6 (pyridoxine)	For metabolism of fats	Nuts, milk, and eggs
VITAMIN B 12	For prevention of anemia	Eggs, milk, yogurt, and liver
NIACIN	For healthy nerves, skin, and digestion	Powdered milk, peanuts, seeds, whole grains, fish, and lean meats
PARA-AMINOBENZOIC ACID	For preventing allergies and graying hair	Fish, fruits, nuts, and whole grains
CALCIUM PANTOTHENATE (Pantothenic Acid)	Essential to every cell in the body, keeps the glands alive and active, and contributes to healthy digestive system	Eggs, molasses, peanuts, lean beef, salmon, potatoes, and vegetables belonging to the cabbage family
INOSITOL AND CHOLINE	Metabolize fats and are essential in preventing the accumulation of cholesterol in the arteries	Whole grains, fruits, seeds, peanuts, liver, yeast, wheat germ, and lecithin (eggs)

WHAT ABOUT MINERALS?

The organic substances in our foods, the proteins, fats and carbohydrates, are constantly forming acids, such as lactic acid and carbonic acid, but in addition to these acid-producing foods, there are seven acid-producing minerals, such as sulphur which forms sulphuric acid, phosphorus which forms phosphoric acid, and others.

Dr. Louis Berman explains in his *Food and Character* that there are seven alkaline minerals which assume a most important role in nutrition by counteracting overacidity. These are sodium, potassium, calcium, magnesium, iron, manganese, and copper, but the most important of these are the first four—sodium, potassium, calcium, and magnesium. The latter three are important to the manufacture of red blood cells in the marrow of the bone. If our bodies are deficient in any one of this important trio, anemia can result.

In addition to balancing the chemical composition of the cells, each of the minerals has other duties to perform. Calcium, for instance, combined with phosphorus and vitamin D makes strong bones and teeth.

Phosphorus soothes nerves and quickens muscular responses through the brain. The intake of phosphorus should not be more than one-third higher than the intake of calcium.

Magnesium is associated with cellular functions and needed to synthesize lecithin. The intake of this mineral should not be more than half that of calcium. The magnesium content in raw foods, however, can be destroyed by the use of chemical fertilizers containing potassium, which prevents plants from absorbing magnesium. It may be further reduced by refining processes, so it is often difficult for this important mineral to be obtained in sufficient quantities from our daily foods.

Iodine is needed to regulate the function of the thyroid gland, while iron increases energy, encourages the body's economy of several of the vitamins, and is necessary for the formation of the red blood-cell pigment.

In general fruits, vegetables, and salad greens furnish most of the alkali-producing minerals, while cereals and animal foods contain mostly acid ones. Milk and milk products are the best sources of calcium and phosphorus (one quart of milk furnishes one thousand mgs. of calcium and nine hundred mgs. of phosphorus). Iodized salt, kelp, fish, and seafood supply adequate iodine, and iron is present in good quantities in liver, eggs, wheat germ, yeast, soybeans, lentils, and molasses.

Eggs are by far the richest source of sulphur, containing the important amino acid methionine, and seafoods and yeast are dependable sources of the trace minerals—copper, manganese, zinc, cobalt, and others that are poorly absorbed by vegetables growing in commercially fertilized soil.

WHAT YOU SHOULD KNOW ABOUT DRUGS

Any drug, even one as mild as aspirin, is toxic to some extent, preventing the absorption of nutrients in the body and increasing their excretion. In large amounts, drugs can cause serious dietary deficiencies and damage to the kidneys and liver.

An adequate diet can do much to offset drug toxicity, and it's not a bad idea at all to accompany any drug with a 250 mg. tablet of ascorbic acid (vitamin C).

During infections or any illness calling for the use of antibiotics, adequate vitamin E is also recommended, and the time-honored practice of serving eggnogs to the ill and feverish should never be forgotten. Nor should we forget to replenish our systems with the yogurt bacteria during illness and the recovery period, for while the twentieth-century miracle drugs destroy many otherwise killing bacteria, they also destroy the beneficial bacteria in the intestines which can be resupplied by yogurt and which, if not replenished, can result in a serious deficiency of the vitamin B complex.

WHAT ABOUT ALCOHOL AND COFFEE?

Alcohol and coffee are both drugs but, just as I believe you can eat whatever you want to eat providing you include essentials to balance the diet, I feel that a quiet, relaxing cocktail before dinner can do much to stimulate the appetite, relax frazzled nerves, and alleviate the stresses and strains of an average busy day, and that alcohol in moderation is probably more beneficial than harmful.

You should know, however, in case you are a heavy drinker that alcohol contains a lot of "empty" calories, which are quickly deposited in the body as fat, and not only slows down the flow of blood but can cause the amount of cholesterol in the blood to double. Alcohol also increases the excretion of all the water-soluble vitamins and minerals, especially magnesium. So, if you are a heavy drinker, at least take the precaution to eat the right foods and supplement your diet with vitamin and mineral pills.

It may be that the caffeine in coffee, especially in the instant varieties, may prove to be more harmful to one's system than alcohol. But, again, I cannot advocate complete abstinence from something as truly wonderful as a good cup of coffee. I can suggest however that you serve and drink only coffee brewed from freshly ground beans, freshly made, and served for breakfast as it is done in France—half hot, strong coffee and half hot milk. And if you add sugar, take a tip from the Latin-American countries and use unrefined crystallized sugar, or brown sugar, or even honey. Honey is a delicious sweetener for freshly brewed tea.

DRINK A LITTLE WINE FOR THY STOMACH'S SAKE

Louis Pasteur said that wine "is the most healthful and hygenic of beverages." Unhappily, in the United States wine is classified as a liquor, whose main purpose is to intoxicate rather than to be used as a food, which is where it should be placed. Throughout the ages man has looked on wine as food. Even Noah cultivated grapes for wine, and Isaiah made the promise, "Until I come and take you away to a land like your own land, a land of corn and wine, a land of bread and vineyards."

The process of fermentation is a natural phenomenon which transforms grape juice into wine, and grape juice is a healthful, fragrant solution of water, grape sugars, acids, vitamins B and C, and many minerals, particularly potassium.

Harold Grossman, in his invaluable *Guide,* writes that wine has been looked upon as a natural remedy for man's ills since earliest days. In ancient times it was invaluable to physicians whose medical knowledge was limited, and European doctors still prescribe various wines in cases of arteriosclerosis, constipation, diarrhea, malaria, pneumonia, and illnesses of the liver, kidneys, and gall bladder.

Fortified wines, such as sherry, Madeira, port, and Tokay, all rich in minerals, are easily assimilated and are most helpful to people who are run down and fatigued. Grandmother knew well the value of red wine as a cure for anemia.

In France, wine is called the "milk of the aged," and claret forms a part of the daily diet of the many octogenarians in the Médoc district of Bordeaux, who attribute their longevity to "half a bottle" of red wine a day.

THE NUTRITIONAL VALUE OF HERBS AND SEEDS

Our remote ancestors were well versed in the magic of herbs and seeds. Whether they learned about the medicinal value of many of our common field plants by experimenting on themselves or by observing the effect of them on birds and animals is not known, but today we know that scientists have proved the medicinal and nutritional value of many of our herbs through chemical analysis and have found that the seeds of many plants contain as perfect a balance of nutrients as can be found in any natural foods.

Seeds are concentrated packets of protein, vitamins, and minerals, containing rich amounts of phosphorus, iron, magnesium, the B complex, vitamins E, and essential fatty acids. And what is the vital element in seeds, such as the seed of the melon, which can sprout into roots, stems, leaves, and fruit, after thirty years of lying dormant? Seeds alone do not form a completely nutritious diet for man, but when combined with eggs, fruit, and milk, the diet is nutritionally complete, perhaps containing the very essence of life itself.

There are excellent dried herbs and seeds available in quality food markets, but as good as they are they cannot come close to the flavor and freshness of home-grown ones. If you have a small plot of ground in a sunny, but partially shaded area, there are many herbs and seed plants that can be grown. Parsley, both curly and Italian, and chervil are easily grown from packets of seeds available in hardware and seed stores. So too are dill, basil, thyme, sweet marjoram, summer savory, sage, the highly-prized French sorrel, which is nothing more than the field weed known as sour grass, cumin, fennel, and coriander. But it takes some of the seedlings of these plants so long to reach usable size that you are farther ahead if you can buy small plants from a nursery. Occasionally, you may be lucky enough to find small pots of dill, sweet basil, and parsley in rural vegetable markets along with pots of chives.

Otherwise seek out a nursery which cultivates root herbs. Here, if you are lucky, you will find tarragon, a hardy perennial once you get it started which grows to a bushy plant about two feet high. You might also want to buy a couple of roots each of rosemary, thyme, mint, winter savory, and sage. Most of these are perennials, but, in very cold climates, will be frosted out, along with your precious tarragon, unless well mulched before the first heavy frost. Parsley and chervil are biennials and can survive one winter if mulched. Sorrel and mint seem to withstand the most severe low temperatures.

Fresh tarragon and sweet basil leaves will give a marvelous flavor to wine or cider vinegar to last you during the winter, but basil leaves lose their flavor easily and are better preserved if packed tightly into a jar and covered with olive oil. In a couple of weeks, strain the wonderfully flavored basil oil off the leaves, and use it for your salads and for flavoring soups, stews, and pasta sauces.

Home-frozen parsley is better than anything you can buy in dried or frozen form. Pick the clusters after a nice rain, when they are clean and have just had enough time to dry off. Spread them on a baking sheet and put them in the freezer for 1 hour. Remove from the freezer and crumble into plastic pouches, and return to the freezer for winter use.

THE BEST WAY TO PRESERVE OTHER FRESH HERBS

Remove the leaves from the stems and pack leaves tightly into small jars with tight-fitting tops. (Empty baby-food jars are perfect.) Cover tightly, drop the jars into boiling water, and simmer for forty-five minutes. Remove jars, cool, and store in the freezer.

TWENTY-SIX EASY WAYS TO GOOD NUTRITION

Eat the foods you like, but eat wisely. Learn moderation in all things and, if you have a weight problem, eat a balanced diet of good foods, but eat a little less and always leave the table just a little hungry. Learn to count protein grams as well as calories.

REMEMBER THE BASICS: Your body needs all the building blocks of *complete proteins,* with their built-in supply of B vitamins, to convert sugar to energy, *natural sugars, natural unsaturated fats* that provide essential fatty acids to put cholesterol into suspension in the blood stream, and the *vitamins* and *minerals* that the body cannot manufacture to regulate and stimulate the body processes.

If you will follow the twenty-six rules for good daily nutrition, such common complaints as high blood pressure, nervous disorders, disorders of the digestive system, and even heart disease may be prevented.

1. EAT LOTS OF RAW FRUIT AND VEGETABLES. Begin each meal with some raw fruit or fruit juice, raw vegetable, or vegetable juice.

2. ENJOY A GREEN SALAD at least once a day.

3. USE NATURAL SUGARS whenever possible. Substitute brown sugar, crystallized sugars, honey, or molasses or maple syrup in place of refined white sugar, which interferes with the absorption of proteins, calcium, and other minerals and retards the growth of valuable intestinal bacteria. Good natural sugars are supplied by bananas, dried fruit, fruit juices, whole grain cereals, and root vegetables.

4. START THE DAY RIGHT by eating a bowl of bran flakes or toasted wheat germ instead of so-called "enriched" cereals. Top it off with one-half sliced banana or fresh berries in season, or with a spoonful of dried prunes or apricots, cooked and sweetened with brown sugar, honey, or maple syrup.

5. AVOID SATURATED FATS. This means the hard fats on meat, hydrogenated fats, such as lard or margarine, or margarine or peanut butter made with "hard" oils. It also means to avoid packaged mixes, deep-fried frozen foods, and whipped toppings.

6. EAT 1 TO 2 TABLESPOONS OF VEGETABLE OILS DAILY. Buy small bottles of fresh soy oil, safflower oil, peanut oil, and olive oil (for flavor), and combine them in one large bottle in equal proportions, or one-quarter of each. Each supplies a different fatty acid needed to put saturated fats into suspension in the blood. Use the combined oils for cooking and for salads.

7. USE DARK GREENS IN SALADS WHENEVER POSSIBLE—spinach leaves, water cress, field salad, and others, and MAKE YOUR OWN SALAD DRESSING. It's so simple! Just salt, freshly ground pepper, lemon juice or vinegar, and your combined oils.

8. USE FRESH CHOPPED GARLIC AND HERBS LAVISHLY. Grow your own fresh herbs if you have a patch of good earth.

9. MAKE YOUR OWN BREADS from whole-grain cereals. The nutrients necessary for energy are supplied in whole grains, while commercial breads and baked goods are "empty" foods, lacking these essential nutrients and causing obesity.

10. ADD WHEAT GERM OR SOY GRANULES to omelets, scrambled eggs, pancakes, muffins, biscuits, croquettes, or loaves.

11. AVOID PROCESSED CHEESES. Eat instead whole or skim-milk fresh cheeses and natural aged cheeses such as Parmesan, Cheddar, Gruyère, Swiss, and Roquefort-type.

12. USE IODIZED SALT (if not on a salt-restricted diet).

13. FORGET BOTTLED SOFT DRINKS and substitute fresh fruit juices, vegetable juices, milk, or a glass of good wine.

14. DON'T ELIMINATE BUTTER, CREAM, AND WHOLE MILK. These are the best way to get vitamin A. Butterfat can be a problem only when other nutrients necessary to utilize it are not supplied.

15. EAT ONE OR TWO EGGS DAILY. Eggs are rich in methionine and lecithin and, according to many food authorities, should not be restricted even in heart diets. Use them in cooking, or poach or scramble them in a little fresh butter, or lightly shirr them in your mixed vegetable oils.

16. EAT ONE SERVING OF LEAN MEAT, FISH, FOWL, CHEESE, OR MEAT SUBSTITUTE DAILY.

17. EAT LIVER OFTEN (if you eat meat), or supplement your diet daily with desiccated liver pills and vitamin D, or with one teaspoon of food yeast stirred into a glass of orange or vegetable juice.

18. EAT YOGURT. Try it plain, or flavored, or frozen on a stick. You just might like it. Or try the recipe for yogurt ice cream (page 320). Delicious! There is no substitute for the cultured bacteria in yogurt so essential for the complete assimilation of nutrients in the digestive system. To make your own yogurt see recipe, page 342.

19. DRINK AT LEAST ONE GLASS OF MILK OR BUTTERMILK DAILY, and supplement homemade baked goods with powdered milk.

20. EAT ONE OR TWO SERVINGS OF FRESH COOKED VEGETABLES DAILY.

21. EAT ONE SERVING OF NATURAL GRAINS DAILY, such as buckwheat grits (kasha), bulgur, natural brown rice or wild rice, or cous-cous.

22. POTATOES ARE A VITAMIN-RICH FOOD, but don't forget other mop-up-the-sauce carbohydrates such as high-protein spaghetti, macaroni, noodles, hominy, or hominy grits, or cornmeal (mush or polenta).

23. KEEP ALL MEALS LIGHT AND EAT A SNACK BETWEEN EACH MEAL. Make the snack a good one. Forget the doughnuts, cookies, candies, and potato chips. Snack on fresh fruit or dried apricots, prunes or dates,

peanuts, almonds with their skins, walnuts, pecans, natural cheeses, yogurt, or sunflower seeds. Peanut butter on crackers supplies high-quality protein, but should not contain hard oils. Buy it at a health store or make your own (page 341).

24. USE SEEDS OFTEN IN COOKING. Poppy seeds, sesame seeds, cumin seeds on buttered vegetables, on top of breads and biscuits and in pie crusts and muffins. Seeds are small packets of concentrated protein and minerals and are especially high in phosphorus and calcium.

25. LEARN TO DRINK COFFEE IN THE FRENCH MANNER, half hot strong, freshly brewed coffee and half hot milk.

26. A HOT MILK DRINK BEFORE BED IS NATURE'S PILL and the best way to assure a good night's sleep.

P.S. Take short and frequent sunbaths during summer and invest in a sun lamp for use during winter months. Supplement your diet with vitamins and minerals whenever a satisfactory diet is not or cannot be consumed daily. This is your best life insurance.

SAMPLE OF BALANCED MEALS FOR A DAY

It's so easy if you just think good health. The following meals supply more than adequate complete proteins (at least 80 grams) with all the essential nutrients.

BREAKFAST

Half a grapefruit or a glass of orange or cranberry juice, or a serving of berries in season, or stewed apricots or prunes.

One-fourth cup of wheat germ cereal or soy granules with brown sugar and milk or half-and-half.

Café au lait.

LUNCH

Cup of homemade soup or vegetable juice.

Two eggs, scrambled in a little butter or an omelet, and a slice of whole-wheat bread or a bran muffin.

or

Egg, salmon, or chicken salad (with mayonnaise) sandwich on whole-wheat bread.

Green or vegetable salad with vegetable-oil dressing, or cole slaw with mayonnaise dressing.

Yogurt topped with fresh or stewed fruit, or homemade ice cream.

Café au lait or, preferably, milk.

DINNER

Raw vegetable or fruit appetizer, or seafood cocktail, or half an avocado with vegetable-oil dressing, or a cooked artichoke vinaigrette, or tossed green salad with vegetable-oil dressing.

Serving of liver, or lamb chops, or steak, or fish, or seafood, or meat substitute.

Serving of a cooked whole grain or pasta, or a potato, plus a slice of whole-grain bread.

Serving of a green vegetable tossed with a little butter.

Glass of good red or white wine.

Maple syrup custard, or crème brûlée, or fresh fruit with an aged cheese, or homemade ice cream.

Coffee, tea, or milk.

HOMEMADE PEANUT BUTTER IN AN ELECTRIC BLENDER

Makes 6 ounces peanut butter. Be sure your blender container is completely dry.

1. Empty *1 cup shelled fresh or vacuum-packed peanuts* into the container. Cover and blend on highest speed for 5 seconds. Turn off motor.

2. Add *1 tablespoon vegetable oil* to the ground nuts, cover container, and blend on medium speed for about 60 seconds, or until nuts are ground and churned into peanut butter.

3. If necessary, stop the motor occasionally and stir down the ground mixture with a thin rubber spatula.

4. Remove peanut butter from container with the spatula and pack into a jar with a tight-fitting cover. Store in refrigerator.

HOMEMADE YOGURT

1. Pour *1 quart milk* into a heavy saucepan and bring to a boil. Watch carefully not to let it boil over the pan. Reduce heat and simmer the milk for 5 minutes, stirring constantly.

2. Remove from heat, and stir in *1 cup instant dried milk* and let cool to lukewarm (110° F.).

3. Stir in *½ cup commercial yogurt*. Cover saucepan with a tight-fitting lid and wrap in a heavy towel. Set it in an oven (heat off) for 6 to 8 hours or overnight. (Or, easier still, pour the lukewarm mixture into a wide-mouthed thermos and seal tightly until the next day.)

4. Spoon the yogurt into pint jars. Store in refrigerator where it will keep fresh for several days.

Index